# Monetizing Your Data

# Monetizing Your Data

**A GUIDE TO TURNING DATA INTO PROFIT-DRIVING STRATEGIES AND SOLUTIONS**

Andrew Wells and Kathy Chiang

Published by John Wiley & Sons, Inc., Hoboken, New Jersey.
Published simultaneously in Canada.

For general information on our other products and services or for technical support, please contact our Customer Care Department within the United States at (800) 762–2974, outside the United States at (317) 572–3993 or fax (317) 572–4002.

Wiley publishes in a variety of print and electronic formats and by print-on-demand. Some material included with standard print versions of this book may not be included in e-books or in print-on-demand. If this book refers to media such as a CD or DVD that is not included in the version you purchased, you may download this material at http://booksupport.wiley.com. For more information about Wiley products, visit www.wiley.com.

*Library of Congress Cataloging-in-Publication Data is Available:*

ISBN 978-1-119-35624-0 (Hardcover)
ISBN 978-1-119-35626-4 (ePDF)
ISBN 978-1-119-35625-7 (ePub)

Cover Design: Wiley
Cover Image: © SergeyNivens/iStockphoto

Printed in the United States of America

10 9 8 7 6 5 4 3 2 1

*Kathy Williams Chiang:*

*To my parents, Si and Patty Jean Williams, who have believed in me longer than anyone else.*

*Andrew Roman Wells:*

*To my loving wife, Suzannah, who is a constant source of encouragement, love, and positive energy. And to my parents, Diana and Maitland, who instilled in me a love of numbers and a spirit of entrepreneurship.*

# Contents

# Preface

The purpose of this book is to enable you to build monetization strategies enabled through analytical solutions that help managers and executives navigate through the sea of data to make quality decisions that drive revenue. However, this process is fraught with challenges. The first challenge is to distill the flood of information. We have a step-by-step process, Decision Architecture Methodology, that takes you from hypothesis to building an analytical solution. This process is guided by your monetization strategy, where you build decision matrixes to make economic tradeoffs for various actions. Through guided analytics, we show you how to build your analytical solution and leverage the disciplines of UI/UX to present your story with high impact and dashboard development to automate the analytical solution.

The real power of our method comes from tying together a set of disciplines, methods, tools, and skillsets into a structured process. The range of disciplines include Data Science, Decision Theory, Behavioral Economics, Decision Architecture, Data Development and Architecture, UI/UX Development, and Dashboard Development, disciplines rarely integrated into one seamless process. Our methodology brings these disciplines together in an easy-to-understand step-by-step approach to help organizations build solutions to monetize their data assets.

Some of the benefits you will receive from this book include:

- Turning information assets into revenue-generating strategies
- Providing a guided experience for the manager that helps reduce noise and cognitive bias
- Making your organization more competitive through analytical solutions centered on monetization strategies linked to your organizational objectives

- Turning your analytics into actionable tactics versus simply "reading the news"
- Monetizing your data to drive revenue and reduce costs

This book is not about selling your internal data to other companies or consumers. Nor is it a deep dive into each of the various disciplines. Rather, we provide you with an overview of the various disciplines and the techniques we use most often to build these solutions.

For Andrew, one of your authors, the process of building monetization solutions started in 2003 when he was the Director of Business Intelligence at Capital One. The standard of that era was to provide analytics that were informational in nature. Whether the reporting was for marketing or operations, the information was automated with the gathering, grouping, and aggregating of data into a few key metrics displayed on a report. What Andrew did not know then, was that these reports lacked the intelligence and diagnostic framework to yield action. During this era, the solutions he developed were assigned an economic value to the analysis as a whole, but not to each individual action to drive quality decisions. Over the past decade, he has worked to refine the analytical solutions brought to his clients that have culminated in many of the methods and techniques prescribed in this book.

Kathy, your other author, over her many years in business planning and forecasting, was continually frustrated by the inability to trace business issues to their root cause. The high cost of IT infrastructure at the time constrained the delivery of analytic information through reporting systems that aggregated the data, losing the ability to explore the character and relationships of the underlying transactional data. She began her journey through the wonderful world of big data in 2009 when she signed on to help the Telecommunications Services of Trinidad and Tobago (TSTT) develop a strategic analytics system with the goal of integrating transactional data into business planning processes. Through this assignment, Kathy learned the power of data visualization tools, like Tableau, that connect managers and analysts directly to the data, and the importance of developing analytic data marts to prevent frustrating dead-ends.

Over the course of the past several years, both Kathy and Andrew have worked together to build a variety of solutions that help companies monetize their data. This includes solutions ranging from large

Fortune 500 companies to businesses that have under $100 million in revenue. When we first started tackling this problem, one of the key challenges we noticed was the siloed approach to the development and distribution of analytic information. The analyst was using a spreadsheet to do most of their analytical work. The data scientist was working on bigger analytical problems using advanced statistical methods. The IT team was worried about distributing enterprise reports to be consumed by hundreds or thousands of users. Small analytical projects that often lead to the biggest returns for the organization would fall into the gaps between the silos, unable to compete for organizational attention.

As we were building our solutions, we noticed several gaps in the current methods and tools, which led us to develop our own methodology building from the best practices in these various disciplines. One gap that is being closed by new tools is the easier access to data for managers. Where in the past, if a manager wanted to build an analytical solution, they were often limited to analysis in MS Excel or standing up an IT project, which could be lengthy and time consuming, today, data visualization and analysis tools such as Tableau, QlikView, and Power BI give the average business user direct access to a greater volume and scope of data with less drain on IT resources.

This move toward self-service analytics is a big trend that will continue for the next several years. Much of the IT role will transition to enterprise scale analytics and building data environments for analysis. This new paradigm will allow for faster innovation as analysts become empowered with new technology and easier access to data.

As the tools have gotten better and business users have direct access to more information than ever before, they are encountering the need to be aware of and deal with data quality issues masked by the cleansed reporting solutions they accessed in the past. Users must now learn data cleaning techniques and the importance of maintaining data standards and data quality.

One benefit that has come with the increased capabilities of these tools is better User Interface (UI) and User Design (UX) functionality. The usability of an analytical solution is often dictated by the ability to understand and interface with the data. We see prettier dashboards now, but not necessarily geared toward usability or guiding someone through a story. As more analysts and managers begin creating their own reporting solutions, they often build an informational solution that helps them "read the news" versus building a diagnostic to help them manage to a decision that drives action.

Another gap we noticed centers around Data Science and Decision Theory, which are not well deployed in analytical solutions. We began integrating these disciplines into our practice several years ago and they are now integral components. These techniques include: choice architecture, understanding cognitive bias, decision trees, cluster analysis, segmentation, thresholds, and correlations.

Few solutions provide *monetization strategies* allowing the manager to weigh the economic value tradeoffs of various actions. In adding this method to our solutions, we noticed a considerable uptick in quantifiable value we delivered to our clients and an increase in usage of these analytical solutions.

Closing these gaps and putting it all together was a process of trial and error. Some things worked in some situations and not others while some things we tried did not work at all. After several iterations, we believe our methodology is ready for broader consumption. It is truly unique in that it brings together a varied set of disciplines and best practices to help organizations build analytical solutions to monetize their data. We humbly share our experience, tools, methods, and techniques with you.

# Acknowledgments

We owe a large measure of gratitude to everyone who has helped contribute to the development of this book and to those who have helped us along our life's journey.

Thank you, Michael Andrews, for welcoming us into your store, walking us through the business of Michael Andrews Bespoke, and serving as an outstanding case study. The way you strive for excellence and provide white-glove customer service is an inspiration to all of us.

Thank you to Amanda Hand, Lloyd Lay, and Jeff Forman for your assistance in developing and editing several of the chapters and conducting the survey. Your guidance and counsel was invaluable.

Thank you to Jason Reiling, Doug McClure, Alex Clarke, Dev Koushik, Alex Durham, and countless others who participated in the interview and survey process. We appreciate the time and energy that you gave to help us understand the current environment and issues that you are encountering.

Bill Franks and Justin Honaman, thank you for your advice and wisdom in the book-writing process and opening up your networks to provide us with an insider's perspective on what it takes to write a great book. In addition, many thanks to the team at Wiley for taking a leap of faith in us.

We would like to thank many of our clients, including: The Coca-Cola Company, The Home Depot, RGA, Grady Hospital, AT&T, TSTT, Genuine Parts Company, Carters, Cox, Turner, SITA, and Macys. We would like to give special thanks to the team at IHG for their support: Quentin, Alex, Tae, Ryan, Jia, Michelle, Ivy, Lisa, Joe, and many others.

Kathy would like to say a few words:

None of us achieve anything of import alone. In the immortal words of John Donne, "No man is an island." And so, in writing this book, I, too, stand on the shoulders of those who went before me, those who mentored me and encouraged me to do my best, to strive for more, to find my own way in the world. It is impossible to name everyone whom I have traveled with but I remember each and every one in my thoughts. I would like to mention a few who have been particularly helpful in my journey. I would like to thank my mentors, AJ Robison, Kinny Roper, John Hartman, Robert Peon, Carl Wilson, Trevor Deane, Linda McQuade, and Stuart Kramer, who believed in me, saw my potential, and invested in my development. I would like to thank my loving husband, Fuling Chiang, who has stood by me from the beginning and makes my coffee every morning. And finally, I would like to thank my children, Sean and Christine, who lovingly accepted their fate with a working mom without complaining.

In addition, Andrew would like to thank the following people:

Thank you to my fellow members of Young Presidents Organization for igniting a spark that gave me the idea and confidence to write a book and the invaluable friendship and advice I received from so many of you. Thank you to Aaron Edelheit and JP James for being an inspiration that anything is possible.

Thank you to the entire Aspirent team for your expertise and hard work every day to deliver outstanding solutions to our clients. In addition, thank you for your help in writing this book and creating our monetization website and collateral.

Thank you to my family, Diana, Jen, Rick, April, Ada, Ayden, Adley, and Wanda. And finally, and most importantly, thank you to Suzannah for supporting me during the many nights and weekends that it took to write this book. I appreciate your loving patience and understanding.

# About the Authors

**Andrew Roman Wells** is the CEO of Aspirent, a management consulting firm focused on analytics. He has extensive experience building analytical solutions for a wide range of companies, from Fortune 500s to small nonprofits. Andrew focuses on helping organizations utilize their data to make impactful decisions that drive revenue through monetization strategies. He has been building analytical solutions for over 25 years and is excited to share these practical methods, tools, and techniques with a wider audience.

In addition to his role as an executive, Andrew is a hands-on consultant, which he has been since his early days building reporting solutions as a consultant at Ernst & Young. He refined his craft in Silicon Valley, working for two successful startups focused on customer analytics and the use of predictive methods to drive performance. Andrew has also held executive roles in industry as Director of Business Intelligence at Capital One where he helped drive several patented analytical innovations. From consulting, to startup companies, to being in industry, Andrew has had a wide variety of experience in driving growth through analytics. He has built solutions for a wide variety of industries and companies, including The Coca-Cola Company, IHG, The Home Depot, Capital One, Wells Fargo, HP, Time Warner, Merrill Lynch, Applied Materials, and many others.

Andrew lives in Atlanta with his wife, Suzannah, and he enjoys photography, running, and international travel. He is a co-owner at Michael Andrews Bespoke. Andrew earned a Bachelor's degree in Business Administration with a focus on Finance and Management Information Systems from the University of Georgia.

**Kathy Williams Chiang** is an established Business Analytics practitioner with expertise in guided analytics, analytic data mart development, and business planning. Prior to her current position as VP, Business Insights, at Wunderman Data Management,

Ms. Chiang consulted with Aspirent on numerous analytic projects for several multinational clients, including IHG and Coca Cola, among others. She has also worked for multinational corporations, including Telecommunications Systems of Trinidad and Tobago, Acuity Brands Lighting, BellSouth International, and Portman Overseas.

Ms. Chiang is experienced in designing and developing analytic tools and management dashboards that inform and drive action. She is highly skilled in data exploration, analysis, visualization, and presentation and has developed solutions in telecom, hospitality, and consumer products industries covering customer experience, marketing campaigns, revenue management, and web analytics.

Ms. Chiang, a native of New Orleans, holds a Bachelor of Science in Chemistry, summa cum laude, with University honors (4.0), from Louisiana State University, as well as an MBA from Tulane University and is a member of Phi Beta Kappa and Mensa. Among the first wave of Americans to enter China following normalization of relations, Ms. Chiang lived in northeast China under challenging conditions for two years, teaching English, learning Mandarin Chinese, and traveling extensively throughout China. Over her career, she has worked in the United States, Caribbean, UK, Latin America, and China.

# Monetizing Your Data

# SECTION I

# INTRODUCTION

# Introduction

The explosion of information is accelerating. This can be seen in our everyday use of emails, online searches, text messages, blog posts, and postings on Facebook and YouTube. The amount of data being created and captured is staggering. It is flooding corporate walls and is only getting worse as the next big explosion is already upon us, the Internet of Things, when our machines talk to each other. At this point, the rate of information growth may go exponential. In his article for *Industry Tap*, David Russell Schilling explained the theory behind futurist Buckminster Fuller's "Knowledge Doubling Curve."

> ... until 1900 human knowledge doubled approximately every century. By the end of World War II knowledge was doubling every 25 years. Today ... human knowledge is doubling every 13 months. According to IBM, the buildout of the "internet of things" will lead to the doubling of knowledge every 12 hours.

According to Gartner, as many as 25 billion things will be connected by 2020. As we try to make sense of this information, of what Tom Davenport calls the "analytics of things," we will need methods and tools to assimilate and distill the information into actionable insights that drive revenue. Having these troves of information is of little value if they are not utilized to give our companies a competitive edge. How are companies approaching the problem of monetizing this information today?

One approach that gets inconsistent results, for instance, is simple data mining. Corralling huge data sets allows companies to run dozens of statistical tests to identify submerged patterns, but that provides little benefit if managers can't effectively use the correlations to enhance business performance. A pure data-mining approach often leads to an endless search for what the data really say.

This is a quote from the *Harvard Business Review* article, "Making Advanced Analytics Work for You," by Dominic Barton and David Court. This idea is further reinforced by Jason Reiling, Group Director of Trade Capability at The Coca-Cola Company, who commented, "If we don't link the business use of the data with the hypothesis and overall objective, we find situations where the data is guiding the analysis, versus the business guiding the data." This sums up one of the biggest challenges that exist in analytics today: organizations are throwing data at the problem hoping to find a solution versus understanding the business problem and aligning the right data and methods to it.

What begins to matter more at this point is not necessarily the amount of data, but the ability to codify and distill this information into meaningful insights. Companies are struggling with this issue due to lack of integrated methods, tools, techniques, and resources. If they are able to solve this challenge, they will have a clear competitive advantage. However, this only solves part of the problem; even with the most relevant information, companies are mired in poor decision making.

## Decisions

The ultimate goal of collecting and synthesizing this information is to provide insights to executives and managers to make better decisions. Decisions are at the heart of your business and the most powerful tool most managers have for achieving results. The quality of the decisions will directly impact the success of your organization. It is no longer acceptable to equip organizational leaders, managers, and analysts with one-off training courses and conferences, expecting them to make quality decisions based on limited knowledge and gut feel. They have more information coming at them than ever before. Distilling the flood of information into actionable decisions that your organization can monetize is the new challenge.

Unfortunately, simply distilling the information is not enough. There are various ways we undermine our ability to make quality decisions, from decision fatigue to cognitive bias. One way to improve decision making is by using best practices and the collective wisdom of the organization. However, this practice is not widely implemented. In a study by Erik Larson of over 500 managers and executives, they found that only 2 percent apply these best practices when making decisions. Furthermore, even fewer companies have solutions in place to improve decision making.

When executives are not applying best practices or data to make a decision, more often than not they are relying on their intuition or "gut." This type of decision making is riddled with flaws and often brings in cognitive biases that influence choice. A cognitive bias is a deviation from the norm in judgment based on one's preferences and beliefs. For example, confirmation bias is the tendency to look for information that confirms our existing opinions and thoughts. These biases distort our judgment and lead to errors in choice.

Another culprit of poor decisions is the hidden influences that can affect our decisions, such as mood. For example, let's take a decision about staffing between two field managers in two different locations. Whom to hire, when to hire someone, when to let someone go are all decisions they make based on little data and not much coaching. The decisions between two managers can vary to a large degree based on years and type of experience, mood on that particular day, and other factors that may be occurring in their life at that moment. These two individuals are likely to make different decisions on staffing even when presented with identical circumstances. This type of discrepancy in decision making is what the authors of "Noise: How to Overcome the High, Hidden Cost of Inconsistent Decision Making" call *noise*.

> The problem is that humans are unreliable decision makers; their judgments are strongly influenced by irrelevant factors, such as their current mood, the time since their last meal, and the weather. We call the chance variability of judgments noise. It is an invisible tax on the bottom line of many companies.
>
> The prevalence of noise has been demonstrated in several studies. Academic researchers have repeatedly confirmed that professionals often contradict their own prior judgments when given the same data on different occasions. For instance, when

software developers were asked on two separate days to estimate the completion time for a given task, the hours they projected differed by 71%, on average. When pathologists made two assessments of the severity of biopsy results, the correlation between their ratings was only .61 (out of a perfect 1.0), indicating that they made inconsistent diagnoses quite frequently.

Along with noise, another impediment to decision making is *decision fatigue*. Decision fatigue is the deteriorating quality of your ability to make good decisions throughout the course of a day of making decisions. For example, scientists Shai Danziger, Jonathan Levav, and Liora Avnaim-Pesso studied 1,112 bench rulings in a parole court and analyzed the level of favorable rulings throughout the course of the day. The study found that the ruling started out around 65 percent favorable at the beginning of the day and by the end of the day was close to zero. Their internal resources for making quality decisions had been depleted through fatigue as the day wore on, resulting in less favorable rulings by the end of the day

Another challenge for decisions is company size. "Internal challenges of large organizations are big barriers to decision making" according to an executive who runs analytics for a Fortune 50 company. She commented that it can take 1.5 years to get an insight to market due to the level of effort associated with disseminating the information throughout a large matrixed environment. The number of hops in the decisioning process impedes speed to market along with the degradation of the original intent of the decision.

How do we solve for these factors that influence our ability to make a quality decision? One way is to automate all or part of the decision process. Later on in their article, "Noise," the authors state:

> It has long been known that predictions and decisions generated by simple statistical algorithms are often more accurate than those made by experts, even when the experts have access to more information than the formulas use. It is less well known that the key advantage of algorithms is that they are noise-free: Unlike humans, a formula will always return the same output for any given input. Superior consistency allows even simple and imperfect algorithms to achieve greater accuracy than human professionals.

Our approach to driving the quality of the decisions higher in your organization is to create embedded analytical solutions to help managers make data-driven decisions of monetary value that generate action for their organization. There is an abundance of evidence to support our approach. In a study performed by Andrew McAfee and Erik Brynjolfsson, they found that "companies in the top third of their industry in the use of data-driven decision making were, on average, 5% more productive and 6% more profitable than their competitors."

## Analytical Journey

Companies are at various stages in their analytical journey, with different levels of capabilities to develop analytical solutions. Over the past 10 years, companies have invested in building teams and leveraging tools to drive insights for a competitive advantage. Those that have progressed furthest are reaping the rewards.

A study on the maturity of analytics inside companies performed by the Harvard Business Review Analytics Services team found that "more than half the respondents who described their organizations as best-in-class also say their organizations' annual revenue has grown by 10 percent or more over the last two years. In marked contrast, a third of the self-described laggards say their organizations have seen either flat or decreasing revenues."

Study after study is finding similar results; companies that leverage data to drive the performance of their organization's decisions are winning at a faster rate than their competition. However, the technology behind most analytical applications is still nascent and lacks the functionality to deliver a complete solution. In an article by Harvard Business Review Analytics Services team, "Analytics That Work: Deploying Self-Service and Data Visualizations for Faster Decisions," they found in a survey of over 827 business managers that there is a sense of frustration with the lack of tool capabilities.

> "Most reporting tools on the desktop only scratch the surface," says Mier of Contractually. "They have limitations in understanding the underlying data structure, so they have not come close to fulfilling their promise. As a result, companies lack a framework for taking a complex issue, forming a hypothesis, and understanding the layers of data."

This is compounded by the fact that most of these solutions simply help managers "read the news," which means that there is nothing actionable about the data presented, it is just informative. The elusive goal to "manage through exception" is still no closer if you rely solely on technology to provide you this functionality.

## Solving the Problem

The purpose of this book is to enable you to build analytical solutions that help managers and executives navigate through the sea of data to make quality decisions. However, this process is fraught with challenges. The first challenge is to distill the flood of information. We have a step-by-step process that takes you from hypothesis to data to metrics to building an analytical solution. We provide techniques to guide an executive through the difficulty of making a decision without influence from bias or noise.

This process is guided by your monetization strategy, where you build decision matrixes to make economic tradeoffs for various actions. Through guided analytics, we show you how to build your analytical solution and leverage the disciplines of UI/UX to present your story with high impact and implement dashboard development to automate the analytical solution.

Lastly, we will provide advice on enabling the solution within your organization through internal capabilities, organizational structure, and adoption techniques. Our methodology, Decision Architecture, provides an approach to solve each of these challenges and build analytical solutions that will help your organization monetize its data.

The real power of our method comes from tying together a set of disciplines, methods, tools, and skillsets into a structured process. The range of disciplines include Data Science, Decision Theory, Behavioral Economics, Decision Architecture, Data Development and Architecture, UI/UX Development, and Dashboard Development, disciplines rarely integrated into one seamless process. Our methodology brings these disciplines together in an easy-to-understand step-by-step approach to help organizations build solutions to monetize their data assets.

Some of the benefits you will receive from this book include:

- Turning information assets into revenue-generating strategies
- Making your organization more competitive through analytical solutions centered on monetization strategies linked to your organizational objectives

- Empowering managers with analytical solutions for better quality decisions
- Providing a guided experience for the manager that helps reduce noise and cognitive bias
- Increasing the analytical maturity of your organization
- Utilizing embedded analytics to gather the collective wisdom of your organization into a reusable analytical solution
- Turning your analytics into actionable tactics versus simply "reading the news"
- Monetizing your data to drive revenue and reduce costs

This book is not about selling your internal data to other companies or consumers. Nor is it a deep dive into each of the various disciplines. Rather, we provide you with an overview of the various disciplines and the techniques we use most often to build these solutions.

## The Survey Says ...

To ground our approach, we performed extensive research into each of the various disciplines. In addition, we interviewed and surveyed over 75 professionals in the analytical community in over 40 companies ranging in size from Fortune 500 to companies with under $100 million in revenue. The results speak to some interesting insights.

The first insight we gained is that the level of maturity for the organizations we surveyed is progressing nicely up the analytical maturity curve. Most organizations fall into the Statistical Modeling level with some firms starting to dabble in greater capabilities. Figure 1.1 shows the levels of maturity mapped to response.

We noticed a variety of insights based on an organization's size. Larger organizations have come to expect less precision when considering their average decisions. This insight was summed up by an executive at a major telecom company who said his people know that he is perfectly satisfied with directional accuracy. He would rather the analytics be 70 percent accurate and actionable than 100 percent accurate and too slow to market.

Midsize organizations were more likely to respond that they have more advanced capabilities. When asked questions about certain capabilities, the midsized companies had an above-average score, greater than larger companies. In Figure 1.2 on the impact of data science in their organization, small companies had an average score

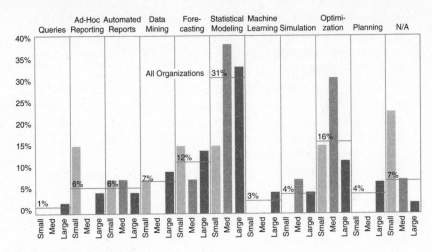

**Figure 1.1    Data Science Maturity**

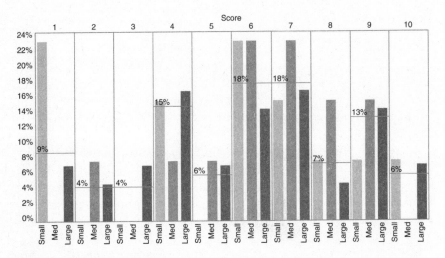

**Figure 1.2    Data Science Impact**

of 5.38, large companies had an average score of 5.81, and midsized companies had an average score of 6.46.

This insight speaks to a general trend we are seeing in the marketplace that the competitive advantage of large companies with respect to the use of analytics is disappearing as the cost of accessing, processing, and housing data along with the costs of analytical tools has decreased to level the playing field. A company no longer has to have large teams of data scientists and millions of dollars to drive insights. Quality tools to mine data are now virtually free. Large communities have sprung up to drive innovation within these tools, providing capabilities to the average company that were not possible 10 years ago. This leveling is providing even the smallest of companies with capabilities that were previously available only to those large enough to afford them.

Another interesting insight came in the use of the various *dashboarding* capabilities by organizations. We found that most companies self-selected that they are utilizing dashboarding tools, but mostly as informational. They are not using advanced techniques to drive revenue through capabilities such as *guided analytics* or *decision matrixes*. Figure 1.3 is a graph of individual capabilities and usage.

Our research further validates that analytical dashboards are producing metrics, but not guidance and structure to interpret the information to drive action. From our respondents, approximately 80 percent have metrics, trends, and graphs, but only 15 percent have guided analytics, decision matrix, diagnostics, thresholds, correlations, monetization strategies, or models imbedded. These important capabilities that help guide a user through a decision process to make a quality decision are still nascent in most

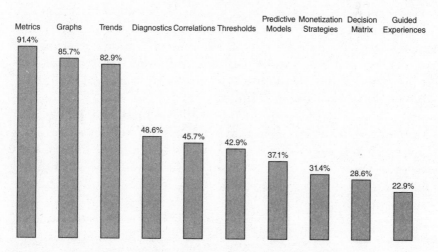

Figure 1.3    Capabilities for Respondent with Higher Data-Driven Decisioning

organizations which further validates the need for the methods, tools, and techniques we prescribe in this book.

Our research, survey, and interviews confirm our hypotheses and validate our experiences of the current state of analytics in most companies. Let's now turn our attention to utilizing this book to solve these challenges and close this gap.

## How to Use This Book

The book provides you with the tools and methods to monetize your data through capturing requirements, building monetization strategies, and developing guided analytical solutions. The book is divided into several sections, each dedicated to a particular capability. Depending on your role, you may want to focus your time on a particular section to assist in building your strategy and solutions. For example, if your role is to help drive requirements for analytical solutions, you will want to focus on the Decision Analysis section of the book to implement in your organization.

Let's cover each of the sections in turn:

### Introduction

Outside of this chapter, the first section starts with a discussion on the Analytical Cycle. The Analytical Cycle provides you with a frame of reference for how to think about solving analytical problems and the steps for each stage. The cycle flows from the business problem statement through the questions you ask yourself to understanding the root cause of an opportunity or issue. It then drills into diagnostics to help determine decision options that lead to actions and finally the need to measure your results.

In this section we also introduce the methodology of Decision Architecture, as presented in Figure 1.4. It is your step-by-step process guide as you build your solution. It is divided into five phases, each with tools and techniques to make you successful. The steps in the methodology serve as the foundation for the book and tie each of the chapters together.

The methodology has five phases: Discovery, Decision Analysis, Monetization Strategy, Agile Analytics, and Enablement. We view

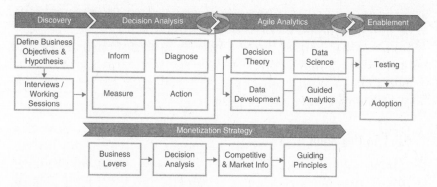

**Figure 1.4    Decision Architecture Methodology**

each of these components, techniques, and tools in the methodology as Lego™ pieces that you can choose from when assembling your analytical solution.

### Decision Analysis

The Decision Analysis section focuses on the techniques that can help you architect a decision and translate these into requirements. This phase of the methodology produces a set of requirements that translates the business problem from a hypothesis to the questions, decision, actions, metrics, and data needed to build your analytical solution.

### Monetization Strategy

The goal of this section of the book is to empower you with the tools and techniques necessary to create winning strategies for your company. The four components of developing your Monetization Strategy are: Monetization Guiding Principles, Competitive and Market Information, Business Levers Framework, and the requirements gathered from the decision analysis. Depending on the type of strategy you are developing, you will need each of these in varying degrees. Lastly, in this section we have a chapter with an example of building a monetization strategy.

## Agile Analytics

The next section of the book is dedicated to building your analytical solution and is the largest section of the book. This section has several components, including Data Development, Guided Analytics, User Interface (UI), User Design (UX), Decision Theory, and Data Science. In this section you build your analytical solution informed by the requirements from decision analysis and monetization strategies.

Guided Analytics is a combination of disciplines that include Dashboard Development and User Interface development. These chapters cover the importance of UI/UX and the role it plays in making your solution user friendly.

This section also covers data development and building analytical structures to support your solution and deliver performance. Lastly, in this section we cover decision theory and data science. These chapters provide a base understanding of the tools you can leverage in each of these disciplines and how to deploy them in your solution.

## Enablement

The final section of the book covers topics on the enablement of the solution and the analytical organization. We start this section by covering the iterative development process and inclusion of end users in the effort to build the final product. This section then goes on to address several key questions: How should you roll out the solution? What type of team will you need to stand up in order to develop these solutions for your organization? What types of skillsets are needed? How should it be governed? What type of mindset should the team and organization have to be successful? As you develop your team, this chapter serves as your guide for the various disciplines needed.

## Case Study

Finally, we bring all of the methods together to look at a case study on Michael Andrews Bespoke, a custom tailor headquartered out of New York City. Through this case study, we show how the techniques we present in this book help the company build engagement and retention monetization strategies to drive revenue. This real-world example brings many of the techniques to life and provides a great reference for you as your build out your analytical solutions.

## Let's Start

Let's start our journey together. By going through each of the chapters you will develop the knowledge to drive significant revenue for your organization. We have been building analytical solutions for over 20 years, helping organizations monetize their information. We hope by sharing our insights and collective wisdom, you will be able to build world-class analytical solutions that help your organization drive a significant amount of revenue and become a better competitor.

We have a companion website, www.monetizingyourdata.com, to continue the dialog with you during and after you read this book. We have exercises to help drive home the concepts along with additional tools, templates, and methods. Visit us and utilize one of our existing tools or post a best practice of your own.

# 2

# Analytical Cycle: *Driving Quality Decisions*

... having troves of data is of little value in and of itself. What increasingly separates the winners from the losers is the ability to transform data into insights about consumers' motivations and to turn those insights into strategy.

This quote is from Frank van den Driest, Stan Sthanunathan, and Keith Weed's article, "Building an Insights Engine." Later on in the same article, they continue with,

Until recently, large firms had an advantage over smaller rivals simply because of the scale of their market research capability. Today research that once took months and cost millions can be done for a fraction of that price and in mere days. What matters now is not so much the quantity of data a firm can amass but its ability to connect the dots and extract value from the information.

Both of these concepts are vital to this chapter and this book. The problem they are referring to is a gap that exists between our ability to define what is relevant information and how to monetize it. We show you how to close this gap through our Analytical Cycle, the focus of this chapter, and Decision Architecture, a methodology comprising Decision Analysis, Agile Analytics, and Monetization Strategy.

The Analytical Cycle provides you with a frame of reference on how to solve analytical problems. The journey starts with the business problem statement and questions you ask yourself as you try to understand how to create an opportunity to monetize. Next, we discuss diagnostics, which is the problem solving that occurs as you look for decisions to make to capture the opportunity. Lastly, we focus on making our solution actionable and measuring our results. This process is enabled through data and informed by the user of the information and the analytical maturity of the organization. Let's start with an overview of the Analytical Cycle.

## Analytical Cycle Overview

As we mentioned in Chapter 1, decisions are often impeded by our personal biases and noise. To raise the level and quality of your decisions, it makes sense to empower your managers with the collective wisdom (best practices) of the organization and provide diagnostic tools with algorithms to make better decisions. When we rely on managers to learn on the job and develop a "gut" instinct for the decisions through learned experiences, we expose ourselves to many traps such as cognitive bias. There is an abundance of evidence that supports this statement and points to the need for a fact-based decision process powered by analytics.

An example of this is from one of the most famous individuals in history, Sir Isaac Newton. In the early eighteenth century, the South Sea Company was granted a monopoly on trade in the South Seas in exchange for assuming England's war debt. The idea that the company had a monopoly was of obvious appeal to investors and the company's stock began a six-month explosive run. Newton got into the investment early and saw his stock nearly double, at which point he decided to exit with a nice return. The stock continued to climb and Newton, feeling that he was missing out while his friends were getting rich, decided to reenter the investment at astronomical prices only to lose the bulk of his life savings. This prompted him to say famously, "I can calculate the movement of stars, but not the madness of men."

Making decisions based on gut feel, intuition, or emotion leaves you vulnerable to the cognitive biases we all carry around with us. In the case of Newton, it was an emotional decision based on the fear of missing out while his friends got rich. In the Decision Theory chapter (Chapter 8), we cover a full range of biases that you need to be aware of as you build out your analytical solutions. For now, let's look at an approach to making quality decisions.

Making a quality decision is harder than ever before. We are flooded with information and are expected to synthesize this information into quality decisions in order to drive results. The first step on our path to utilizing this information is to distill it into what is accurate and relevant for our organization and job function. Once we have more accurate and relevant information, the next step is to diagnose or spot an opportunity in order to make a quality decision. With a better *decision*, we get higher quality actions that we can execute on to capitalize on an opportunity. The higher quality *actions*, the better our results and measurements. We are able to take these *measurements* as information to inform our next decision, and the cycle continues. Figure 2.1 depicts this concept.

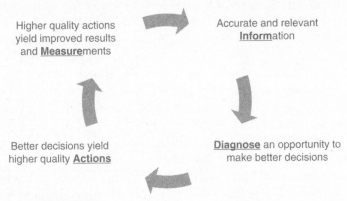

Higher quality actions yield improved results and **Measure**ments

Accurate and relevant **Inform**ation

Better decisions yield higher quality **Actions**

**Diagnose** an opportunity to make better decisions

**Figure 2.1    Analytical Cycle**

We refer to this virtuous cycle as the Analytical Cycle, which is broken down into four components: Inform > Diagnose > Action > Measure. The foundation for the entire process is *data*, and we should probably stress, quality data. Figure 2.2 is an abstracted version of the Analytical Cycle.

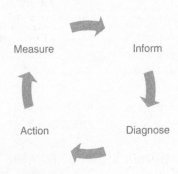

Measure

Inform

Action

Diagnose

**Figure 2.2    Analytical Cycle in the Abstract**

This analytical cycle is structured very similarly to that of a doctor or scientist trying to diagnose an issue. Let's look at a hypothetical example. A patient walks into the doctor's office and the doctor is trying to diagnose a course of treatment based on verbal and visual information provided by the patient.

In Figure 2.3, the first step is for the doctor to take the patient's vitals and then proceed with a set of questions to narrow down the potential issue. We see that the patient has a rash and the doctor is going through a set of Inform questions to determine the potential cause of the rash. In this case, the doctor was able to get to a root cause in five questions and determine the issue must be associated with a poisonous plant.

| | | Doctor | Patient | |
|---|---|---|---|---|
| | Inform | What are the patient's vitals? | Blood pressure, heart rate, weight all look normal | |
| | | What seems to be the problem? | I have a rash | |
| | | How long have you had the rash? | 2 days | |
| | | Where is the rash located? | On my forearm | Determines issue is probably associated with a poisonous plant |
| | | Where did you get the rash? | In my garden | |
| | Diagnose | Let's look at the rash. | Small red spots | |
| | | Are there blisters? | Yes | Poisonous Plant Diagnostic |
| | | Are rash & blisters severe? | Yes | |
| | | DECISION: What should I treat for? | Poison Ivy | |
| | Action | ⟋ Prescribe a topical steroid, call pharmacist, explain treatment to patient | | |
| | | ⟋ Recommend OTC pain medication if itching is bad | | |
| | | ⟋ Patient follows doctor's instructions for prescribed duration of treatment plan | | |
| | Measure | ⟋ Patient to visually inspect rash and blisters, should see signs of improvement in 2–3 days | | |
| | | ⟋ If rash improves, no follow-up needed | | |
| | | ⟋ If no improvement within 5 days, call doctor for a follow-up visit, may need a more aggressive treatment | | |

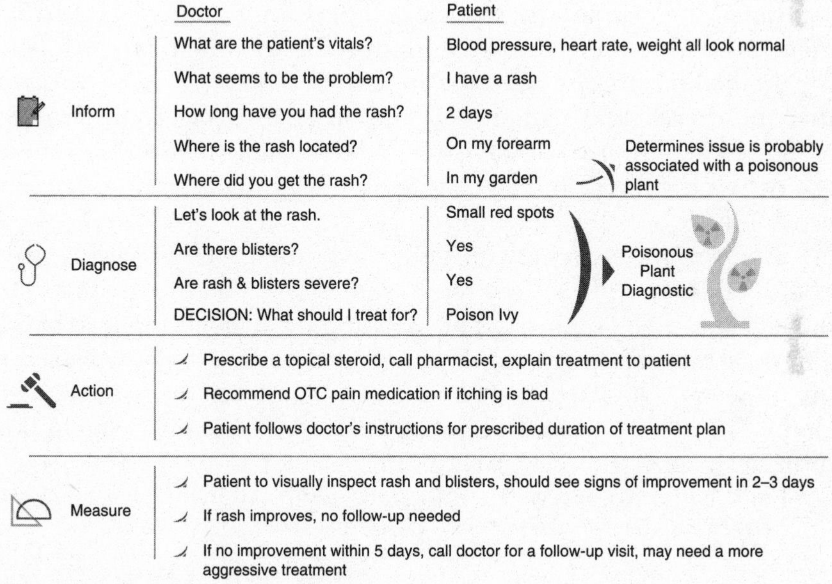

Figure 2.3   The Analytical Cycle in Action

Once the doctor knows the root cause of the issue, the next step is to determine the type and severity of the rash to make a decision on what type of treatment plan. After a visual inspection and a few additional diagnostic questions, the doctor is able to make a decision. From the decision we have an *action*, which in this case is the treatment plan and the patient's application of medication in the prescribed amounts and duration. Finally, to *measure* the results, the patient is to monitor if the rash improves to determine the effectiveness of the treatment plan. If there is no improvement, a return visit will be needed.

We can see from the example that each of the analytical steps helps drive to a better quality decision. The doctor starts with a line of questioning to understand the issue and develops a hypothesis to narrow down the possible types of rashes. This is the Inform stage of the process and is driven by an initial hypothesis and a line of questions that perform a root cause analysis.

Once the doctor narrows the problem down to a poisonous plant, she begins a poisonous plant *diagnostic* to determine the type and severity of the rash in order to make a decision on the type of treatment. Once this information is understood, a treatment is prescribed for the patient. In our case, the treatment plan is the set of *actions* that the doctor and patient will take to resolve the issue. Finally, *measuring* the progress of the issue to determine effectiveness is necessary to see if the rash heals or if a more aggressive treatment plan is needed.

The Analytical Cycle helps guide us in the problem-solving process. By following these four steps with quality data, we enable our managers to make higher quality decisions. The next step is to build analytical solutions on top of this framework to empower the broader organization. Our Decision Architecture methodology in the next chapter picks it up from here to provide a deep dive into each of the individual steps.

Let's drill into each of the four steps of the Analytical Cycle, starting with the spark to the cycle, Inform.

### Inform

Distilling the troves of information that our organizations collect starts with understanding what business problem we are seeking to solve. This is where we start our journey to let the business problem dictate the right information needed.

The Inform stage starts with a business problem statement and one or more hypotheses. The business problem statement should be in alignment to an overarching business objective or goal. Anchoring your hypothesis to a business problem statement creates alignment and focus.

A *hypothesis* is an educated guess or proposition to explain a potential outcome and guide an analysis. Your hypothesis should help solve the business problem statement. To form a hypothesis, take your knowledge of the business environment, market cycles, industry knowledge, current issues, and specific area of expertise to generate a set of statements you believe will solve the business problem. Your hypothesis guides the focus of your investigation. The more specific you can be with your hypothesis, the greater the direction you will provide the analysis.

Let's review an example. We have a Business Problem Statement to "grow revenue by 10 percent while focusing on our best customers" and want a few candidate hypotheses. Below are a few potentials:

*Hypothesis 1*—If we can target marketing activities focused on segmented outlets likely to purchase the "organic/green retail" product, then we can achieve a 5% lift.

*Hypothesis 2*—If we sell in our new innovated product line "strength and flexible" to the industrial trash container segment with a small price increase, then we can achieve a $10 million increase in revenue over the next 12 months.

*Hypothesis 3*—If we attrit poor customers that are unprofitable, we can save $5 million in costs.

The Inform stage starts with a hypothesis or question to ignite the analytical process. The next step in this stage is focused on asking questions to drive to a root cause to perform a diagnostic. These questions lead us to understand what is the core opportunity or issue we will use to develop our action plan. The questions asked during this stage also help us determine what datasets are needed to support the questions. This can come from existing reporting systems that are in place, onetime ad-hoc analysis, or new analytic environments to be developed.

For example, let's see what questions we have for Hypothesis 1:

*Initial Analysis:* The initial analysis gives us a market size for trash bags of $5 billion. Our current market share is $850 million or 17 percent. We have 10 different products, package, pricing variations that we leverage based on store type and format, large store versus small store versus specialty store.

**Inform Questions/Answers:**
- What are the top five most profitable product segments?
  - Industrial—Heavy Duty
  - Industrial—Small Bags
  - Office
  - Home Kitchen
  - Recycling/Composting
- What is our market share in each of those product segments?
  - Industrial—Heavy Duty—12%
  - Industrial—Small Bags—9%
  - Office—22%
  - Home Kitchen—16%
  - Home Recycling/Composting—29%
- What are the three fastest growing product segments and their respective growth rates?
  - Office—12%
  - Home Kitchen—16%
  - Home Recycling/Composting—32%
- What are the average profit margins for each of these product segments?
  - Office—40%
  - Home Kitchen—36%
  - Home Recycling/Composting—45%

As we can see, after about the fourth question, we start to narrow down a potential opportunity to help solve our hypothesis. The goal is to get to a probable root cause. At this point we can begin to develop a plan as we further diagnose the opportunity. From our example, we see that the Home Recycling/Composting segment is one of the fastest growing segments that also has the highest margins. We may want to focus our energy for our diagnostic on how we can improve this segment.

## Diagnose

Merriam-Webster defines *diagnosis* as "investigation or analysis of the cause or nature of a condition, situation, or problem." The intent of the diagnostic stage is to finalize the root cause analysis and make a decision on a course of action. Where the Inform stage is the filtering of information to drive to an issue or opportunity, the Diagnose stage takes the issue or opportunity and adds specificity to it along with a course of action to make a quality decision.

The Diagnose stage is where managers will spend their time analyzing and diagnosing opportunities or issues that translate into actions. They bring the actions to life through detailed analysis of information, usually driven by specific metrics that guide their analysis.

Let's take a look at our example from the last section and how it relates to the Diagnose stage. In our prior example we determine that the Home Recycling/Composting segment is an attractive segment to pursue as it has high margins and a high growth rate.

In the diagnostic stage we want to understand trends, forecasts, correlations, opportunity, and metrics that are more specific to the diagnostic. In this case we are going to perform a *product diagnostic* based on price and package combinations in the Home Recycling/ Composting segment (Tables 2.1–2.4).

### Diagnostic Questions/Answers
- What are the Package Price Combinations in the Home Recycling/Composting product segment?
  - Tall Kitchen Compostable Bags—45 count ($8.89)
  - Recycling Tall Kitchen Drawstring Clear Bags—45 count ($8.49)
  - Recycling Large Trash Drawstring Blue Bags—45 count ($14.99)
- What is our Competitor Pricing for each of these product lines?

Table 2.1  Competitor Pricing

|  | Competitor A | Competitor B | Our Price |
|---|---|---|---|
| Tall Kitchen Compostable Bags | $8.45 | $9.50 | $8.89 |
| Recycling Tall Kitchen Drawstring Clear Bags | $8.07 | $9.15 | $8.49 |
| Recycling Large Trash Drawstring Blue Bags | $11.52 | $15.68 | $14.99 |

- What has been the order volume trend for each of the products in the Home Recycling/Composting product segment for the last six months?

**Table 2.2    Order Volume Trend**

|  | Month 1 | Month 2 | Month 3 | Month 4 | Month 5 | Month 6 |
|---|---|---|---|---|---|---|
| Tall Kitchen Compostable Bags | 11,091 | 12,099 | 11,441 | 11,789 | 11,273 | 11,804 |
| Recycling Tall Kitchen Drawstring Clear Bags | 5,928 | 6,003 | 6,189 | 6,224 | 6,431 | 6,577 |
| Recycling Large Trash Drawstring Blue Bags | 4,334 | 4,729 | 5,035 | 5,632 | 6,101 | 6,871 |

- What do the next 90 days look like for our Order Pipeline to Forecast and Budget for the Recycling Large Trash Drawstring Blue Bags product line?

**Table 2.3    Order Pipeline to Forecast**

| Recycling Large Trash Drawstring Blue Bags | 0–30 days | 31–60 days | 61–90 days |
|---|---|---|---|
| Orders on Books | 7,896 | 5,199 | 3,388 |
| Forecast | 7,536 | 8,265 | 9,065 |
| Budget | 5,000 | 5,250 | 5,512 |

- If we want to target a marketing campaign focused on the purchase of Recycling Large Trash Drawstring Blue Bags with a $.50-off instore coupon for a total purchase price of $14.49 ($14.99 minus $.50) to create awareness in underperforming outlets, what is the total opportunity by outlet type?

**Table 2.4    Total Opportunity by Outlet Type**

| Outlet Type | Number of Stores | Current Penetration | Product Profit by Outlet Type | Opportunity Potential | Ability to Achieve |
|---|---|---|---|---|---|
| Large Grocery Store | 38,000 | 28,553 | $5.79 | $54,698.13 | Med |
| Convenience Retail | 64,500 | 5,211 | $6.75 | $400,200.75 | Low |
| Large Retail | 11,200 | 9,837 | $5.07 | $6,910.41 | Low |
| Organic Specialty Stores | 24,000 | 3,027 | $7.97 | $167,154.81 | High |

As you can see, the Diagnose stage has a different flavor than the Inform stage. In the Inform stage we filter information to get to a potential opportunity. In the Diagnose stage, we ask questions to solve for specifics around the opportunity in order to take action.

In the first part of the diagnostic we review Package Price combinations and how they compare to our competition. Next we want to know historical volume information for the past six months and forecast volume for the next three months. This analysis gave us an understanding of what products are growing the fastest. In addition, it tells us if the growth is a onetime occurrence or a trend that we believe will continue.

In our final analysis we look at the market share for the Recycling Large Trash Drawstring Blue Bags product line along Outlet Types. We are able to perform an opportunity analysis from this based on profitability and market potential. In addition, we rate each of the outlet types in terms of ability to achieve the opportunity amount based on type of channel and market share. Based on our diagnostic, we are ready to make a decision to focus on Organic Specialty Stores with a marketing campaign and sales force sell-in initiative.

The diagnostic process is enabled through decision analysis, data science, and decision theory. In this example, our Decision Analyses are the questions and thought processes that lead us to an opportunity. We leverage a decision matrix from the Decision Theory discipline to structure the analysis to determine which decision to make. Finally, we utilize Data Science to provide a confidence factor in our ability to achieve the results. We cover more on these topics in future chapters.

## Action

The Action stage is about execution. Based on the *action levers* we develop in the Diagnose stage, it is time to execute in the marketplace. The ability to execute may vary depending on the type of action. If the action is to develop a pricing strategy, it might involve getting organizational buy-in at many levels and departments before you are able to act. If the action is developing marketing collateral, you may need to work with your marketing department. These dependencies with other departments in your organization are an important consideration. If your actions are too complex to commercialize, they have a low chance of succeeding.

When developing your actions, it is important to consider how to measure each action. Some actions are measured by simply executing on the activity. Others need the ability to correlate a response from a customer back to the particular action. For example, a coupon code on a marketing piece that has a specific marketing ID associated with it enables us to tie it back to a specific action.

In our example, the action is associated with the decision to generate marketing campaigns for the Organic Specialty Stores. At this point, our analysis may be complete as we have provided direction to the marketing department on a focused campaign strategy. We may also choose to take the next steps in our solution and provide marketing initiatives tied to the campaign.

### Measure

Measuring is often the hardest step in the Analytical Cycle. Often, the time from analysis to measure is months, if not years, apart, making continuity difficult as people shift jobs, organizational changes occur, or business interests change. When the timelines are closer together, measurement gets easier as long as the action and the intent are recorded. There are two methods for measuring an action: *direct* or *inferred responses.*

A direct measurement is a link back to the original action. This can be from code on a webpage that links back to a marketing email showing a click-through occurred. The code is usually parsed with specific information that links back to any number of items that can include specific action type, date, category, and/or marketing campaign.

An inferred measurement is what the name implies; you do not have a direct link and need to infer that the sale was linked back to a specific action. This is much more common and also much more prone to error or interpretation.

An example of an inferred response would be reviewing sales of a specific product for up to six weeks after an action has been taken to see if there was a spike in sales. To be more specific in the example, if we choose to increase prices on a product, we want to measure the post-six-week time period to see if we sold more or less of that product with the new pricing structure. While we can't directly link a sale back to a particular action via a code, we can infer that the amount of sales is a result, for better or worse, from the price increase.

Measurement also gives us the lessons learned from the action to understand what is or is not working. This helps us when we develop our next set of hypotheses in the Inform stage. To extend our example, if we increase our price and it did not have any effect on the sales volume during that time, then we have a successful hypothesis. We are able to generate more money by increasing the price and not lose customers. This may lead to a hypothesis that the demographics in that outlet has shifted and other products may be ripe for price increases or new upscale product lines might be a better fit. These insights would start the analytical cycle over again.

### Data

Data is at the heart of the Analytical Cycle. There are many facets to data, some of which include the quality of the data, ability to find relevant data, ability to stitch data together, knowing where to find the data, and internal versus external data.

The quality of the data, in our opinion, is one of the most important factors. It is the one component that either severely hinders or enables the analytical process. Without quality data that is meaningful to the business, you have tremendous difficulty driving insights.

The ability to quickly link relevant information together is another important factor. Information often sits in the various siloed data islands throughout the organization. One system may contain financial forecast information, the company enterprise data warehouse may contain sales transaction information, and a marketing database may contain customer segmentation information. Our ability to find and stitch these together drives what capabilities we can bring to the analytical solution.

This point is further validated in the article, "Building an Insights Engine," in which the authors discuss the results of an i2020 research study. The article points to the results in which certain firms have built the capability to amass large amounts of information quickly in order to make quality decisions.

> This capability differentiates successful organizations from less successful ones: According to the i2020 research, 67% of the executives at overperforming firms (those that outpaced competitors in revenue growth) said that their company was skilled at linking disparate data sources, whereas only 34% of the executives at underperformers made the same claim.

Another key component is finding the right individuals who can provide business context to the data. If your organization has a good master data program, this might be an easier task. In most organizations, individuals often have to relearn the business rules applied to certain data sets or find subject matter experts with tribal knowledge.

Lastly, various types of data can provide a competitive advantage. This might mean internal data or external data to drive specific insights. For example, in the same article, "Building an Insights Engine," the author discusses an insights group called CMI at Unilever who leverage social information to solve a stockout problem.

> CMI's approach to data gathering and analysis is often technology-intensive. For example, while monitoring Twitter chatter in response to a Ben & Jerry's "free cone" promotion, a CMI team noticed a strong relationship between chatter and sales increases in most regions—but not all. A real-time analysis of the slow spots revealed that stockouts there were inhibiting sales, allowing Unilever to head off similar problems with future promotions.

Once you have the right data, your analysis can take life. In the chapter on Data Development (Chapter 10), we cover additional concerns, including the concepts of *data quality, data transformation,* and *data structure.*

## Hierarchy of Information User

Another key concept when building an analytical solution is to know your user. Tailoring the analytics and diagnostics to the right user group is important. Imagine giving an executive an operational report that shows line item detail of purchases for a particular store in a particular city, when what the executive really wants is a summary of sales across regions. Please see Figure 2.4 for the level of detail that the various information users desire.

For an executive user, high-level metrics, aggregations, and alerts are probably more interesting. These can be displayed in a executive dashboarding format that allows the executive to easily interpret information to figure out if there are any major issues or

High level

Level of Information Detail

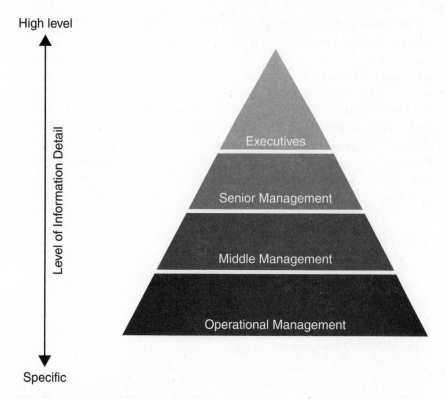

Executives

Senior Management

Middle Management

Operational Management

Specific

**Figure 2.4    Hierarchy of the Information User**

opportunities. They may look for answers such as what products are performing well or what markets are underperforming.

For senior management, a dashboard may be the first place they start before drilling into the next level of information to gain an understanding of divisional, product, channel, or geographic issues. They may choose to drill deeper, but rarely at an operational level.

Middle managers, which would also include analysts, spend the bulk of their time in the data trying to understand how their division or product is doing and developing insights for action. The ability to translate an insight into action is best understood by the group that lives with the process, operation, or data on a day-to-day basis.

Operational managers are usually less interested in the high-level dashboard view and more interested in operational-level reports that will assist them with decisions in their day-to-day jobs. These might be decisions such as product replenishment, labor schedules, and detailed product sales figures.

Knowing your user helps you determine the right level of information and decisions to include in your analytical solution.

## Next Steps

We are excited to start our journey together with the Analytical Cycle as backdrop for your monetization strategy. Over the next couple of chapters, we will go deep into the Decision Architecture methodology, Guided Analytics, and Monetization Strategy that will provide a step-by-step approach to building your analytical solution.

The important points to remember from this chapter are the four stages of the analytical cycle:

1. Inform
2. Diagnose
3. Action
4. Measure

The stages are enabled through quality data. We can enhance our analytical solution by working with a variety of data sets that improve our decisions. In addition, we also need to be aware of our audience and the level of detail the information consumer will require.

For additional tools, templates, examples, and workbooks, please visit us at www.monetizingyourdata.com.

CHAPTER

# 3

# Decision Architecture Methodology:
## *Closing the Gap*

One approach that gets inconsistent results, for instance, is simple data mining. Corralling huge data sets allows companies to run dozens of statistical tests to identify submerged patterns, but that provides little benefit if managers can't effectively use the correlations to enhance business performance. A pure data-mining approach often leads to an endless search for what the data really say.

This quote from the *Harvard Business Review* article, "Making Advanced Analytics Work for You," by Dominic Barton and David Court, sums up one of the biggest challenges that exist in analytics today: organizations are throwing data at the problem hoping to find a solution versus understanding the business problem and aligning the right data and methods to it. The premise of this book addresses this shortcoming and we focus on the importance of connecting data to decisions in order to truly monetize the wealth of business data accessible.

The Decision Architecture methodology laid out in this chapter helps you make practical use of the waves of information flooding your desktop. The methodology provides a framework to translate the business problem into hypotheses, questions, decisions, action levers, metrics, and data needed to build an analytical solution tied to a monetization strategy. The monetization strategy is a major component to the overall methodology and has its own dedicated section.

The frameworks, techniques, and tools in the Decision Architecture methodology are similar to Lego™ pieces you can select to assemble the analytical solution appropriate to the problem or opportunity at hand. Putting the Lego pieces together is a complex task, not always occurring in a straight line; accordingly we have found that an iterative approach delivers the best solutions. As you build your analytical solution, you should expect to iterate through components of the methodology several times.

Your solution may vary in the level of automation, from an spreadsheet to a fully automated solution. The degree of automation that will work for your case depends on the desired repeatability and scale of deployment. As each of these steps in the methodology are repeated, templates and tools can be built, accelerating the process for subsequent projects.

In this chapter we describe how the Lego pieces fit together in the Decision Architecture methodology. This book pivots around three core concepts—Decision Analysis, Agile Analytics, and Monetization Strategy; accordingly in this chapter we provide an overview of the Decision Architecture methodology that encompasses the three concepts.

## Methodology Overview

The Analytical Cycle, from the previous chapter, guides us in the problem-solving process (Figure 3.1). Cycling through the Inform,

Measure    Inform

Action    Diagnose

**Figure 3.1    The Analytical Cycle**

Diagnose, Action, and Measure steps, supported by quality data at each step, empowers managers and analysts to make better-quality decisions.

To build solutions that empower the analytical cycle, we developed the Decision Architecture methodology. The five phases include: Discovery, Decision Analysis, Monetization Strategy, Agile Analytics, and Enablement. Since the majority of the phases are iterative in nature, you may find yourself cycling through them several times during the life of the project. Additionally, you will notice in the Decision Analysis phase we spend significant energy capturing requirements centered on each step in the Analytical Cycle (see Figure 3.2).

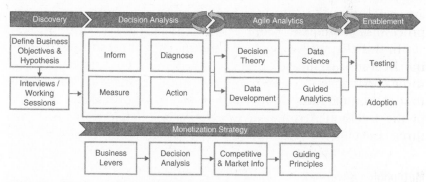

**Figure 3.2    High-Level Decision Architecture Methodology**

Our approach is novel because we integrate several traditionally siloed disciplines into a continuous process comprising Decision Theory, Decision Analysis, Data Science, Data Development, Monetization Strategy, Dashboard Development, and UI and UX Development. We have found integrating these disciplines into a common methodology delivers superior results when building analytical solutions that monetize data.

Your final solutions may have varying degrees of automation. On one end of the spectrum, your solution may be a spreadsheet with a well-formed decision matrix and monetization strategies that produce clear decisions for a manager or analyst. The other end of the spectrum might include a fully automated application with embedded analytics driving automated actions. A few suggestions for you to consider when you think about the appropriate degree of automation to implement for your organization:

- **Quick Wins**—We are a big fan of getting something in people's hands sooner rather than later. Small, quick wins are far better than a big-bang approach. Iterate your way through the solution and get tons of feedback as you go.
- **Results**—As you are developing your solution, get early reads on whether the results align back to the original hypothesis and are impactful enough to continue. If the end result delivers only a meager improvement in performance, it may not be worth the cost and organizational energy to move forward.
- **Repeatability**—Is this a one-off exercise or is it something that can be repeated many times by various groups and users? In order to automate, your solution should have a high degree of repeatability.
- **Scalability**—The solution needs to be scalable to many users. Does the solution focus on two or three individuals or 20–30 or 200–300? You will generally want a larger base of potential users for the automation to be worth the costs. However, if the solution is impactful enough to the organization in driving revenue, it may make sense to automate even for only two or three people.
- **Technology Footprint**—Depending on the technology footprint of your organization, there can be many paths to automation, such as through an enterprise business reporting platform, an embedded analytical solution in your Enterprise Resource Planning (ERP) system, or a highly flexible data visualization tool like Tableau.
- **Data Plumbing**—If you have to patch the data together with duct tape and bubble gum, it might not be a candidate for a high degree of automation. If the data sources are delivered through repeatable or automated processes and the quality of the data is high, then it may be a good candidate.

We also want to emphasize the iterative nature of the analytical exercise. You will find yourself going back and forth between the phases as you iterate through development of your analytical solution. We often find ourselves starting with a metric that drives a decision in the Decision Analysis phase and by the time we get to the Agile Analytics phase we may determine that some of the data does not exist or the quality of the data is so poor we cannot use it. At this point, we will iterate through Decision Analysis again to find relevant information that is actionable and supported by quality data. There are several disciplines in play and the dance between them causes rework as each discipline continues to refine their part of the solution.

A high-level overview of each of the phases may be in order before we go too deep into the specific areas. Let's begin with the Discovery phase. The Discovery phase starts with aligning your project goals to organizational objectives to ensure alignment. Next we identify the business priority, which may be a problem or opportunity. From our business priority we develop one or more hypotheses we believe articulate the priority in an actionable manner. Once we know what we are looking to address, we conduct interviews and working sessions to ramp up on the subject matter, understand existing systems, and fine tune the hypothesis and scope.

Decision Analysis, the next phase, is designed to capture questions, key decisions, action levers, metrics, data needs, and a category tree. We leverage specific facilitation techniques in working sessions designed around topics and compile this information into the various Decision Analysis components. This information drives the building of *category trees, key decisions, action levers,* and *success metrics,* providing requirements for the Agile Analytics and Monetization Strategy phases.

During the Decision Analysis and Agile Analytics phases, you build and refine your monetization strategy. In this phase you develop specific strategies, identify business levers, and assign actions from the earlier phases to deploy to drive revenue or reduce costs.

The Agile Analytics phase encompasses building a solution from the requirements gathered in the Decision Analysis and Monetization Strategy phases. This phase is composed of several process steps: Data Development, Analytical Structure, Decision Theory, Data Science, and Guided Analytics. These components may vary in size and length depending on the level of automation and technology.

Finally, in the Enablement phase, once a solution has been developed, it is rolled out to the user base. Adoption, a key theme in this phase, only occurs if adequate testing and training have been successfully conducted.

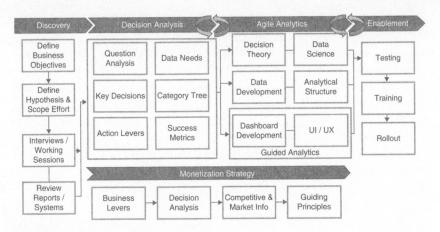

**Figure 3.3 Decision Architecture Methodology**

Figure 3.3 lays out the complete methodology. We describe each of the process steps in detail in the following sections and chapters but first let's go through a high-level overview of the primary phases.

## Discovery

The Discovery phase starts with defining business objectives and aligning these to corporate goals. For example, the objective may be to "Grow Revenue by 10% through marketing activities focused on the Millennial generation." If the end analytical solution does not align to the company's objectives and goals, you may want to question whether the project is worth doing.

Once you know your business objective, it is time to define the hypothesis and scope the overall effort, a necessity in any analytics project. Your goal is to confirm or reshape the hypothesis from your learnings as you progress through the project. An example hypothesis is that by combining social media data with our existing customer data, we can drive more relevant and targeted marketing activities, achieving an 10 percent lift in our Millennial Segment credit card campaigns.

In order to develop a monetization strategy, anticipating the business levers that will drive your strategy is important. It will impact the development of your hypothesis and the levers that should align to your actions. Our chapter on Monetization Strategy (Chapter 5) introduces the *business lever* concept and provides more information on the topic.

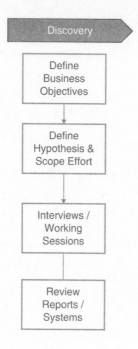

**Figure 3.4    Discovery Phase**

Figure 3.4 is a visual of the steps within the Discovery phase.

Along with developing a hypothesis, we need to scope the effort. In the Scoping process step we develop our project plan, project charter, and scoping document. The project plan should include scope, schedule, budget, and project team. The schedule provides an overall timeline for completing various phases in the project. While the process is agile in nature, some stakes should be driven into the ground to help with prioritization and to push the team toward a completion date knowing that they will learn and adjust along the way.

The next process step is the Interviews and Working Sessions step. To complete our discovery of the possible solutions paths, we conduct interviews and working sessions to get an understanding of the current state. What are the existing processes, business practices, and business rules? Do they leverage data science and in what capacity? What data do they normally use? The answers to these questions help us narrow our scope and get the team up to speed on the particular subject matter.

The final process step in the Discovery phase is to Review Reports and Systems. In this step we review each of the existing reports and the various information systems to gain an understanding of the current state of the analytics in use. This step helps us understand what data is currently available and the capabilities that currently exist.

Each of the components in the Discovery Phase feeds our Decision Analysis phase, which is where we explore and document the details of the decision process.

## Decision Analysis

We cover the Decision Analysis phase in depth in the Decision Analysis chapter (Chapter 4), but present here a high-level review of the information so you can see how everything fits together. This phase maps to our Analytical Cycle: Inform, Diagnose, Action, and Measure. In this phase there are six process steps: Data Needs, Category Tree, Question Analysis, Key Decisions, Action Levers, and Success Metrics. Figure 3.5 is a visual of how the four stages in the Analytical Cycle map to the six process steps in Decision Analysis.

In the Discovery phase we uncover a rich background of information that enables us to execute focused interviews and working

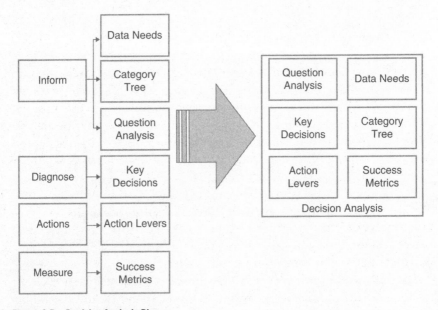

Figure 3.5   Decision Analysis Phase

sessions in the Decision Analysis phase. The Inform process step determines the questions that the manager asks when considering a problem. The output of this step, the Question Analysis, points us to the data and data sources needed to support the analytic effort. In addition, in this process step we produce the Category Tree, a diagram outlining the various information and diagnostic categories. We view the nodes in the Category Tree as groupings of like information such as sales performance or a particular diagnostic like call center performance.

If we go back to our doctor's example from the prior chapter, also repeated later, the Inform section covers the questions that help us get to the root cause of the issue. Once we get to a narrow enough understanding of the issue, the questions then turn to more of a Diagnostic exercise. We can see that the initial questions in the Inform section help us narrow down what is wrong with the patient so we get to a final diagnosis and treatment plan (Figure 3.6).

The Diagnose stage in the Analytical Cycle focuses on questions associated with the root-cause issue and determines the final diagnosis that enables a quality decision. The decisions that someone takes during this process step are important to uncover and

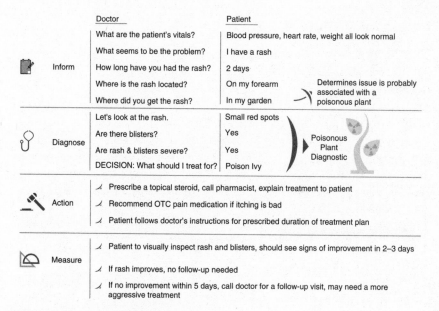

**Figure 3.6    The Analytical Cycle in Action**

are captured through Key Decisions. For example, once the doctor determines that the rash has something to do with a poisonous plant, she then goes into a diagnostic about poisonous plants to determine severity and treatment plan. Once the doctor narrows down the probable cause of the rash to poison ivy and the severity of the rash, she knows what decision to make.

The Action stage in the analytical cycle takes the Key Decisions and maps Action Levers to each of them. These Action Levers are specific initiatives that you can take to capture an opportunity or resolve an issue. This step also ensures that our Success Metrics are actionable. In the doctor example, we see the action is to prescribe medication and explain the treatment plan to the patient. It is important in this step for the patient to agree with the diagnosis and fully understand the treatment plan. By taking this final step, we can have a higher confidence that the plan will be acted on.

Lastly, the Measure stage of the analytical cycle captures the success metrics that help drive our decisions and measures our outcomes. From our example, the Measure stage determines if the treatment plan is effective. If it is effective, there is nothing more to do. If the treatment is not effective, the patient will need to go back to the doctor to get a more aggressive treatment.

## Monetization Strategy

The Monetization Strategy phase runs concurrent with Decision Analysis and Agile Analytics phases and employs data science and decision theory to structure the actions that guide you to the best decision. We utilize the requirements from our Decision Analysis to formulate our strategy. This phase has four process steps: Business Levers, Decision Analysis, Competitive and Market Information, and Guiding Principles (see Figure 3.7). It is important to apply an economic benefit to an action which enables someone to make a more informed decision. We devote an entire section to this topic

**Figure 3.7   Monetization Strategy Phase**

later in the book and provide a framework and case study to help you adopt these concepts.

## Agile Analytics

The Agile Analytics phase has five components: Data Development, Analytical Structure, Decision Theory, Data Science, and Guided Analytics (see Figure 3.8). Each of these components interlink with each other during the development phase. For example, as data is sourced and integrated, it is provided to the Data Science team to analyze and discover correlations and thresholds. After reviewing the data, the data scientist may need additional data, which in turn involves Data Development work. This interplay between the process steps occurs often through the life of the project.

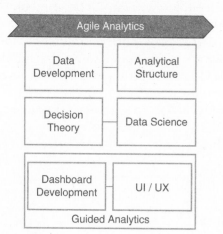

**Figure 3.8    Agile Analytics Phase**

Let's review the components of the Agile Analytics phase:

### Data Development/Analytical Structures

The Data Development and Analytical Structures process steps involve the preparation of a dataset that can be used for analytics. The data process step starts with the data sources identified in the Inform and Diagnose process steps along with the metrics, business rules, transformations, and calculations. At this point, your job becomes sourcing and transforming quality data to answer the questions and decisions you have identified. Some of this data may come from within the walls of the company; other data you may need to purchase to round out the picture.

Extracting data may involve various source systems, internally and externally, and is often one of the most complicated steps. Once you have extracted the necessary data, you need to stitch it together into an Analytical Structure via some type of key value relationship between the datasets regardless of whether the data is structured or unstructured.

Ensuring the data correctly represents the subject of analysis is critical; as the saying goes, "Garbage in, garbage out." You will be hard pressed to derive any meaningful analytics from a poor-quality dataset.

Finally, an analytical structure needs to be developed that encompasses the values, transformations, and aggregations to answer the various questions and decisions. For example, if the doctor wants to build a report to understand the most effective treatment options based on the historical performance of various medications for the treatment of poison ivy, she may have to combine several datasets. First she looks at patient records and then combines them with efficacy data for each of the medications. The ability to combine both datasets, the quality of the data, and the structuring of the data for analysis is the focus for this process step.

The Data Development process step drives the Data Science and Guided Analytics process steps. Without a solid dataset to analyze, you cannot perform the Data Science process step. Likewise, without the right analytical structure, dashboard development is not possible.

We will go into depth on this process in the Data Development chapter.

### Data Science/Decision Theory

The Data Science and Decision Theory process steps help you find insights and then structure the insights into a decision process to drive the best actions for the company.

The Data Science process step comprises descriptive and predictive analytics techniques. The inputs into this process step are the Data Development process step and requirements from the Decision Analysis phase, which include the Question Analysis, Key

Decisions, Action Levers, and Success Metrics process steps. With further analysis of our metrics, informed by our Question Analysis, we can specify particular Data Science studies we want to perform to further develop the solution.

For example, having identified a particular metric that drives a decision, we will want to establish thresholding for the metric to determine when it has hit a boundary. This boundary serves as a signal that there may be an opportunity or issue. To continue with our poison ivy example, our doctor wants to know the threshold for blister sizes and treatment options. When the blisters reach over a certain threshold, she knows a more aggressive treatment is needed. If the blisters are within range or below, it might warrant a less aggressive treatment. This is a perfect exercise for a data scientist and we cover this in greater detail in the Data Science chapter (Chapter 9).

Whereas data science helps you turn information into insights that are actionable, we need tools that help us structure the decision process to guide a person to the correct decision. Decision Theory, along with Behavioral Economics, focuses on understanding the components of the decision process to explain why we make the choices we do. It also provides a systematic way to consider tradeoffs among attributes that helps us make a better decision. There are several tools and techniques in the Decision Theory chapter (Chapter 8) that help you structure your analytical solution.

### Guided Analytics

Guided Analytics is the process you use to take your users through the analytical journey to make effective decisions. Guided Analytics depends on a solid foundation of User Interface (UI)/User Experience (UX) and Dashboard Development. We discuss these concepts in depth in the Agile Analytics section.

For now, let's give an overview of some of the key concepts as well as describe two experiences, one unguided and one guided.

> **Unguided**—This is the state most analytical solutions are in today. For now, let's assume that we have a report that has been developed that has Sales by Region, Sales by Product, and Sales by Channel. There are pie charts that break out each of

these dimensions to let us know our sales mix. After we view the information, we begin to wonder, How does this information compare with last month? Are we trending up or down? Do we have any opportunities or issues that we need to be aware of? What decisions are we supposed to make from this report? The issue we run into with unguided solutions is that the data on the report is simply informative and does not guide us to an opportunity or issue.

**Guided**—You log onto your dashboard to see how the organization is performing today and over the past year. Your eyes are drawn to the Northeast region as a threshold has been triggered on the metric associated with your Electric Car division sales volume. You click on the metric and are taken to another dashboard to view the metric over a period of time to see if the spike in sales is a onetime occurrence or a trend. You notice that it seems to be a short-term trend that has been in place for the last several months. You also notice that sales have increased to the point where you are having out-of-stock issues, so you then drill down to the sales volume diagnostic. In the diagnostic you are presented several metrics and a decision matrix that has been formulated into a monetization strategy. In the decision matrix you have five decisions presented to you of various opportunities to help close the shortage gap. Each decision has a monetary value and probability score associated with it so you can determine which decision has the highest chance for success to return the largest amount of revenue to the company.

Which of these experiences did you prefer? The first experience simply helps you "read the news." It tells you the current state of things but does not help you tease out any opportunities or issues. Nor does it provide a diagnostic experience to help you weigh alternative decisions based on monetization factors. In the guided experience, you are taken on a journey to uncover an opportunity and several decisions you can make to resolve it.

We hope you learn how to build these guided experiences, or stories, through the techniques in this book and that by doing so you empower your organization to be more competitive and drive revenue.

Storytelling is becoming a bigger movement in analytical circles. This is evidenced in Frank van den Driest, Stan Sthanunathan, and

Keith Weed's *Harvard Business Review* article, "Building an Insights Engine." Below is an excerpt from the article:

> The i2020 research imparts a final lesson about what makes for a strong insights engine: good storytelling. At overperforming firms, 61% of surveyed executives agreed that people in their insights functions were skilled at conveying their messages through engaging narratives; at underperforming firms, only 37% agreed.
>
> At Unilever, CMI has embraced storytelling. Traditionally its presentations were data-intensive, built on the assumption that a fact-filled talk would be more persuasive than a fact-based one with less data and more narrative. Although data has its place, CMI has moved away from charts and tables and toward provocative storytelling, embracing an ethos of "Show, don't tell."

These types of analytical stories are brought to life through UI/UX and analytics elements such as metrics, trends, patterns, diagrams, alerts, and decision matrixes. A big part of the story is how a user engages with the solution, which is done through thoughtful deployment of UI/UX standards. In Tom Davenport's article, "How P&G Presents Data to Decision-Makers," he argues that visual design commonality is more important than creativity. If you establish a common visual standard, it is easier for people to interpret the information. As a user navigates from dashboard to dashboard, they can spend their energy interpreting the data versus learning how to reinterpret the visual cues. These standards and guidelines help create consistent look and feel as well as better overall usability.

UI and UX development is part art and part science and iterative in nature. You will work with your users to see what is meaningful to them and how they interpret information. Next you create the visual elements that help the users answer questions and make decisions to drive actions. For example, what are the thresholds for a particular metric and what color should we choose to help draw the user's eye to an issue or opportunity? An easy-to-use interface that is intuitive and guides a user through the analytic story to a decision promotes usability and, therefore, adoption.

The Guided Analytics solution often deploys a dashboard tool, but not always. The inputs to the process step are the Decision Analysis, UI/UX Development, Data Development, Decision Theory, and Data Science. The Decision Analysis greatly influences the Dashboard Development process step. A major influence is the Category Tree, which maps out the thought process of how a user asks questions to diagnose an issue and then take action through an informed decision. This is your "story" that draws the user to engage with the solution. It is one of the most important components to get right.

Lastly, the Guided Analytics process step is one of the most user-engaged steps in the methodology. Working with the users to cycle through the various options in a dashboard tool and your Decision Analysis is time consuming, but a process that ensures you get it right. We recommend frequent checkpoints with the end user to review progress and adjust accordingly. This level of engagement results in an analytical tool guaranteed to meet user expectations as they have seen the end product evolve and are invested in its success.

## Enablement

The Enablement phase is the last phase in the methodology and can vary in duration (Figure 3.9). It is also iterative in nature between earlier phases. For example, once you get to Testing, you may discover an issue that needs to be addressed in the Dashboard Development process step. You may find yourself repeating through these two steps until all the issues are resolved.

*Continuous improvement,* or the "good-enough" principle, is the recommended guidance during this stage. The solution will never be perfect but rather should be regarded as one that is constantly evolving on the path to perfection. At some point, the analytical solution is good enough to start providing value to the business and should be rolled out. Once rolled out, you can begin to develop the next wave of capabilities on your path to perfection.

Let's review each of the steps in the Enablement phase.

Testing involves each of the analysts/developers testing their components individually and as an integrated group. The testing process is focused on ensuring the functionality is correct, the data and calculations are accurate, and the solution responds as intended. It is the last step for the individual developers to make sure they get their piece of the solution correct before the users test the solution.

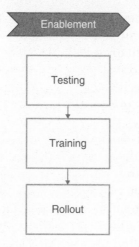

**Figure 3.9 Enablement Phase**

A component of testing is User Acceptance Testing (UAT). This component engages users of the solution to test it to make sure it meets the requirements laid out in Decision Analysis. During this phase the users of the solution are testing overall functionality, accuracy, and performance and finally accepting the solution before it goes live.

The Training process step involves a few activities geared toward helping users understand the solution and generate adoption. Training can involve the building of online, electronic, and paper training materials. These materials help walk a user through the functionality, usability, and often the decisions and actions that should be taken.

Executing on training can involve self-study, in-person, or online training classes. You need a plan with many options to help users absorb the material in a way that best suits them. Tailoring the type of material and delivery medium to the user base helps with the Rollout process step, adoption, and usage.

The Rollout process step is the deployment of the solution to the end users and is the last step in the methodology. After the user base is trained on the solution, you can flip the switch to have them begin using the analytical solution in a production environment. Adoption can often be a big issue and you will need to take special care to engage the user community early and often in the process. In their article, "Making Advanced Analytics Work for You," Dominic Barton and David Court talk about the importance of adoption of an analytical solution:

> Managers must come to view analytics as central to solving problems and identifying opportunities—to make it part of the fabric of daily operations. Efforts will vary depending on a company's goals and desired time line. Adult learners often benefit from a "field and forum" approach, whereby they participate in real-world, analytics-based workplace decisions that allow them to learn by doing.
>
> At one industrial services company, the mission was to get basic analytics tools into the hands of its roughly 200 sales managers. Training began with an in-field assignment to read a brief document and collect basic facts about the market. Next managers met in centralized, collaborative training sessions during which they figured out how to use the tools and market facts to improve sales performance. They then returned to the field to apply what they had learned and, several weeks later, reconvened to review progress, receive coaching, and learn about second-order analysis of their data. This process enabled a four-person team to eventually build capabilities across the entire sales management organization.

Let's review some techniques that can assist you in getting a high adoption level.

- **Coaches**—Typically, an analytical project can be complex; we recommend having coaches in the field to answer questions and ensure usage of the solution. Coaches can be peers or supervisors of the user of the solution. The frequency of coaching can be as often as daily and as far apart as monthly. We encourage a high frequency of touchpoints at the beginning of the rollout process.
- **Performance Management**—Another way to encourage adoption is performance management. If you can tie something in the employee's yearly goals to the solution, that encourages adoption. For example, if you have deployed an analytical solution that helps people solve for the best marketing campaign, you can layer into the person's yearly goals that they

have to find a certain amount of revenue-generating initiatives from the solution.

- **Embed the Process**—Embedding the analytical solution as a step in a broader process helps with adoption. If we know we need to use this tool before we are able to take the next step in the process, it is ingrained in how we work. Take care to ensure that the right handoffs are available in the solution to the next step in the broader process.
- **Create a Community**—Ongoing engagement and continuous improvement help build a user community that is engaged in the features and functionality for subsequent phases. Seek out feedback through newsletters, town halls, and ongoing meetings about the solution. During these meetings, encourage ideas around additional functionality that may be needed, maybe a new analytical function or new dataset that would support a new metric. These new features generate a backlog of work for the next phase and excitement about the expansion of the system.

## Summary

We reviewed a lot of concepts in this chapter. You may have to refer to it often as you build out your solution. Do not feel obligated to use all of the methodology. If your situation does not require Data Science efforts, you can skip that process step. In addition, this is not intended to be a one-size-fits-all methodology and can be tailored to meet your specific needs. For example, you may need approval steps for funding in the Discovery phase or a data governance step for any new metrics created in the Data Development process step.

The book's website (www.monetizingyourdata.com) is a resource for you to review tools, templates, and research articles that might assist you if you are stuck in a given situation. Leverage this site as a community to post information to as well as seek out advice.

# DECISION ANALYSIS

# 4

# Decision Analysis: *Architecting Decisions*

In their 2012 study, Andrew McAfee and Erik Brynjolfsson found that "companies in the top third of their industry in the use of data-driven decision making were, on average, 5% more productive and 6% more profitable than their competitors."

In this book we focus on data-driven decisions over process because we believe it is the anchor point that drives actions. If we focus on process alone, we miss what is truly driving a person's ability to act, which is the ability to make a quality decision. This viewpoint is further elaborated on in Brad Power's article, "Drive Performance by Focusing on Routine Decisions," where he states:

> Process is about action. When we talk about processes, we're talking about everything an organization does in its ongoing operations. And so, it makes sense that in order to improve operational performance, many organizations use process improvement techniques such as process mapping to get a handle on all the actions that make up their process flow.
>
> The problem is, in this explicit focus on process-as-action, organizations overlook a much more powerful process performance lever—day-to-day operational decisions.

Later in the article he quotes Rob Moon:

> The biggest payoff of focusing process improvement on individual decisions and the overall decision architecture is that it engages and empowers workers. As we clarify interdependencies,

ownership, risk tolerances, and the skills we need, we are putting performers at the center of the operation.

In this chapter we introduce the tools and techniques to conduct your Decision Analysis to empower managers with data-driven decisions. The Lego pieces you choose to bring together may vary depending on the business problem and type of analytics. At the heart of this phase in the methodology are six components: Category Tree, Question Analysis, Key Decisions, Data Needs, Action Levers, and Success Metrics. These techniques help you elicit and gather requirements for your analytical solution.

Before we discuss the techniques, let's review where we are in the methodology. Figure 4.1 is the Decision Architecture methodology with the Decision Analysis as the second phase. Note that this is the beginning of an iterative cycle between Decision Analysis, Agile Analytics, Monetization Strategy, and Enablement. We find ourselves cycling back and forth between these phases. For example, if you have a requirement for a certain metric in the Decision Architecture phase but are unable to source the data during the Data Development process step, you may decide to briefly cycle through the Decision Analysis phase again to gather a new set of metrics.

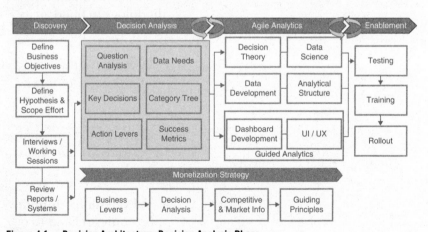

**Figure 4.1    Decision Architecture: Decision Analysis Phase**

## Category Tree

Let's start our discussion with the Category Tree, which serves as our story for how an executive will leverage our analytical solution.

The Category Tree is a grouping of like questions and decisions fit into a business context. It is a hierarchical structure that provides the subjects or topics that the manager will want to analyze codified into the Inform > Diagnose > Action > Measure framework. For example, if many of the questions we are uncovering during requirements involve knowing the performance of a particular division, we will want to group those questions together into a category node called "Performance."

We will cover the Category Tree several times within the Decision Analysis phase. The first time relates to scoping the project and structuring working sessions and interviews to draw out requirements. We cover it a second time after we complete the Question Analysis and Key Decisions process steps when we have additional information to help us complete a fuller picture of the Category Tree. The last time we address it is to finalize its structure when we bring all of the requirements together to develop our solution.

To determine the groupings and structure for the Category Tree, we review existing reports, conduct interviews, and/or facilitate workshops. We find the interviews and working sessions in the Discovery phase are a great place to start.

Let's begin with an example of the Edison Car Company, which wants to use the Decision Architecture methodology to build an analytical solution that helps them increase revenue 10 percent over last year.

In performing our discovery process we develop two hypotheses that are still a little vague at this point, but help us start our journey. The two hypotheses are:

1. Increase revenue through targeted promotional campaigns.
2. Drive revenue through data science helping to understand out-of-stock incidents and inventory levels.

In our discovery interviews, we ask several questions to understand how they solve various issues and opportunities related to our hypotheses. We are able to determine that the first set of questions they ask are related to how the company is performing from an overall sales perspective. Next, they drill into specific product lines looking for trends, and finally they look at product sales by geography.

From there we ask for common analytics that they currently perform. We find they do a lot of work to diagnose issues with their

"Budget to Forecast" sales figures to see if they are on target for the year. "Pricing" is another area they spend time analyzing the optimal price for a particular product line. Finally, we uncover an "Inventory" diagnostic where they look into the supply chain to provide visibility to manufacturing on the number of cars they are selling, overall demand, out-of-stock issues, and excess inventory.

From our Discovery phase, we were able to compose the Category Tree in Figure 4.2 aligned to the Inform and Diagnose stages in the Analytical Cycle.

With the Category Tree in place we have a general scope for the project. In the Decision Analysis phase, we structure sessions for each node to continue to develop the tree. Our first session focuses on Performance with the goal of uncovering the Questions, Decisions, Actions, and Metrics they currently ask themselves when solving for an opportunity or issue. The techniques in the following sections help us unearth each of these components and provide a structure for capturing them.

The Category Tree is broken out into the Inform and Diagnose stages. We label nodes 1 through 3 as part of the Inform stage and nodes 4a to 4c as part of the Diagnose stage. The first part of the tree structure is hierarchical and then breaks out into various branches once the diagnostics process begins. This is not always the case, as the branches may occur during the Inform stage as well.

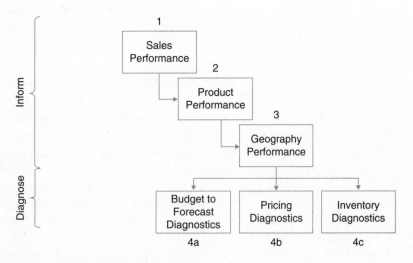

**Figure 4.2   Edison Car Company Category Tree**

When navigating the tree, we begin with the Inform stage, asking questions about Performance of the company. The managers use the topic Performance to understand how well they are doing relative to their goals. An example of the questions might be the following:

Q1: Are sales down for the United
States, Canada, or Mexico?     (Sales/High-Level Geography)
Q2: What product lines were down
for the month?               (Product/Time)
Q3: What regions were sales down
for?                         (Sales/Detailed Geography)

Once we answer these three questions, the manager may want to break off to perform specific diagnostics. A *diagnostic* is a specific component of the analytical solution with a narrow focus on solving a specific issue. Examples of a diagnostic include:

D1:  Pricing—Should we increase the price for the Electric car product line?
D2:  Inventory—Should we slow down production for the SUV product line?

We see that in the diagnostic realm, the questions turn to decisions. This is a vital component we use when we map actions to specific diagnostics.

## Question Analysis

When trying to understand how a manager utilizes information to make a decision, we need to understand the questions they ask themselves. The questions, along with decisions, are the threads that guide the manager through the Decision Analysis phase. In the Question Analysis process step, our goal is to elicit the questions the manager asks when trying to solve an opportunity or issue.

Before going into the Question Analysis process, let's cover types of questions that we ask to facilitate the process of gathering questions. The techniques we use most often are the following:

- **Open Ended**—These questions are typically broad-based questions designed to elicit a range of responses. Examples: Tell me about how you measure sales productivity. What are the top 3–5 questions you ask yourself to understand opportunity in your area?

- **Closed Ended**—These questions are designed to shut down a conversation or get to a final answer. They are often yes-or-no questions or asking for a final result. Example: Do you measure sales productivity as Number of Total Units Sold or Total Revenue amount?

- **Clarifying**—These are usually statements of fact that one is looking to validate or leverage to continue a deeper line of questioning. Examples: Is sales productivity only measured in the Number of Total Units Sold metric? What did you mean when you said the competitor metric is correlated to units shipped?

- **Root Cause**—This question type is one of our favorites for soliciting questions. The premise of this type of questioning is to find if there are a deeper set of issues or concerns for a particular symptom or line of reasoning. It entails asking 5–7 questions in succession around a particular topic to uncover the root cause of an issue. We'll provide an example of a root cause question later in this section.

We think the most important factor when asking questions is to just be curious. Take a keen interest in the interviewee's business problems, issues, decisions, and actions. You do not have to become the expert, but it helps to get a deep understanding of how their business works, their role, and how they utilize data.

An interview that deconstructs the Question Analysis for a role is usually the starting place for the exercise. To elicit the questions, one can review existing reports, conduct interviews, or facilitate workshops.

When eliciting questions from the user, we find it useful to stick with a particular subject thread and perform a root cause analysis. This usually entails asking a series of questions, five to seven of them, that drill into a particular subject area. For example, let's look at a root cause analysis for the Edison Car Company.

With a problem statement presented, we perform a working session to uncover the questions, decisions, actions, and metrics. We guide this process with a root cause analysis of questions and answers.

The following is a set of questions the managers ask themselves, along with associated answers, when diagnosing the issue:

**Example Problem Statement**: Sales for North America are down last month in March for the Edison Car Company.

Q1: Are sales down for the United States, Canada, or Mexico?

*Answer 1:* US is down by 2 percent, Canada is flat, and Mexico is slightly up.

Q2: What product lines are down for the month?

*Answer 2:* Sedan, Economy, and mostly SUV.

Q3: Which regions were sales down for?

*Answer 3:* Northeast is 5 percent off forecast for March, which is the biggest offender.

Q4: Were there any seasonal concerns, events, or weather issues last month for the Northeast?

*Answer 4:* There was a blizzard in the Northeast that shut down several cities for the second week of the month.

Q5: Which product line's sales were hurt the most by the blizzard?

*Answer 5:* We normally sell 500 SUVs in that region in a given month; we sold only 350 due to the weather issue.

As you can see, after about five questions, we are able to get to the root cause of the sales issue for the month. We are also able to glean how the team thinks through the process of troubleshooting issues. They go from performance at an overall level, to product, to geography before they diagnose the weather as the root cause. You can see how something informational is turned into the start of a diagnostic exercise.

The root cause analysis helps us determine current state. We want to challenge this to make sure it is the best approach as well as iterate through additional questions and decisions that a manager might ask as we compose our final solution.

To continue our example, what can we decide from this line of questioning? We might determine to slow down production in order to not overproduce given the drop-off in sales. We may also start looking into moving some of the inventory in the region to other regions. However, just looking at sales figures during this snapshot in time might be a false indicator. Let's see what happens when we add data science and metrics to the process with two additional questions.

Q6: What is the Actuals Sales to Forecast Indicator (AFI) for the region year-to-date?

*Answer 6:* The AFI is reading .98, which equates to 98 percent of actuals to budget.

Q7: What is the Product Velocity Metric (PVM) for the region?

*Answer 7:* The PVM reads 1.05, which means that the volume has been increasing for the past three months and is forecasted to accelerate over the next two months.

When we add Data Science to the process, the conclusion changes. We see two important data points that are hidden if we only look at the raw sales numbers.

First we see that our forecast to budget looks good through the AFI metric with our actual sales at 98 percent to our forecast. This tells us that we had a great January and February, but March was the issue due to the weather. This leads us to conclude that the event is probably an anomaly.

The next metric, PVM or velocity, is really interesting. PVM tells us that volume of sales had actually been on the increase until the incident in March.

It is interesting how the conclusions change with a few key metrics in place to provide a broader context of performance of the region over a period of time versus a single snapshot in time.

Let's start to record our results in the Decision Architecture template:

| | |
|---|---|
| **Business Objective** | Increase revenue by 10 percent over last year using Decision Architecture methodology. |
| **Hypothesis** | Increase revenue through targeted promotional campaigns. <br> Drive revenue through data science helping to understand out-of-stock incidents and inventory levels. |

**Decision Architecture**

| | |
|---|---|
| Questions | Q1: Are sales down for the US, Canada, or Mexico? |
| | Q2: What product lines are down for the month? |
| | Q3: Which regions were sales down for? |
| | Q4: Were there any seasonal concerns, events, or weather issues last month for the Northeast? |
| | Q5: How much did the blizzard impact sales volume for the month for SUV product line? |
| | Q6: What is the Actuals Sales to Forecast Indicator (AFI) for the region year to date? |
| | Q7: What is the Product Velocity Metric (PVM) for the region? |
| Decisions | TBD |
| Metrics | TBD |
| Actions | TBD |

## Key Decisions

Another key process step in the Decision Analysis phase is to understand the types of decisions that the manager needs to make on an ongoing basis. Key Decisions help us understand what a manager will do with the information. Will the analyst act on a piece of information or is it just a nice-to-have metric? Will the information drive a particular action or event?

Typically, at the end of our Question Analysis, we have enough information to start to tease out decisions based on the answers to the questions. For example, from our working sessions we uncover a great set of questions as well as the following decisions that the team may make:

- **Should we increase marketing spend for the Northeast Region?**

    With the Actuals Sales to Forecast Indicator (AFI) metric of 98 percent, we decide to increase our marketing budget for the Northeast to assist in making up for our deficit by offering a dealer rebate to generate additional sales. The AFI metric is a key indicator for us to determine marketing spend. Since we are below forecast, the region needs more energy in order for sales to catch up to plan.

- **Should I redirect inventory from the Northeast to other regions?**

  Based on the information provided in the last section, we decide to redirect new inventory shipments of SUVs to other regions until current capacity levels decrease in the Northeast. However, we know that Product Velocity Metric (PVM) is increasing and need to dig more to determine if this is a good decision and for which product lines.

By leveraging the root cause analysis questions technique, you can drill into the opportunity or issue until you arrive at a decision that leads to an action. We are also able to uncover the metrics that drive each of the decisions, which are important pieces of information.

What is interesting about this approach is that we are able to elicit the actions associated with the decisions. This will help us build out the overall Decision Analysis to tie together the pieces of Inform, Diagnose, and Action. There will be more to come on this topic.

Another approach to finding the Key Decisions is to start by asking the manager about the major decisions they make on a routine basis. If we perform the exercise of Key Decisions without performing a Question Analysis first, the path might be a little different. What we are looking to gather is the top five to eight Key Decisions the person wants to make to perform effectively in their role. For example, we ask the interviewee what are the Key Decisions they make when thinking about Sales for North America.

**Subject Area: Sales for North America**

- Key Decision 1—Should I increase or decrease marketing spend?
- Key Decision 2—Should I change my sales forecast to slow down or increase production for a particular product line?
- Key Decision 3—Should we develop any specific rebates or promotions to help increase sales?
- Key Decision 4—Should I talk to specific salespeople about their performance?
- Key Decision 5—Should I go on a dealer roadshow to boost sales performance?

For each of the decisions, try to understand if there is a key piece of information or metric that would drive the decision. If not, keep probing using a root cause analysis to unearth the metric. For example, let's deconstruct Key Decision 1.

**Key Decision 1—Should I increase or decrease marketing spend?**
- Q1: What would help you determine whether to increase or decrease marketing spend?

    *Answer:* There are several factors that might help me with the decision:
    - AFI for the region by product line
    - New promotional events that are not on the marketing calendar
    - Specific dealer issues or promotions
    - Product issues
    - Safety emergency events
- Q2: What would you look for in the AFI metric to determine the allocation of marketing spend?

    *Answer:* If AFI was down for a particular product line we might decide to run a campaign to help boost vehicle sales for that region.
- Q3: What level would the indicator need to read to tell you there is an issue?

    *Answer:* If AFI was more than 5 percent off, we would probably want to look deeper and take actions.

The approach with Decisions as the primary driver for decomposing the Key Decisions leads us to a very similar place as the Question Analysis process. Here again we see that AFI is an important metric for the Edison Car Company and a major lever they pull when the need to make up a revenue gap arises.

Let's fill in more of our Decision Architecture document with the decisions we have gathered:

| | |
|---|---|
| **Business Objective** | Increase revenue by 10 percent over last year using Decision Architecture methodology. |
| **Hypothesis** | Increase revenue through targeted promotional campaigns. Drive revenue through data science helping to understand out-of-stock and inventory levels. |

**Decision Architecture**

| | |
|---|---|
| Questions | Q1: Are sales down for the US, Canada, or Mexico? |
| | Q2: What product lines are down for the month? |
| | Q3: Which regions were sales down for? |
| | Q4: Were there any seasonal concerns, events, or weather issues last month for the Northeast? |
| | Q5: How much did the blizzard impact sales volume for the month for SUV product line? |
| | Q6: What is the Actuals Sales to Forecast Indicator (AFI) for the region year to date? |
| | Q7: What is the Product Velocity Metric (PVM) for the region? |
| Decisions | Key Decision 1—Should I increase or decrease marketing spend? |
| | Key Decision 2—Should I change my sales forecast to slow down or increase production for a particular product line? |
| | Key Decision 3—Should we develop any specific rebates or promotions to help increase sales? |
| | Key Decision 4—Should I talk to specific salespeople about their performance? |
| | Key Decision 5—Should I go on a dealer roadshow to boost sales performance? |
| | Key Decision 6—Should I redirect inventory from the Northeast to other regions? |
| Metrics | TBD |
| Actions | TBD |

At this point, we have more information to fill out our Category Tree with a fuller set of diagnostics. From the line of questions in the prior section, we can see a general pattern beginning. As you interview 4, 5, 6+ people, the pattern begins to become more apparent. From our interviews so far, we add several new diagnostics to the Category Tree (see Figure 4.3).

## Data Needs

One of the major outputs of the Question Analysis and Key Decisions process steps are the data sources necessary to answer the questions. This is a valuable piece of information that we derive from

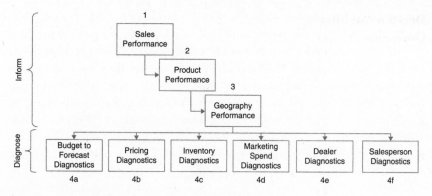

**Figure 4.3    Edison Car Company Category Tree: Diagnostics**

the techniques. We also use this information to start our data analyst looking into the various systems to see if good-quality data exists to support an analytical solution, specifically the questions, decisions, and metrics.

Based on the data review, we may decide to add elements to our Decision Analysis or remove them due to lack of data or data-quality issues. Without the right data or quality data, we are not able to perform the analysis to develop our analytical solution. Our suggestion is to repeat this process step once you finish each session to determine if you have the right data to support the analysis.

In our example, we determine we need the following data subject areas for our data analyst to source:

- Sales data
- Product data
- Budget data
- Forecast data
- Pricing data
- Inventory data
- Marketing spend data
- Dealer data
- Salesperson data

This information may come from one place, like an enterprise data warehouse, or from other reporting systems that house your Sales or Financial data. Since the data analyst has a big job on their hands with these types of projects, this role is engaged very early on in the life of the project.

In the Data Needs process step, we try to challenge the business in their current thinking about what data they have available to them. There is the ability to purchase external data as well as leverage unstructured data. An example of this comes from Harvard Business Review Analytical Services, which published the article, "Analytics That Work: Deploying Self-Service and Data Visualization for Faster Decisions." The article is based on a survey conducted with over 827 business managers and posits:

> One big reason for the excitement over analytics is the explosion of available data. In many industries, external data—whether from analyst reports, social media, or elsewhere—has become just as important as internal data. Overall, about two-thirds (65 percent) of survey respondents say the ability to access and integrate both internal and external data is critical to decision-making. This view is held even more strongly by best-in-class companies.

A good example of using unstructured data comes to us from the luxury hotel business. In this case study, hotel management was spending their time and energy focused on making their dinner service to be a fine dining experience on which to build the hotel's reputation. Leveraging social media information and text mining, they discovered that breakfast is the most important meal when travelers choose hotels. In her article, "Using an Algorithm to Figure Out What Luxury Customers Really Want," Ana Bryant says,

> [Metis] pointed out that one in every three reviews of The Dorchester hotel mentions breakfast, far more than cite dinner. Indeed, Metis told us that breakfast defines our guests' perception of our entire food and beverage division.
>
> In our minds, there were three distinct breakfast offerings at The Dorchester. Guests could have breakfast in their rooms, at the Promenade, or in The Grill restaurant, and the menus—and experience—were different in each location.
>
> Guests, Metis told us, don't make those distinctions. No matter where breakfast is served, they simply use the menu as a guide

to ingredients. Each guest wants something particular; they want what they are accustomed to. Breakfast, it seems, is not a time for experimentation or discovery; its purpose is to comfort us and make us ready for the day.

This is a powerful example of how stretching the current sources of data to include external unstructured data leads to a change in strategy for the hotel. One of our goals as a decision architect is to work with the managers and analyst to understand their current situation and challenge them on new techniques and methods that analytics and data can provide.

## Action Levers

The actions, or Action Levers, are the output of a decision. What is interesting about this exercise is that by understanding someone's decisions we are able to quickly see what levers the person has available to manage their business. The decisions they make and actions that stem from these decisions drive their business results.

From the working session in our example, we were able to determine that the manager has three main levers to effect change in their role:

1. Production—Slowing down or increasing via sales forecast
2. Marketing Spend—Rebates, promotions, advertising, dealer roadshow
3. Sales Management—Working with sales teams to drive deal volume

Actions are an important component of the methodology as we want our analytical solutions and monetization strategies to be actionable. If our solution simply provides good information, we have missed the mark.

In the working session we identify the important pieces of information we need to take action for each decision. It is important that we drive down to this level of detail in our working sessions to understand the Action Levers available to the manager to determine how to best align metrics with each of the actions.

We make note of the Action Levers when we hear them raised during the interviews or working sessions. If Action Levers are not surfacing, we push for them when we discuss the Key Decisions. For example, if we are not getting the actions associated with the decision, we ask the following question:

Q: What are the key business levers you have at your disposal in order to drive actionable results?
*Answer:* I have four main levers that I can pull to influence the results of my role:
1. Production—Slowing down or increasing via sales forecast
2. Marketing Spend—Rebates, promotions, advertising, dealer roadshow
3. Sales Management—Working with sales teams to drive deal volume
4. Pricing—Working with our revenue management team to change the pricing structures

By asking the question, we uncover a fourth important lever, Pricing. These are four powerful Action Levers that we want to dig deeper into to understand how our analytics can support the decisions associated with them.

Action levers should tie back to business levers that drive the monetization strategy. If we are unable to map our selected action levers to a business lever, we need to revisit the decisions we are solving for to determine if it is the right set of decisions. We discuss business levers in further detail in the Monetization Strategy chapter (Chapter 5) of this book.

## Success Metrics

Success Metrics help drive an organization's decisions. In this section we refer to *metrics* as something that drives a decision or something that we can measure. We use the word *success* because an organization can flood itself in measuring every aspect of the business. In our experience the top 10 to 15 metrics make the difference and should be used to drive behavior; otherwise we can quickly get lost in the noise.

When managers attempt to use a large number of metrics to manage their business, more often than not, analysis paralysis sets in and the value of each additional piece of information diminishes. This is true, especially, in the Inform stage of the analysis. Additional metrics may come into good use during the Diagnose stage when trying to pinpoint specific issues, but outside of specific diagnostics, less is more. There is a lot of eloquence in simplicity.

We need to ask ourselves, does the metric drive any action or measurement? If not, it is probably just informative and should be reconsidered. Our key point is to rationalize our metrics to the top 10 to 15 that are the most impactful and directly related to the business problem we are trying to solve.

In the example above, we use two Success Metrics:

1. *Actuals to Forecast Indicator (AFI)*—The AFI helps to quickly identify if actuals are meeting forecast. This metric is simple math, but helps managers determine if they are on or off target with a single number versus doing the math in their head.

2. *Production Velocity Metric (PVM)*—The PVM metric is based on data science and provides the information user with an understanding of the direction of production volume. The indicator is a moving average of the last three months, helping a user understand if things are trending up or down. In addition, it has a forward-looking component, leveraging the last three months to forecast the next two months to determine the upcoming trend. The data gets really interesting at this point; it can help a manager determine if the velocity of production will increase or slow down in the weeks ahead. This demand signal might affect several decisions and would need to be watched closely.

Thresholds are another key concept we cover in detail in the Data Science chapter (Chapter 9). We discuss them at a high level here because thresholds help bring metrics to life. They assist the manager or analyst in determining when metrics fall outside a normal or expected distribution and require a closer look. Thresholds are the signal for action.

Thresholds enable a manager to focus on the metrics with a signal that points to an issue or opportunity and not divert valuable attention to metrics that are going well.

In our Success Metrics above, examples of thresholds might include the following:

*Actuals to Forecast Indicator (AFI)*—After analysis by the data scientist, we determine the threshold for the AFI is 5 percent of forecast. Therefore, we want a signal that indicates when the AFI is outside of this range, telling the information user to look further into this issue.

*Product Velocity Metric (PVM)*—The PVM might have a higher or lower tolerance due to the variance for a particular product line or production schedule. The PVM may not read out of variance until you reach 1.1 or .9 (a 10 percent variance) for a particular car product. However, at an aggregate product level, the tolerance might be tighter, closer to a 5 percent variance, or 1.05/.95.

The individual threshold may be a combination of insights from the data found by the data scientist and/or subject matter experts. In addition, thresholds are rarely one-size-fits-all. The data scientist will need to perform an analysis to determine if the threshold for a particular product line or geography can be set to a standard or if it should be modified due to unique circumstances. We do not want to throw off a false positive with a threshold that is too narrow or broad in a particular instance.

Now, let's finish our Decision Architecture template to make sure we have captured all of our requirements.

| | |
|---|---|
| **Business Objective** | Increase revenue by 10 percent over last year using Decision Architecture methodology. |
| **Hypothesis** | Increase revenue through targeted promotional campaigns.<br>Drive revenue through data science helping to understand out-of-stock and inventory levels. |

**Decision Architecture**

| | |
|---|---|
| Questions | Q1: Are sales down for the US, Canada, or Mexico?<br>Q2: What product lines are down for the month?<br>Q3: Which regions were sales down for?<br>Q4: Were there any seasonal concerns, events, or weather issues last month for the Northeast? |

|  | Q5: How much did the blizzard impact sales volume for the month for SUV product line? |
|---|---|
|  | Q6: What is the Actuals Sales to Forecast Indicator (AFI) for the region year to date? |
|  | Q7: What is the Product Velocity Metric (PVM) for the region? |
| Decisions | Key Decision 1—Should I increase or decrease marketing spend? |
|  | Key Decision 2—Should I change my sales forecast to slow down or increase production for a particular product line? |
|  | Key Decision 3—Should we develop any specific rebates or promotions to help increase sales? |
|  | Key Decision 4—Should I talk to specific salespeople about their performance? |
|  | Key Decision 5—Should I go on a dealer roadshow to boost sales performance? |
|  | Key Decision 6—Should I redirect inventory from the Northeast to other regions? |
| Metrics | M1—Actuals to Forecast Indicator (AFI) |
|  | M2—Production Velocity Metric (PVM) |
| Actions | A1—Production—Slowing down or increasing via sales forecast |
|  | A2—Marketing Spend—Rebates, promotions, advertising, dealer roadshow |
|  | A3—Sales Management—Working with sales teams to drive deal volume |
|  | A4—Pricing—Working with our revenue management team to change the pricing structures |

This may not be the complete set of requirements but it is a good start. As we meet with more managers, analysts, and subject matter experts, we will get a fuller set of requirements.

## Category Tree Revisited

Let's continue on with our Category Tree, having completed requirements for the Decision Architecture. We go through two exercises to accomplish this task. First we map our Success Metrics, Question Analysis, Key Decisions, and Action Levers to each of the applicable categories on the tree. Second we map the Category Tree to dashboards to gain an understanding of how many dashboards we want to develop in our automated solution. This process may require many iterations. The end product of this alignment is our roadmap for development.

Let's use the example of the Edison Car Company to map the questions, decisions, metrics, and actions to the Category Tree. Below is the list from our requirements documentation that we have developed in the last few sections:

- Questions (Q)
  - Q1: Are sales down for the US, Canada, or Mexico?
  - Q2: What product lines are down for the month?
  - Q3: Which regions were sales down for?
  - Q4: Were there any seasonal concerns, events, or weather issues last month for the Northeast?
  - Q5: How much did the blizzard impact sales volume for the month for SUV product line?
  - Q6: What is the Actuals Sales to Forecast Indicator (AFI) for the region year to date?
  - Q7: What is the Product Velocity Metric (PVM) for the region?
- Key Decisions (D)
  - Key Decision 1—Should I increase or decrease marketing spend?
  - Key Decision 2—Should I change my sales forecast to slow down or increase production for a particular product line?
  - Key Decision 3—Should we develop any specific rebates or promotions to help increase sales?
  - Key Decision 4—Should I talk to specific salespeople about their performance?
  - Key Decision 5—Should I go on a dealer roadshow to boost sales performance?
  - Key Decision 6—Should I redirect inventory from the Northeast to other regions?
- Success Metrics (SM)
  - SM1: AFI—Actuals to Forecast Indicator
  - SM2: PVM—Product Velocity Metric

- Action Levers (AL)
  - AL1: Production—Slowing down or increasing via sales forecast
  - AL2: Marketing Spend—Rebates, promotions, advertising, dealer roadshow
  - AL3: Sales Management—Working with sales teams to drive deal volume
  - AL4: Pricing—Working with our revenue management team to change the pricing structures

Taking all of these items together, we have the Decision Architecture. From Figure 4.4 we can see the mapping of the various questions, decisions, actions, and metrics to Category Tree.

In Figure 4.4 we observe several Questions (Q), Decisions (D), and Metrics (SM) that get repeated often. We also notice a new section added to the Category Tree, our Actions. Each of the actions is aligned to a particular diagnostic that is focused on helping the manager make a particular decision.

When we go through the process of aligning each of the elements to the Category Tree, we test each item to assess if it is truly a fit and drives an action. For example, when going deeper into the Pricing diagnostic, we may decide to include five additional metrics necessary for a complete diagnosis. At the same time, we take out metrics that are no longer needed. The decision architect, subject matter

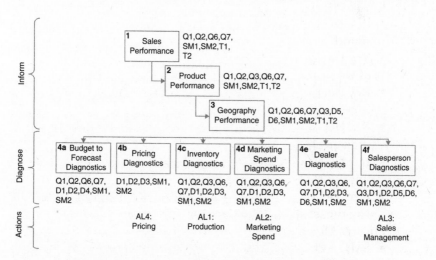

**Figure 4.4   Category Tree Mapped to Questions, Decisions, Metrics, and Actions**

experts, and team cycle through an iterative process to get the best analytical solution by adding and removing elements to each node in the tree. Once the elements of the Category Tree come to life on a dashboard, the manager may choose to make additional revisions. At this point they are better able to determine if the right elements are in place to solve the purpose of that node in the Category Tree.

If the plan is to automate the analysis, an important point to consider is that each node may map to an individual dashboard or many dashboards. Figure 4.5 is an example of this type of mapping.

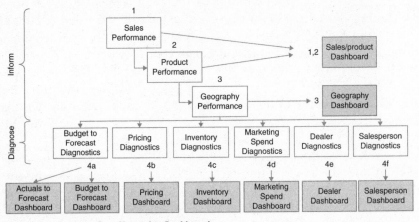

**Figure 4.5    Category Tree Mapped to Dashboards**

The number of nodes in a Category Tree can map one to one with the number of dashboards or can be many to many. For example, in Figure 4.5 we see that nodes 1 and 2 in the Inform stage map to one dashboard, Sales/Product dashboard, while node 3 maps to one dashboard, Geography dashboard. In addition, node 4a maps to two dashboards, Actuals to Forecast dashboard and Budget to Forecast dashboard. We take our cues from the Category Tree when assembling the dashboards, but it is not always a direct one-to-one relationship.

## Summary

We covered a lot of ground in this chapter and it could easily be its own book. We reviewed the components of the Decision Analysis phase: Category Tree, Question Analysis, Key Decisions, Success Metrics, and Action Levers. These components make up your Decision Architecture.

The process of composing your Decision Architecture takes practice and may not be apparent when you first start the interview process. Our recommendation is to get through all of the interviews, take copious notes, and assemble your initial thoughts on the Category Tree and Decision Architecture template from the elements you collect.

If they are not fitting together, develop a few straw models to run by your SMEs for counsel. After you have created a model you feel is worth sharing, hold a working session with the stakeholders to review. It is helpful to repeat often and early. In addition, it is helpful to narrow the scope of subject areas to get quick wins to begin gaining momentum.

# MONETIZATION STRATEGY

# CHAPTER 5

# Monetization Strategy: *Making Data Pay*

The power of a good monetization strategy is the ability to take a good decision and make it a great one. A Monetization Strategy is a plan to achieve one or more business goals through several tactics (actions) that have a quantified benefit. The strategy will most likely be deployed under conditions of uncertainty and your Monetization Strategy will leverage Decision Theory and Data Science to reduce this risk and provide a greater level of confidence to the decision.

Monetization strategies are unique to your business and are not one-size-fits-all. These are your proprietary tools and methods that you can utilize to drive value from your data. Your company probably already has several monetization strategies within its walls that live in siloed functions, such as Marketing, Finance, Revenue Management, and Sales, to name a few. These groups have analyses they perform to assist them in making decisions which are, more than likely, one-off exercises performed only a few times a year. The challenge for your organization is to integrate existing strategies and the ongoing development of new strategies into analytical solutions that become scaled throughout the organization.

Let's take a look at a real-world example from Unilever that has a team called Consumer and Market Insights (CMI) that builds monetization strategies for various business units. In the following excerpt from Frank van den Driest, Stan Sthanunathan, and Keith Weed's article, "Building an Insights Engine," they discuss two analytical solutions, Growth Scout and Growth Cockpit, that were built to drive better decisions through monetizing strategies. What strikes us about this article is the number and variety of decisions the analytical solutions influence. In addition, these solutions have economic benefits from the actions they prescribe.

> A typical application might be to gauge the impact of, say, increasing the penetration of shower gels by 10% in Thai markets. The results could help Unilever prioritize growth opportunities and decide where it could most profitably invest additional marketing or product-development resources. Recently, the CMI home-care team used Growth Scout to uncover potentially lucrative new markets for Unilever detergent brands by identifying demographic segments with weak penetration.
>
> Additionally, CMI employs other tools to help answer questions about which product benefits marketing should emphasize, which ads are most effective, what marketing budget allocations will yield the highest return on investment, and what pricing is optimal. CMI then plays a central role in tracking the performance of marketing initiatives against targets and advising on tactical adjustments that may improve performance.
>
> Once decisions have been made about where to play, another custom-built software tool, called Growth Cockpit, helps guide "How to win?" strategies. The tool provides a one-screen overview of a brand's performance in a market relative to the category. By rapidly building a visual picture of how the brand compares on a host of metrics—market share, penetration, pricing, media spending, and more—it points managers to growth opportunities.

Just in this small excerpt, there are several really good examples of how effective the tools are in driving decisions. In each of these cases, the analytical solution, whether Growth Scout or Growth Cockpit, helped business managers make better quality decisions through monetization strategies. Our goal in this section of the book is to empower you with the tools necessary to create winning strategies for your company. There is nothing stopping you from empowering your company with its own Growth Scout or Growth Cockpit.

The four components of developing your Monetization Strategy are the Monetization Guiding Principles, Competitive and Market Information, Business Levers, and the requirements gathered from Decision Analysis. Depending on the type of strategy you are

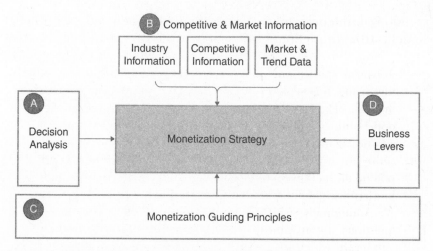

**Figure 5.1    High-Level View of the Monetization Strategy Framework**

developing, you need each of these in varying degrees. Figure 5.1 is a high-level picture of the Monetization Strategy Framework showing how the components fit together.

## Business Levers

The goal of developing a monetization strategy is to provide a manager with the ability to drive revenue or reduce costs. In order to do this, we need to know what our business levers are so we can understand the tools we have at our disposal. For example, if you develop a strategy to optimize the utilization of assets in a company that is asset light, you may not be applying the method against the best business lever.

Your business levers will drive your monetization strategy and should be included in your business objective and aligned to your hypothesis and actions. The analytical solution you develop will flow from these statements.

One of the best places to start is with your company's profit and loss (P&L) statement. Understanding what drives growth and costs, and ultimately profit, will help you determine which business levers are available for you to use. Depending on your role and the size of your organization, you will need to adapt this to be specific to what you can practically achieve in your department or company.

In Figure 5.2 we have developed an example set of business levers partially aligned to a P&L of a fictitious company. The business levers you deploy will shape the decisions available in the monetization strategy. From this you can develop specific strategies to drive revenue or cut costs. You will need to develop a similar set of levers, as in Figure 5.2, for your organization, which will be used as a key input for your monetization strategies.

The business levers are high level in nature and the detail behind them needs to be specific to your industry and company. It is your job to work through the specifics to make it actionable. For example, the Customer Acquisition business lever can mean different things if you are a business-to-business company or a business-to-consumer company. Customer acquisition can also mean different things if you are a product or service company. See where we are heading? We leave these details in your capable hands, but completing your Business Levers is a vital component as you develop strategies to monetize your company's data.

Let's review some examples of monetization strategies you might be able to build leveraging your Business Levers:

- **Cash Cow**—We are in an enviable situation of having high market share but low market growth. This could be a utility company or dominant players in a sector. The business levers we want to deploy are centered on protecting our market share and managing costs. Therefore, price and market share may be two business levers we focus on to build our monetization strategies.
- **Asset Optimization**—In this scenario, our company might be an asset-heavy organization, like a trucking company, that produces greater profit when its assets are highly utilized. Based on the type of company, we want to focus our energy on the bottom portion of the framework centered on Capital Costs and Equipment.
- **Market Share**—Let's assume we are in a slow-growing sector and want to grow our market share. We decide acquiring competitors would be the best strategy and choose to leverage our Customer Acquisition Strategy business lever. We develop a monetization strategy that shows the economic value of acquiring different companies.
- **Channel Optimization**—In this scenario we might be a retailer that sells our products to consumers in third-party retail outlets, direct online through various websites, and direct

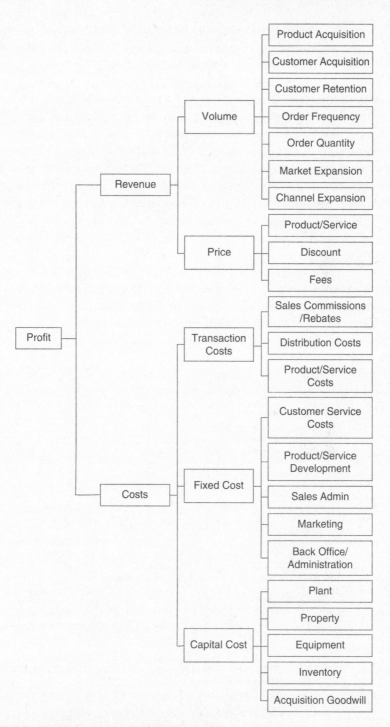

**Figure 5.2 How Business Levers Partially Align to a P&L**

online mobile. We want to develop a monetization strategy to maximize Marketing Spend against each of the channels based on our optimal channel mix.

The choices you make with respect to business levers will dictate which decisions are available for your strategy. Spend the energy to develop your business levers and brainstorm several strategies you can deploy to begin your journey. In the next section, we cover an equally important topic, the requirements for your strategy. This includes aligning your business problem to your hypothesis and generating the questions and decisions that you will enable through your solution.

## Monetization Strategy Framework

In this section we focus on putting the Lego pieces together on what makes a good Monetization Strategy. To start, let's reference our Decision Architecture methodology. Each of the components in the methodology have some degree of interdependence on each other; let's discuss the ones that impact the Monetization Strategy the most, highlighted in Figure 5.3. In each of these steps there are several requirements you want to capture as inputs into your Monetization Strategy.

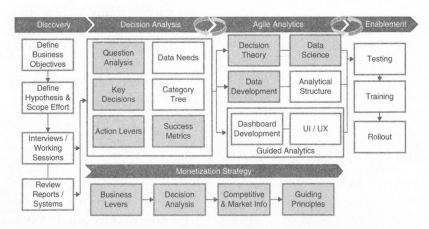

Figure 5.3    Decision Architecture Components with Impact on the Monetization Strategy

From the process steps highlighted under the Decision Analysis phase, we have our decision requirements, but that is not all we are going to need. Assembling the Monetization Strategy takes more than just decision requirements. Overall, there are the four input components to the Monetization Strategy:

1. Business Levers
2. Decision Analysis and Agile Analytics
3. Competitive and Market Information
4. Monetization Guiding Principles

To develop your strategy, you will start by building your Business Levers to determine what impact the strategy will have on the organization. The next step will be to utilize decision analysis to drive monetization requirements (Questions, Decisions, Metrics, Actions). Once you have the requirements, along with your business levers, you will need to determine what competitive and market information will impact the solution. The Guiding Principles will act as your guidepost throughout the journey. At this point, you have a full set of requirements needed to build your Monetization Strategy.

We covered a lot of ground in the previous paragraph and will explain this in detail through the rest of this and the next chapter. To bring this concept together visually, Figure 5.4 depicts our detailed Monetization Strategy framework.

We covered the Business Levers topic earlier in this chapter. The Monetization Guiding Principles will be a separate chapter as there is a lot to digest on that topic. The other two topics, Decision Analysis and Agile Analytics and Competitive and Market Information, are the discussion points for the remainder of this chapter. To get started, let's begin with the Decision Analysis and Agile Analytics and how the process steps map back to our strategy.

## Decision Analysis and Agile Analytics

There are eight process steps in both the Decision Analysis and Agile Analytics phases that have a high degree of importance for your Monetization Strategy: Hypothesis and Scope Effort, Question Analysis, Key Decisions, Action Levers, Success Metrics, Data Development,

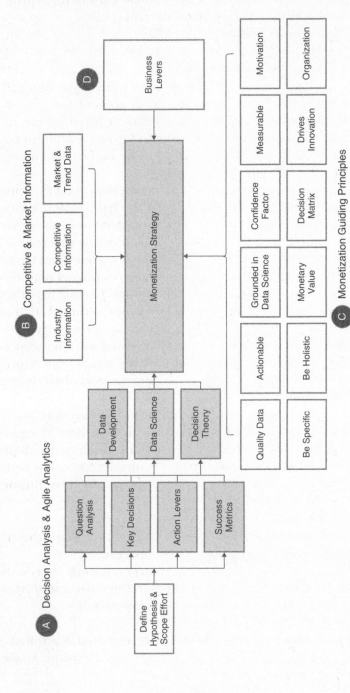

**Figure 5.4   Monetization Strategy Framework in Detail**

Data Science, and Decision Theory. Let's cover each of these process steps and how they map to your monetization strategy.

### Define Hypothesis and Scope Effort

In the Discovery phase, the Define Hypothesis and Scope Effort process step enables you to capture the overall goals of the analytical solution. With these goals comes an alignment to an overarching business objective. Our Monetization Strategy drives revenue or costs savings with measurable outcomes that can be tied back to a larger corporate initiative.

The hypothesis and problem statement are important to capture because they will provide you direction on the type of Monetization Strategy to deploy. It is our recommendation that you leverage your business levers in the development of your business objective and hypotheses. The business levers serve as a great anchor point to align to your corporate, individual department, and/or project objectives. In addition, they are very useful in the creation of your hypothesis and finally your actions. They should be one of the threads that ties your solution together.

You may find that after going through several working sessions, you have more than one hypothesis to solve your business problem, which is perfectly okay. If you start to have more than three or four, you need to prioritize them.

Let's use an example from the Business Levers section. We are in a high-growth sector and are racing with competitors to sign up as many customers as possible for our software product. We deploy a Customer Acquisition strategy through our sales force, leveraging Commissions and Rebates and Sales Reps as the two Business Levers.

- *Business Objective:* Grow revenue and market share through aggressive customer acquisition campaigns.
- *Hypothesis:* We can achieve 25 percent growth in revenue through optimizing our sales rep workforce size and territory along with changes in sales commission structure.

These two statements are enough to get us started. We will need to work to narrow our hypothesis through our Decision Analysis phase, but for now it is a good start.

The three main items to capture out of this process step for your Monetization Strategy are:

1. Alignment to or the creation of your business objectives
2. Development of your hypothesis
3. Utilizing the business lever to tie the solutions together

### Question Analysis

The Question Analysis process step captures the questions you will want to understand to diagnose the opportunity or issue. These questions help yield the type of data that we want to source from various systems. In addition, by understanding the manager's line of questioning, we get a view into their thought process of how they diagnose an opportunity or issue.

More often than not, we develop more questions than we can answer, so we need to prioritize the list of questions to the most important ones that fit our strategy. Once we have the list of questions, our job turns to understanding the various data sources associated with the questions to ensure we can build an analytical solution.

As an example, let's take our business objective and hypothesis above and deconstruct them in a working session with several managers, analysts, and subject matter experts. In this session we uncover the Questions, Decisions, Actions, and Metrics associated with the sales rep workforce size and territory. Let's start with the Question Analysis by performing a root cause:

Q1: When you look at the sales team size and territory, what is the first question you ask yourself?
*Answer:* What is the productivity of each of my sales reps?
Q2: What is the second question you ask yourself?
*Answer:* What is the potential sales for each of their territories?
Q3: What is the next question you ask yourself?
*Answer:* Based on the productivity of my sales rep, I ask, Can they handle the size of their market/territory? Is it too big or small?
Q4: What is the next question you ask yourself?
*Answer:* Based on the answer above, I might decide to redistribute territory between sales reps or add new sales reps.

By the time we got to the third question we found an area or root cause that might need further diagnostics. In the fourth question, we got to a potential decision that the team may make, which is usually the stopping point for that line of questioning. Each of these questions leads us to data sources that we need.

The two main items to capture out of this process step for your Monetization Strategy are:

1. Question Analysis, prioritized
2. Data subject areas

### Key Decisions

Along with the Question Analysis process step, the Key Decisions are a major input into the creation of the Monetization Strategy. From the Key Decisions process step, we gather the decisions to make as a result of the Question Analysis. These decisions typically occur in the Diagnose phase of the analytical cycle.

During the Key Decisions process step, usually resulting from the same working session as the Question Analysis, we typically generate too many decisions and metrics. With each decision that is captured, we also record Success Metrics that enable the decision. We cover this in the section ahead on Success Metrics.

As an example, let's use our working session above to identify the decisions that the team will make. There are two decisions wrapped in question 4 above, which are:

1. Should I redistribute territory?
2. Should I hire new sales reps?

The main point to capture out of this process step for your Monetization Strategy is:

• Key Decisions, prioritized

### Action Levers

The Action Levers process step is one of the most important steps for your Monetization Strategy. The objective is to find the associated actions (or tactics) with each decision. These are the actions you will execute to capture the desired benefit. Recording the actions in this process step helps us determine what we can enable in our Monetization Strategy.

A decision may have multiple actions; it will be our job to prioritize them and determine the key actions to enable. Prioritization is important as well as anchoring back to the business objectives, hypothesis, and business levers. Each action should tie back to our business levers and these should tie back to both our hypothesis and business objective. If they do not, we may need to change our actions.

As a reminder, one of the key components of a Monetization Strategy is the fact that it is an actionable strategy. If our actions are too high level, vague, or not feasible to execute within your organization, you need to rethink alternative actions.

To continue on with our example, there may be several actions associated with each decision. We concluded with two decisions; let's look at possible actions:

- Should I redistribute territory?
  - *Action 1:* Redistribute territory to the most productive sales reps.
  - *Action 2:* Give sales reps with big territories a smaller territory to make room for additional sales reps.
- Should I hire new sales reps?
  - *Action 3:* Hire sales reps for newly created territory.

The key input into our Monetization Strategy from the Action Levers process step is:

- Action Levers, prioritized

### Success Metrics

With each decision that is captured, we also record Success Metrics that enable the decision. These Success Metrics will be used in our Monetization Strategy through a Decision Matrix. Since the metric is driving the decision, displaying the metric in the Decision Matrix along with a monetary value provides greater relevancy to the metric and drives up the quality of the decision.

Another key component of our Monetization Strategy is the ability to measure the outcome to determine performance. The Success

Metrics process step also defines how we are going to measure our actions. We want the ability not only to take action on our strategy but also to measure and learn from it. A Success Metric may serve as both one that drives a decision and one that can be measured, but not always.

Let's continue on with our example. We understand our two decisions and need to know what success metrics drive each decision. Below are the two decisions along with the potential associated metrics:

1. Should I redistribute territory?
   • Market Potential by territory
   • Market Share by territory
   • Actual Sales per sales rep
   • Quota by sales rep
2. Should I hire new sales reps?
   • Current number of sales reps

From these metrics, we should be able to derive the number of new sales reps needed if we find that the existing territories can support additional bandwidth.

The key input into our Monetization Strategy from the Success Metrics process step is:

• Success Metrics that enable decisions
• Success Metrics that enable measurement of actions

### Data Development

From the Question Analysis process step, we determine the data sources needed for our strategy. In the Data Development step, we build out data structures to support the various analytical needs, including our Monetization Strategy.

The process for building out the Analytical Structures to support the Monetization Strategy is iterative in nature. As we continue to refine the strategy, metrics, thresholds, and actions we want to deploy, we need to work with the data development team to support the needed changes.

The solution may range from a large de-normalized table to a star schema with dimensions and facts or something in between.

Work with your data team to find the right Analytical Structure for your solution that is performant and easy to maintain.

In our example, what are the data sources we would need to source from? From our Question Analysis and Key Decisions, we see that they include the following subject areas:

- Sales
- Sales rep
- Market share
- Territory
- Commissions

The key input into our Monetization Strategy from the Data Development process step is:

- Data sources
- Additional metrics

### Data Science/Decision Theory

To bring your Monetization Strategy to life, the deployment of techniques associated with Data Science and Decision Theory are needed. Data Science helps us determine the insights associated with the metrics. Decision Theory helps to determine the best way to structure the decision for the end user. You will want to leverage techniques such as *segmentation, profiling, propensity, velocity, opportunity, choice architecture,* and *decision matrix* to generate insights and structure the decision to drive your strategy.

Many of our guiding principles, which we will review in the next chapter, are rooted in data science and decision theory. These include:

1. Grounded in data science
2. Monetary value
3. Confidence factor or probability
4. Decision Matrix
5. Measurable

Spending significant time working through which techniques you will utilize requires working with a data scientist to vet the applicability of the technique and the supporting dataset for the strategy. Like the Data Development process step, this step is iterative and requires many cycles to finalize. Another output of leveraging data science is that the method is based in science, which engenders trust from the users of the solution. They are more likely to utilize the analytical solution if they trust the outcome of the Monetization Strategy for making a decision.

Let's finish our example by applying some new metrics leveraging data science and utilizing decision theory to compose a decision matrix. To assist in answering the question of how many sales reps we should hire, we are going to add a new metric, Market Velocity. This metric takes into account how many sales reps we have in a market and the time it will take them to mature the market based on their quota. We also add a Number of New Sales Reps Needed metric, which takes the velocity metric along with number of sales reps and market share to determine the number of new sales reps needed to mature the market.

Since we are in a race to capture market share, we set an aggressive goal to get to 50 percent market share in the next two years. How many reps do we need to accomplish this task?

Let's put all of our information into our requirements template and then create our decision matrix. Note that we refined our hypothesis at this point to reflect our updated goals.

| | |
|---|---|
| **Business Objective** | Grow revenue and market share through aggressive customer acquisition campaigns. |
| **Hypothesis** | Grow market share to 50 percent in the next two years by hiring additional sales representatives and splitting current territory. |

**Decision Architecture**

| | |
|---|---|
| Questions | Q1: What is the productivity of each of my sales reps? |
| | Q2: What is the potential sales for each of their territories? |
| | Q3: Based on the productivity of my sales rep, can they handle the size of their market/territory? Is it too big or small? |
| | Q4: How should I redistribute territory between sales reps or add new sales reps? |

| Decisions | Should we redistribute territory? |
|---|---|
| | Should we hire new sales reps? |
| Metrics | Market Potential by Territory |
| | Market Share by Territory |
| | Actual Sales per sales rep |
| | Quota by sales rep |
| | Market Velocity |
| | Number of New Sales Reps Needed |
| Actions | Action 1: Redistribute territory to the most productive sales reps. |
| | Action 2: Give reps with big territories a smaller territory to make room for additional sales reps. |
| | Action 3: Hire sales reps for newly created territory. |

From our requirements, we put together a decision matrix and completed our Monetization Strategy with specific tactics to deploy (see Table 5.1). Based on our decision matrix, we can see that the average quota per rep is $10 M and our current rep total is 28. We need to decide how many sales reps we need to hire to meet our goal of 50 percent market share assuming each sales rep achieves 100 percent of quota every year.

With the Market Velocity metric, we can see how many years it takes to capture 50 percent of the market share for that territory with our current number of reps. To accelerate this and capture 50 percent market share in two years, we look at the Number of Rep Hires Needed metric to help us make our decision. Overall, the Northeast

**Table 5.1  Decision Matrix**

| Territory | Potential Market Size in Two Years | Current Market Share of Potential Market | Current Number of Sales Reps | Quota per Sales Rep | Current Market Velocity (in years) | New Sales Rep Hires Needed | Sales Potential of Additional Hires |
|---|---|---|---|---|---|---|---|
| Southeast | $ 450,000,000 | 8% | 4 | $10,000,000 | 4.73 | 5.45 | $109,000,000 |
| Mid-Atlantic | $ 325,000,000 | 11% | 6 | $10,000,000 | 2.11 | 0.34 | $ 6,750,000 |
| Northeast | $ 750,000,000 | 4% | 2 | $10,000,000 | 17.25 | 15.25 | $305,000,000 |
| Midwest | $ 500,000,000 | 15% | 6 | $10,000,000 | 2.92 | 2.75 | $ 55,000,000 |
| Northwest | $ 425,000,000 | 11% | 6 | $10,000,000 | 2.76 | 2.29 | $ 45,750,000 |
| Southwest | $ 800,000,000 | 9% | 4 | $10,000,000 | 8.20 | 12.40 | $248,000,000 |
| Total | $3,250,000,000 | 9% | 28 | | | 38.48 | $769,500,000 |

territory has one of the biggest potential opportunities to accelerate with 15 hires needed.

In total, the sales manager needs to hire 38 sales reps, more than doubling the size of the sales team, to reach the goal. The new sales reps, at full quota, should have a sales contribution of $769,500,000 in market share to the firm. This along with their existing market share and the existing sales reps' production over the next two years accomplishes the goal of 50 percent market share.

While doubling your workforce and meeting full quota for all reps is a tall order, the Monetization Strategy may point to specific tactics the sales manager needs to deploy for underserved territories like the Northeast and Southwest.

Depending on your solution, you may have many inputs into your Monetization Strategy from the Data Science and Decision Theory process steps, some of which may include:

- Decision Matrix
- Choice architecture
- Correlations
- Thresholds
- Trends and forecasting
- Segmentation
- Cluster analysis
- Predictive and explanatory models
- Probability factor
- Velocity

## Competitive and Market Information

When composing your Monetization Strategy, knowing your competitive information, market data, and industry information can be vital to understanding your company's current positioning. Some of this information may exist in the public domain, some may be known through competitive situations or third-party data brokers, and some of the information may not be attainable.

Each of the three areas has a plethora of information types that you can gather. Let's look at a few:

**Competitive Information**
- Leadership
- Customers

- Products
- Pricing strategy
- K1, 10Q
- Unique intellectual property
- News, press releases

**Market Data**
- Market share
- Market trends
- Customer demographics
- Segmentation
- Economy trends
- Stock market

**Industry Information**
- Industry growth
- Industry publications
- Regularity and compliance
- Legislative activities
- State information
- Federal information

If this information does not exist within your organization, it can often be acquired as most industries have competitive datasets that can be purchased for analysis. For example, third-party companies often scrape pricing information from industry-specific websites in order to resell back to companies in a particular industry. This information can be as specific as a given price for a particular product during a certain day/time combination.

In addition, many companies in an industry provide a level of information about themselves to third parties so the industry as a whole can measure market share and perform competitive analysis. These datasets are typically higher level sets of information on overall market share, trends in the industry, and general growth rates.

Industry and demographic datasets collected from surveys, publicly disclosed information, and company-provided information can also be purchased. When composing your Monetization Strategy, knowing your competitive information, market data, and industry information is important to determine your relative position with your competitors and in your market.

## Summary

We covered a lot of ground in this chapter, which includes the four components of developing your Monetization Strategy: Monetization Guiding Principles, Competitive and Market Information, Business Levers, and the requirements gathered from Decision Analysis and Agile Analytics. We also went through the Decision Architecture methodology and how several of the process steps serve as input into your strategy through the requirements gathered.

In the next chapter, we will cover the final framework component, the Monetization Guiding Principles. We will outline the 12 key principles that serve as guideposts for your solution.

CHAPTER 6

# Monetization Guiding Principles:
## *Making It Solid*

I love the man that can smile in trouble, that can gather strength
from distress, and grow brave by reflection. 'Tis the business of
little minds to shrink, but he whose heart is firm, and whose
conscience approves his conduct, will pursue his principles unto
death.

**Thomas Paine**

Guiding principles can serve a variety of functions for corporations. Some companies leverage them as strict guidelines by
which their organization operates and their culture is driven. Other
organizations use them as guideposts that evolve as the organization
grows. In our case, we use our Monetization Guiding Principles as
guideposts to monitor over time as you integrate and refine your
strategies.

Our principles are general rules of engagement that act as guidelines for your Monetization Strategy. Understanding what makes a
good monetization strategy is specific to each organization. It will be
your job to apply the Guiding Principles to fit your situation. You
may develop your own set based on your organization and lessons
learned from implementing your strategies. Our intention is to give
you a strong starting point.

In this chapter, we cover 12 guiding principles (see Figure 6.1):

1. Quality Data
2. Be Specific
3. Be Holistic
4. Actionable
5. Decision Matrix
6. Grounded in Data Science
7. Monetary Value
8. Confidence Factor
9. Measurable
10. Motivation
11. Organizational Culture
12. Drives Innovation

These principles are not intended to serve as a checklist, rather more as guidepost that may or may not impact your strategy; not all principles will apply in every situation. For example, if your division is more focused on operations and does not do much innovation, Drives Innovation may not be a principle your monetization strategy utilizes. If developing a Confidence Factor is not available due to lack of data science resources, push that to a phase-two effort. Leverage these principles to make your strategy better, but don't over-engineer or force-fit them and risk developing a bad strategy.

## Quality Data

"The dirty little secret of big data is that most organizations spend the vast majority of their time cleaning and integrating data—not actually analyzing it," says Tom Davenport, a professor of IT and management at Babson College and thought leader in analytics with such books as *Competing on Analytics* and *Only Humans Need Apply: Winners and Losers in the Age of Smart Machines.*

We talk about the quality of the data often throughout this book and we want to stress it again. The quality of your data is table-stakes for any analytical exercise. Without good data, you will not be able to produce meaningful analysis for a monetization strategy. More importantly, though, the end consumer of this information will not trust the output of the analysis.

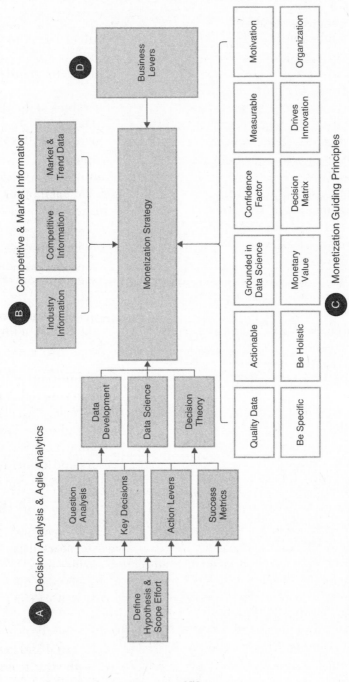

**Figure 6.1   Monetization Guiding Principles**

There are some key standards you want to make sure the datasets you use adhere to:

- **Completeness**—The completeness of the data refers to any missing or partial data in the dataset.
- **Conformity**—How well the dataset adheres to standards reflects its conformity.
- **Consistency**—Data consistency refers to the values of the data, which must be consistent throughout the dataset.
- **Accuracy**—The accuracy of the data is focused on the data being consistent, non-duplicative, and complete.
- **Duplication**—Data duplication refers to multiple records in a database that are exact or partial duplicates of each other.
- **Integrity**—The integrity of data refers to the accuracy and consistency of the data over its lifecycle.
- **Timeliness**—How often the data is updated defines its timeliness.
- **Availability**—The availability of the data refers to how often you will be able to access the data for analysis.
- **History**—How much history is available for analysis will determine how you are able to perform analysis like trends or linear regression.

The variety of data sources and types of data is important as well. We encourage you to think outside the box when utilizing data both within your organization and outside. In their article, "Analytics That Work: Deploying Self-Service and Data Visualization for Faster Decisions," the team at Harvard Business Review Analytical Services conducted a survey of over 827 business managers and came away with several insights into the importance of varied data sources. One such use of external data comes from Belk's department store:

> At department-store chain Belk Inc., business analysts use geographical information—along with customer feedback data from online surveys, social media, call centers, emails—to get a full customer view. "Analyzing that view helps us determine the customer's 'path to purchase,'" says Anu Brookins, Belk's VP of customer insights and analytics.

Insights gained from a variety of sources, both internal and external, are translating to real dollars for Belk. Work with your team to understand all data sources available to enhance your solution. The more insights you are able to deliver that are actionable, the better decisions you will empower and the more competitive your organization will be in the marketplace.

## Be Specific

The more specificity you can apply to your Monetization Strategy the higher the likelihood that the actions can be executed. If your monetization strategy is too high level or abstract, the ability to derive actions and deploy them throughout the organization will be difficult. In addition, if your strategy does not fit into your team's ability to execute, it will not be actionable. This is especially true if you work in a large organization that requires you to navigate many internal groups before the action reaches a consumer.

For example, if you are an airline company, pricing may be a key focus of your strategy. You have developed a monetization strategy to price coach seats. This strategy may be difficult to deploy because it is too broad. However, if your strategy focuses on price by a particular route for a particular time period, that may be more actionable. Better yet, if you focus on a specific route, for a particular time of day, for a particular day of the week, your chances for an actionable strategy are very likely.

Limiting the scope of your monetization strategy will depend on your circumstances. Below are some suggestions to help you narrow your monetization strategy:

- **Channel**—What are the various selling channels your organization uses? Maybe you start with just one channel to narrow the focus.
- **Geography or Region**—Picking a specific country or region can help limit the options and add a layer of specificity to your strategy.
- **Time Period**—Choosing a daily or weekly view versus a quarterly or yearly might make the strategy more actionable.
- **Customer Segment**—Can you focus on just one customer type? This is a great option for providing incremental value for an underserved segment or a growth segment.
- **Product or Service Category**—Limiting the strategy to one product or service can provide more focus.

## Be Holistic

Not to contradict ourselves, but you need to be *specific* and also *holistic*. What do we mean by this? The Monetization Strategy needs to fit into the broader organization and, therefore, it needs to be holistic. This means knowing your constraints, being collaborative, and aligning to the overall corporate goals of your company.

Knowing constraints both within and outside your organization helps you determine your guardrails. We recommend building a list of possible constraints at the beginning of your project to determine if you have a risk that needs consideration before you get too far into your efforts.

Constraints can come in all sizes and shapes. Time constraints on getting something out to market during a major selling season is a big one to consider. For example, if you are a retailer, to launch something in time for the fall season can be a time window you want to hit.

Resource constraints is another boundary you want to make sure you understand. Do you have a limited budget or number of employees who can participate? Maybe the data scientist group has low bandwidth and they will be a constraint for your effort. Other constraints include historical precedence, regulatory, internal policies, and organizational.

Collaboration is another consideration for being holistic. If you are not collaborating with other departments, they may not give the okay to move forward with any actions that come from the strategy. A great example of this comes from Aditya Joshi and Eduardo Giménez's article, "Decision-Driven Marketing," where a firm's marketing department was building marketing collateral for the sales team. They discuss the divide that existed between marketing and sales:

> It's almost a business cliché that these two functions frequently go their separate ways, with little communication—let alone collaboration—between them. That was the situation at one global technology company a few years ago. Like most business-to-business companies, this one relies heavily on its skilled salespeople to close deals and grow revenue with its largest customers. Marketing is responsible for conducting campaigns and creating collateral materials to support the sales reps. In the past,

unfortunately, those materials often didn't meet the reps' needs, so many reps would revise what they were given or create their own materials. In fact, an internal survey revealed that they were spending an average of nearly one day a week digging around in the company's systems to find or develop what they felt they needed, instead of spending time with customers. Not only was this wasteful, but it resulted in materials that varied widely in appearance, tone, and consistency of message, chipping away at the company's investment in creating a distinct brand.

To help close the gap with other departments, look to engage them early in the process. Should they be a stakeholder on the project? How is what you are doing going to benefit them? Why should they care? Spend some energy reaching out to other departments and getting them excited about your efforts and how it will benefit them.

Another key concern regarding being holistic is making sure what you are doing fits into the broader strategy of the company. If you align your hypothesis and business objective back to corporate objectives, you should be fine. However, you don't want to be caught going in one direction while the firm is pivoting in another. Maybe your firm sells services and products and has decided to get out of the services business. If your monetization strategy deals with the service side of the business, it may not get legs in the organization.

Along with fitting into the broader strategy of the company, leveraging other departments' work will often be necessary if you are in a large organization. As an example, if in developing your monetization strategy for the airline industry, your strategy charges higher baggage fees, it may not fit the overall pricing strategy for baggage fees for your company. In this case, the strategy is unlikely to be adopted as the one-off in pricing will be difficult to support.

Be careful to get input along the way as you develop your strategy and leverage other departments' good work to inform your work.

## Actionable

The ability to take action on the decision from the Monetization Strategy is paramount. So many of the analytics developed today simply help someone "read the news." They are informative, but do not guide you to a specific action they should take to capture an opportunity. Your monetization strategy needs to be actionable and should consider this guiding principle as *not* optional.

As you develop the actions that someone will execute on, consider the following points:

**Specific**—The level of specificity associated with each action often determines your ability to execute. We discussed this in depth earlier in this chapter.

**Resources**—The level of resources, both human and budget, is important to understand to determine if the strategy is actionable. Does your strategy require a skillset to develop a model that does not exist internally? Does the strategy involve increasing your salesforce in order to execute? Think big when you are developing your strategy, but make sure the resources are available to make it actionable.

**Senior Management Buy-In**—Attaining consensus from senior leadership about the monetization strategy and the actions it recommends can make or break the strategy. If leadership has bought into the idea, they can provide resources from various parts of the organization to assist in making the strategy successful. If they have not bought in, they can be significant roadblocks. We recommend having a stakeholder group of senior leaders who walk the journey with you to obtain buy-in as you go.

**Complexity**—The level of complexity to execute both within your organization and outside will be a big factor to consider. If your strategy requires a lot of hoops to jump through—for example, regulatory change—it may be overly complex and not a great candidate.

**Holistic**—The action needs to fit into the broader organization structure. We discussed this in depth in the prior section.

**Organizational Energy**—Regardless of the size of your company, organizational energy is key. It is particularly true if you are a small company. Taking on too many initiatives and priorities can often lead to getting nothing accomplished. Be sure that the monetization strategy fits within the energy level of the organization. The good strategy that is easy to implement is better than the best strategy in the world that is never implemented.

**Business Lever**—The action needs to be tied to a business lever and business objective. This will ensure organizational support and that the company will get behind the action. We discuss this many times as it is worth repeating.

## Decision Matrix

Displaying the actions available to a manager is best deployed through a Decision Matrix. As you will learn in the Decision Theory chapter (Chapter 8), a Decision Matrix reflects the outcome and values of various decision scenarios in a grid format.

The matrix is useful for looking at a large quantity of decision factors and assessing each factor's relative significance. It allows the manager the ability to quickly analyze the relationship between the decision factors in order to come up with the optimal decision. The values within the matrix can be numerical or descriptive in nature.

The four building blocks of a decision matrix are: *acts, events, outcomes,* and *payoffs.* Acts are the actions or decisions that a person may take. Events are the occurrences taking place, usually with some level of uncertainty. Outcomes are the results of the occurrences, and payoffs are the values the decision maker is placing on the occurrences.

In Table 6.1, we see a Decision Matrix for a Customer Acquisition Monetization Strategy. The acts in this scenario are the channels we

**Table 6.1    Decision Matrix for a Customer Acquisition Monetization Strategy**

|   | Channel | Marketing Spend in Channel | CPM | CTR | Conversion Rate | Sales Volume | Revenue | Profit Margin (22%) | ROI |
|---|---------|--------|------|-------|-------|--------|------------|-----------|------|
| 1 | etsy | $100,000 | $3.80 | 2.40% | 1.20% | 7,579 | $930,255 | $204,656 | 205% |
| 2 | pinterest | $100,000 | $4.10 | 3.10% | 1.10% | 8,317 | $1,020,854 | $224,588 | 225% |
| 3 | ebay | $100,000 | $2.80 | 1.50% | 0.90% | 4,821 | $591,792 | $130,194 | 130% |
| 4 | silkfair | $100,000 | $2.50 | 1.10% | 0.60% | 2,640 | $324,039 | $71,289 | 71% |
| 5 | artfire | $100,000 | $1.50 | 0.09% | 0.50% | 300 | $36,823 | $8,101 | 8% |
| 6 | dawanda | $100,000 | $2.10 | 1.05% | 0.90% | 4,500 | $552,339 | $121,515 | 122% |
| 7 | bonanza | $100,000 | $1.80 | 0.88% | 0.30% | 1,467 | $180,022 | $39,605 | 40% |
| 8 | zibbet | $100,000 | $1.90 | 1.10% | 0.60% | 3,474 | $426,367 | $93,801 | 94% |
| 9 | amazon | $100,000 | $2.40 | 0.70% | 1.40% | 4,083 | $501,197 | $110,263 | 110% |
| 10 | google adwords | $100,000 | $2.30 | 1.60% | 2.30% | 16,000 | $1,963,872 | $432,052 | 432% |

want to spend our marketing dollar on. In this example, we have $100,000 to spend on one channel. The events are the Click-through (CTR) and Conversion rates. The outcome is the Sales Volume. Finally, the payoffs are the Revenue and ROI metrics.

Decision matrixes are our preferred structure for displaying monetization strategies, but there are several cases where we leverage graphical techniques to depict similar messages.

## Grounded in Data Science

Along with confidence in the quality of the data, trusting in the method used to calculate the expected results of the monetization strategy is important. If the consumer of the strategy feels like the results are not achievable or accurate, they are not likely to take action to achieve them. However, if you ground your strategy in data science that the manager trusts, you are likely to get buy-in for the prescribed actions.

For example, you are putting together a monetization strategy for attachment products purchased at a convenience drugstore. These are companion products that people purchase with an anchor product, like cereal and milk. Your task is to help your marketing department and merchandizing teams understand which products are most likely to be companion products for major purchases. Your goal is to provide a lift by solving for correct pricing of these products, placement in stores, and how they are advertised. Your initial analysis does not produce obvious attachments. But with exploratory data visualization, you discover that diapers and Tylenol are two purchases that are often made together and that you can achieve a 5 percent lift in revenue by offering a coupon for the companion purchase. If you went to the various groups with this insight, without additional analysis, you might get strange looks. However, if your data scientist is able to prove, through some basic profiling and market basket analysis, that 20 percent of the time when a consumer purchases diapers they also purchase Tylenol, the marketing manager will probably listen.

Due to the nature of a monetization strategy having a financial value and some type of implied mathematical function to determine a revenue increase or cost saving, data science will often be a part of your solution. This bring us to our next section, applying some monetary or economic value to the action.

## Monetary Value

Every monetization strategy will need some type of economic value associated with it, whether a cost savings or revenue increase. The goal of the monetization strategy is to assign a value to an action in order to determine the most optimal decision.

Anchoring back to your Business Levers is a great place to start when trying to depict an economic value for a particular action. We covered this topic in the Monetization Strategy chapter (Chapter 5), but let's do a quick recap. The Business Levers should be aligned to your company's P&L statement and are the levers by which you can drive monetary value to your organization. Examples of business levers to drive revenue include: Price, Volume, Number of Sales Reps, Market Share, Customer Acquisition, and Frequency of Customer Visits. The Business Levers provide you with plenty of fodder to align an action to your strategy.

Our primary recommendation for showing an economic value that provides a tradeoff in decisions is a dollar amount, a value showing revenue increase, profit increase, or cost saving. These are tangible numbers by which the manager can make a direct impact on the organization and clearly understand the tradeoff between actions.

Another way to depict an economic value is through a metric like Return on Investment (ROI). While this metric can provide guidance, we still suggest showing an actual dollar amount as well. An ROI of 200 percent that returns $1 million to the company is not the same as an ROI of 25 percent that returns $100 million to the company. Depending on what is important to the business objectives, either option could be correct.

Let's take a hypothetical example involving a productivity saving strategy through optimization that translates to revenue. In this case we are a trucking company looking to optimize our maintenance schedules for a fleet of trucks. By determining when a truck should be scheduled for general maintenance and proactively looking for maintenance issues that occur in trucks with similar mileage, haul loads, and repair histories, we are able to conclude the optimal schedules for repairs and maintenance.

**Table 6.2   Decision Matrix for a Maintenance Analysis**

| Truck Number | Current Mileage | Next Scheduled Service | Optimal Scheduled Service | Reason Code | Projected Productivity Saving |
|---|---|---|---|---|---|
| 35–2287 | 54,322 | 100,000 | 60,000 | Heavy Loads | $3,500.00 |
| 35–1012 | 122,412 | 125,000 | 135,000 | Recent Engine Overall | $500.00 |
| 35–0025 | 174,900 | 200,000 | 200,000 | N/A | $0.00 |
| 35–9001 | 35,000 | 50,000 | 40,000 | Weather Routes | $ 4,000.00 |
| 35–8334 | 72,399 | 75,000 | 85,000 | Light Loads | $1,500.00 |

This analysis can generate millions in revenue by delaying unnecessary maintenance and keeping trucks more productive. It can also save millions in costs by determining when a truck is most likely to need service or a major repair. By getting ahead of any maintenance issues, we can reduce costly outages and extensive repairs. Table 6.2 is an example of this analysis in a decision matrix.

If you are the fleet manager managing thousands of vehicles, this level of specificity can assist in driving actions to select which vehicles to schedule for maintenance. Based on the Optimal Schedule Service for mileage and Projected Productivity Savings, you conclude that truck numbers 35–2287 and 35–9001 should be scheduled for early service. If you multiply this analysis across thousands of vehicles in productivity savings, the numbers add up quickly.

We could have stopped our analysis and not included the Projected Productivity Savings metric, but the monetary value associated with the decision helps us determine priority as well as urgency. Monetary value may be one of the most important aspects of your monetization strategy. Put the time and energy to solving for the economic value you apply to each action and your analytical solution will have a bigger impact on the organization and drive managers to better decisions.

## Confidence Factor

As we will discuss in the Decision Theory chapter (Chapter 8), a *confidence factor* or *probability* can help navigate an executive to the action with the highest likelihood to achieve the desired results. There are several ways to depict opportunity; a probability score or descriptive measure are the two most prominent methods.

A probability score is an assigned numerical value attributed to an outcome, such as 95 percent. A descriptive measure may be the use of High, Medium, Low, or it could be a relative score of 1 to 5 where 1 is difficult to achieve and 5 is easiest to achieve.

Let's look at examples of both. In Table 6.3, we have a Propensity to Purchase score that has been calculated as a confidence factor of a particular consumer's ability to purchase a product from our company.

The second method we recommend is a descriptive measure or relative score. These are typically associated with higher level monetization strategies versus specific targeted customers. In Table 6.4, we see the Ability to Achieve as a relative score that can be applied where 5 is the easiest to achieve and 1 is the hardest.

Calculation of the Probability score depends on a number of factors. We recommend working with your data science team to come up with the best method that is most likely to be adopted and accepted by your organization.

**Table 6.3   Confidence Factor Analysis**

| Email | Name | Propensity to Purchase |
|---|---|---|
| bcho@gmail.com | Beddy Cho | 22% |
| suz@gill.com | Suzannah Gill | 88% |
| jwells@yahoo.com | Jen Wells | 75% |
| wzimbi@outlook.com | Wanda Zimbinski | 64% |
| dianaw@yahoo.com | Diana Wells | 87% |
| ada@gmail.com | Ada Wells | 35% |
| awells@outlook.com | Ayden Wells | 34% |
| theomontague@outlook.com | Theo Montague | 39% |
| beine@gmail.com | David Beine | 56% |
| mysuit@mab.com | Michael Mantegna | 65% |
| smallhands@gmail.com | Greg Sitkiwitz | 82% |
| mriad@yahoo.com | Magd Riad | 44% |
| hussmoo@apple.com | Hussian Moosajee | 25% |
| matty@google.com | Matt Mason | 64% |

**Table 6.4  Descriptive Measure Matrix**

| Segment | Emails to Send | Click-Through | Expected Click-Through Rate | Expected Conversion Rate | Total Expected Revenue | Cost per Email | ROI | Ability to Achieve |
|---|---|---|---|---|---|---|---|---|
| Northeast | 500,000 | 23,000 | 4.60% | 3.20% | $ 84,640 | $0.12 | 141% | 4 |
| Southeast | 500,000 | 31,000 | 6.20% | 3.50% | $ 37,966 | $0.05 | 152% | 2 |
| Midwest | 500,000 | 19,000 | 3.80% | 2.40% | $ 46,512 | $0.05 | 186% | 5 |
| West | 500,000 | 25,600 | 5.12% | 1.20% | $ 44,544 | $0.06 | 148% | 3 |
| Canada | 500,000 | 24,000 | 4.80% | 4.00% | $102,720 | $0.15 | 137% | 3 |

## Measurable

To know whether your actions are working, you need the ability to measure them. This is one of the hardest guiding principles to achieve. It is based largely on the level of automation an organization is able to achieve and the channels in which your organizations sells through. If these actions are mostly through offline channels, they are considerably harder to measure than online channels.

With offline channels like advertising, connecting an action to an outcome can be difficult. If one of your channels is billboard advertising where an inferred response is needed, it is difficult to measure. If the action has a promotion code associated with it that is captured at the time of sale, we can make a direct link back to the action to measure the results. Depending on your organization, the action type, and the various selling channels, you may or may not be able to measure a particular action.

If the channel is online or fully automated, measurement gets considerably easier. If the campaign involves a banner ad placement on a website, we can measure impressions and click-throughs. If the action is associated with a recorded event, for example, a truck stopped for service within a particular mileage window, the service systems should be able to provide us with this information. If the action is to see if our churn rate decreases, we can measure this through the number of customers that canceled service over a period of time. The better the automation, the easier it is to measure the outcome.

We suggest you determine up front how you plan to measure your actions when considering your monetization strategy. Measurement of actions impacts the metrics you put in your decision matrix along with the level of specificity you apply to the actions.

## Motivation

Motivating individuals to align their actions with your strategy may be necessary depending on the type of monetization strategy you deploy. People have busy agendas and often have too much work to do already. Taking on yet another task is not something most people do lightly unless there is some incentive.

For example, one of your actions is to deploy a sell-in strategy for additional space inside of a retail outlet. Your strategy will compete with the selling of major product lines that produce the bulk of the salesperson's salary along with other sales initiatives from other departments. The field sales team is not likely to jump at the chance at selling in your strategy if they don't see value in the effort. You will need to get senior management support and most likely a financial incentive for the sales reps to execute on your plan.

Here are three ideas on incentives to create an environment for a higher execution rate:

1. **Corporate Initiative**—Align your strategy to a major corporate initiative to give it energy as other groups will also be working on projects to implement this initiative. Your work efforts may help them progress their efforts, creating a winning scenario for both teams.
2. **Performance Management**—Another effective approach is getting the work effort associated with the strategy included as a key goal for the individual's performance review. This ensures that the person will get credit for their participation.
3. **Financial Rewards**—Providing a financial incentive is a powerful motivator. If someone is rewarded financially for their participation or execution of an action, they are more likely to act.

Depending on your monetization strategy and organization, adding an incentive to the strategy can drastically increase the probability that the actions are executed upon.

## Organizational Culture

According to Robert E. Quinn and Kim S. Cameron in their book, *Diagnosing and Changing Organizational Culture: Based on the Competing Values Framework*, there are four types of organizational culture:

1. **Clan**—Consensus and collaboration drives the organizations that fit into this grouping. They are internally focused and flexible. These organizations have cultures that are family-like with a focus on facilitation, mentorship, and team building.
2. **Adhocracy**—The adhocracy culture is defined by being creative. They are externally focused and flexible in nature. Innovation, entrepreneurial, and visionary are the focus of their leadership style.
3. **Market**—Competition is the focus of this organizational group. They are hard driving and focus on results. They are externally focused and controlled.
4. **Hierarchy**—Controlled with a focus on operations best describes hierarchy-oriented cultures. These cultures are internally focused and controlled in nature. Their leadership is focused on monitoring, organizing, and coordinating the various aspects of the company.

Which culture does your company fall into? Knowing how to navigate your organization's culture will help you figure out how to get support for your monetization strategy. If your organization is an *adhocracy*, then you will have more autonomy to drive a strategy through to the consumer. If you are in a *clan* organization, building consensus every step of the way will be vital. Leverage these four organizational types as you build your plan to gain the right type of support for your monetization strategy.

## Drives Innovation

The last of the Guiding Principles is the ability of the strategy to drive innovation. This is not a necessity as many of our strategies are associated with normal blocking-and-tackling of day-to-day business. However, a good percentage of our energy when building our monetization strategies is centered on driving growth for our organization, often through some type of new product introduction or innovative technique.

There are several avenues to drive innovations, many of which come from within the walls of your company. In their article, "The New Patterns of Innovation," authors Rashik Parmar, Ian Mackenzie, David Cohn, and David Gann ask the question, "How can we create value for customers using data and analytic tools we own or could have access to?" They write about the coming wave of innovation that will be created through the new data that will be generated with the upcoming technology of the Internet of Things, where machines talk to each other:

> … using data that physical objects now generate to improve a product or service or create new business value. Examples of this include smart metering of energy usage that allows utilities to optimize pricing, and devices installed in automobiles that let an insurance company know how safely someone drives.

Innovation can take many forms. Product innovation can include launching a brand-new product to the marketplace. Other product innovations can include package innovations or bundles of products to sell together. It can also include an understanding of when to innovate as a particular product may have reached its end of life.

The ability to drive innovation is an important component to consider when developing your monetization strategy. It may not be necessary for all the various types of strategies you deploy, but it can help in situations where product or service growth are key goals.

In the next chapter we will cover an example of using the Monetization Strategy framework to solve a hypothetical challenge to reinforce many of the concepts we have discussed.

# Product Profitability Monetization Strategy:
## *A Case Study*

In this chapter we will cover an example of Monetization Strategies related to product profitability. If this strategy does not fit your organization or situation, following are several monetization strategies that may spur thoughts on how you can develop custom strategies for your organization.

- Pricing strategy
- Cost opportunity
- Yield strategies
- Revenue lift
- Marketing investment
- Cross-sell/up-sell
- Inventory management
- Retention/churn
- Asset utilization
- Fleet management
- Customer acquisition
- Big data/social analytics
- Channel strategy

## Background

The example for this case study will be the fictional Edison Furniture company. Edison Furniture is a 75-year-old, highly respected office furniture supplier. It is the market leader in terms of quality, volume, and revenue. While there is a fashion veneer to office furniture design that changes with the times, at its core it is a utility, almost commoditized business. High-end, niche players have carved out space for businesses desiring an "exciting, innovative" edge for their employee workspace. However, Edison Furniture is the undisputed supplier of choice for Fortune 500 companies that office 17 percent of the workplaces in the United States.

In order to defend its leading market position, Edison Furniture offers configurable options for its core product items, such as color, size, and accent styles like desk-drawer handles. For this case study we will focus on a standard business desk with options for color and desk-drawer handles.

Furniture wood or laminate color is a slowly changing design preference. In the late 1900s, deep-wood colors such as dark cherry or mahogany dominated the market. In the 2000s, lighter colors such as ash, maple, or white on steel have become more fashionable. In the late 1900s, drawer handles were thicker and more angular. In the 2000s, slimmer, rounder handles are preferred. Style preferences change gradually as new generations climb the ladder and take their seats at the executive desk. Accordingly, as the market leader, Edison cannot pick and choose its clients' tastes; it must be able to serve new, upcoming executive tastes as well as the seasoned leader.

Cost volume is a well-established relationship in the business field; the higher the volume, the lower the cost per unit. Edison Furniture's challenge is to navigate the changing of styles and preferences, satisfying customer preferences while managing price and costs to maintain profitability.

Edison Furniture's primary channel for product orders is an online order form. The client purchasing agent can order items directly, or the sales agent may enter the order on behalf of the client. When choosing desks, clients are presented with a desk style to choose from, then a selection of colors and accent styles for the desk-drawer handles. Upon completion of the online order form and payment confirmation, a work order is sent to the distribution center to ship the selected item.

Edison Furniture's executive management has noted that although revenues have been increasing with the rate of increase of business spending, gross margins and inventory turns have been decreasing to alarming levels. Gross margin measures the profitability of items sold after transactional costs, such as cost of goods sold and inbound shipping, have been deducted from revenue. Inventory turns are calculated by dividing cost of goods sold by average inventory value. With revenues increasing and margins and inventory turns decreasing, Edison Furniture has an operations management problem.

The Executive Team commissions a cross-functional team, drawing from Finance, Sales, Marketing, Product Development, and Operations, to study the issue and recommend solutions. We structure our presentation of this case study using our Monetization Strategy Framework.

## Business Levers

In order to confirm that the business objectives, hypothesis, and actions are in line and will deliver the expected business performance, the team develops their Business Levers (see Figure 7.1). The levers articulate what will be impacted to drive revenue or reduce costs.

## Discovery

During the discovery phase, the team finalizes the Business Objective and Hypothesis. Following several working sessions and interviews with key departmental stakeholders, the team determines they have a "long-tail" product complexity problem. That is, on average, 70 percent of business profits are derived from 40 percent of 100,000 product configurations ordered each month. The top movers have a higher gross margin of 40 percent, whereas the long tail has a gross margin of 25 percent, implying that the long-tail products account for 40 percent of revenue.

Operations would love to chop off the tail and concentrate on the high-moving products but 40 percent of revenue is too much to sacrifice. The team determines they need to dive into the long tail to determine how they can improve productivity without sacrificing sales.

| | |
|---|---|
| **Business Objective** | Improve gross margins and increase inventory turns. |
| **Hypothesis** | Low-volume product configurations are dragging down profitability and productivity. |

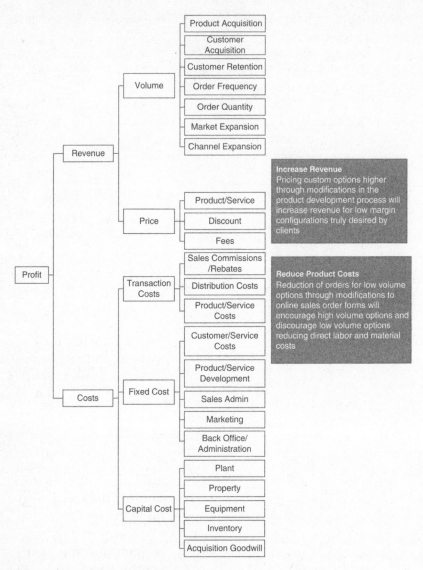

Figure 7.1    Edison Furniture Business Levers

## Decide

### *Category Tree*

The team determines the Category Tree they will use to navigate the Decision Architecture. As the market leader, maintaining top-line

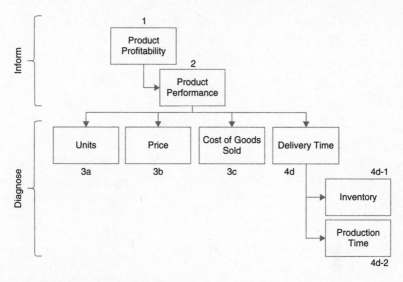

**Figure 7.2 Edison Furniture Company Category Tree**

revenue share is a key objective for Edison Furniture. While the Executive Team objectives are focused on profitability and productivity, the team does not want to lose sight of the revenue impact resulting from decisions and actions they consider. In Figure 7.2 we show the Category Tree the team develops.

### Question Analysis

Following a working session focused on flushing out the questions and decisions, the team identifies the key questions their analysis and solution should address. Following is a recap of the session:

Q1 Which product configurations account for the bottom 30 percent of annual profits on a monthly basis?

Q2 Which product configurations are the poorest performers?

Q2.1 How many units are sold per month? per year?

Q2.2 What is the price relative to other similar configurations?

Q2.3 What is the cost of goods sold per unit?

Q2.4 What is the average delivery time?

Q2.5 What is the average time to produce one unit or production cycle time?

Q2.6 How many units are in inventory on average?

### Key Decisions

With the diagnostic questions identified, the team pulls some sample data that reveals that a number of product configurations have negative gross margins. Others have unusually long production cycle times. Based on the diagnostics uncovered and the working session the team determines the key decisions they will need to make.

**Should we discontinue low-profit or unprofitable configurations?**
Discontinuing unprofitable configurations on the surface appears to be an easy answer. However, the sales team member points out that some of these products may be part of a package that could be highly profitable. Eliminating an option may put the larger package at risk.

**Should we raise prices for these configurations?**
Raising price is certainly an option but a marketing team member notes that there is nothing particularly expensive about the configuration; rather looking at a few examples, several of the cases are configurations of a newer style color with older style accents. In these cases, the individual components are not costlier, making it difficult to set a higher price when the option is selected in one configuration and not in another.

**Can we reduce production costs to make these items profitable?**
The operations department adopted Lean production techniques several years ago and, while there is always room for improvement, they believe that the current production processes are already world class. Since there is not much improvement in this area, we decide not to pursue this decision at this point.

Having evaluated these options, the team realizes that while the solutions appear simple, the decisions are difficult. They move on to determine the metrics and data they need to determine the best course of action.

| **Business Objective** | Improve gross margins and increase inventory turns. |
|---|---|
| **Hypothesis** | Low-volume product configurations are dragging down profitability and productivity. |

**Decision Architecture**

| Questions | Q1 Which product configurations account for the bottom 30 percent of annual profits on a monthly basis? |
|---|---|
| | Q2 Which product configurations are the poorest performers? |
| | Q2.1 How many units are sold per month? per year? |
| | Q2.2 What is the price relative to other similar configurations? |
| | Q2.3 What is the cost of goods sold per unit? |
| | Q2.4 What is the average delivery time? |
| | Q2.5 What is the average time to produce one unit or production cycle time? |
| | Q2.6 How many units are in inventory on average? |
| Decisions | D1 Should we discontinue low-profit or unprofitable configurations? |
| | D2 Should we raise prices for these configurations? |
| Metrics | |
| Action Levers | |

### Success Metrics

The team realizes that this problem has escaped management's attention because the business reports they use to manage performance are aggregated and analyzed by product groups. It would be impossible to analyze 100,000 individual product configurations. The problem arises because the unprofitable configurations are spread among all product types and not concentrated in one that would be easier to spot. The unprofitable configurations hide in the averages. When analyzed from a customer order or package perspective, the situation remains the same.

While the team has identified 60,000 out of 100,000 potentially problematic product configurations, they are not easy to spot due to the low unit volumes compared with the high-moving configurations.

The team selects the following success metrics to accompany each of the following decisions:

D1 Should we discontinue low-profit or unprofitable configurations?

SM—Retail price per configuration

SM—Cost per configuration

SM—Gross margin per configuration

D2 Should we raise prices for these configurations?

SM—Retail price per configuration

SM—Competitor price per configuration

SM—Total units sold per configuration

There are a total of five unique success metrics that drive our decisions that we will add to our monetization requirements.

| | |
|---|---|
| **Business Objective** | Improve gross margins and increase inventory turns. |
| **Hypothesis** | Low-volume product configurations are dragging down profitability and productivity. |

**Decision Architecture**

| | |
|---|---|
| Questions | Q1 Which product configurations account for the bottom 30 percent of annual profits on a monthly basis? |
| | Q2 Which product configurations are the poorest performers? |
| | Q2.1 How many units are sold per month? per year? |
| | Q2.2 What is the price relative to other similar configurations? |
| | Q2.3 What is the cost of goods sold per unit? |
| | Q2.4 What is the average delivery time? |

|              |                                                                                    |
|--------------|------------------------------------------------------------------------------------|
|              | Q2.5 What is the average time to produce one unit or production cycle time?         |
|              | Q2.6 How many units are in inventory on average?                                   |
| Decisions    | D1 Should we discontinue low-profit or unprofitable configurations?                |
|              | D2 Should we raise prices for these configurations?                                |
| Metrics      | SM—Retail price per configuration                                                  |
|              | SM—Cost per configuration                                                          |
|              | SM—Gross margin per configuration                                                 |
|              | SM—Retail price per configuration                                                 |
|              | SM—Competitor price per configuration                                             |
|              | SM—Total units sold per configuration                                            |
| Action Levers |                                                                                   |

## Action Levers

The team next turns its attention to the business marketing, selling, ordering, and production business processes to determine what action levers could be used to address the issue. Below are the action levers the team developed.

D1 Should we discontinue low-profit or unprofitable configurations?

A1 For product configurations with negative profitability that have no impact on other configurations and low sales volume, discontinue selling.

D2 Should we raise prices for these configurations?

A2 For product configurations with negative profitability and high sales volume, raise prices to achieve a 40 percent margin.

A3 For product configurations with low profitability and medium-to-high sales volume, raise prices to achieve 40 percent margin.

A4 For product configurations with low profitability and low sales volume, consider discontinuing.

| | |
|---|---|
| **Business Objective** | Improve gross margins and increase inventory turns. |
| **Hypothesis** | Low-volume product configurations are dragging down profitability and productivity. |

**Decision Architecture**

| | |
|---|---|
| Questions | Q1 Which product configurations account for the bottom 30 percent of annual profits on a monthly basis? |
| | Q2 Which product configurations are the poorest performers? |
| | Q2.1 How many units are sold per month? per year? |
| | Q2.2 What is the price relative to other similar configurations? |
| | Q2.3 What is the cost of goods sold per unit? |
| | Q2.4 What is the average delivery time? |
| | Q2.5 What is the average time to produce one unit or production cycle time? |
| | Q2.6 How many units are in inventory on average? |
| Decisions | D1 Should we discontinue low-profit or unprofitable configurations? |
| | D2 Should we raise prices for these configurations? |
| Metrics | SM—Retail price per configuration |
| | SM—Cost per configuration |
| | SM—Gross margin per configuration |
| | SM—Retail price per configuration |
| | SM—Competitor price per configuration |
| | SM—Total units sold per configuration |
| Action Levers | A1 For product configurations with negative profitability that have no impact on other configurations and low sales volume, discontinue selling. |
| | A2 For product configurations with negative profitability and high sales volume, raise prices to achieve a 40 percent margin. |

A3 For product configurations with low profitability and medium-to-high sales volume, raise prices to achieve 40 percent margin.

A4 For product configurations with low profitability and low sales volume, consider discontinuing.

## Data Science

In order to identify the specific options or combination of options that give rise to unprofitable configurations, the team will rely on data mining to analyze the bill of materials for the 60,000 configuration and then sort the key component parts by cost and frequency of use. They will also use market-basket analysis to determine if there are patterns of order packages that might trigger an unprofitable configuration. There may be instances where the loss of profitability on the configuration is justified by the value of the package.

For each product configuration, the team will produce a profitability number along with an impact metric. The impact number will let us know how many other profitable configurations this configuration impacts. Lastly, the Data Science team will produce a velocity metric that will provide insight into sales volume for the configuration. A number over 1.0 lets us know that the sales volume for that product has been on the increase. Anything below 1.0, and the sales volume has been on the decrease.

## Monetization Framework Requirements

The final step in completing the requirements is to review the guiding principles to see which ones the team plans to utilize.

| | |
|---|---|
| **Business Objective** | Improve gross margins and increase inventory turns. |
| **Hypothesis** | Low-volume product configurations are dragging down profitability and productivity. |

**Decision Architecture**

| | |
|---|---|
| Questions | Q1 Which product configurations account for the bottom 30 percent of annual profits on a monthly basis? |
| | Q2 Which product configurations are the poorest performers? |

Q2.1 How many units are sold per month? per year?

Q2.2 What is the price relative to other similar configurations?

Q2.3 What is the cost of goods sold per unit?

Q2.4 What is the average delivery time?

Q2.5 What is the average time to produce one unit or production cycle time?

Q2.6 How many units are in inventory on average?

| | |
|---|---|
| Decisions | D1 Should we discontinue low-profit or unprofitable configurations? |
| | D2 Should we raise prices for these configurations? |
| Metrics | SM—Retail price per configuration |
| | SM—Cost per configuration |
| | SM—Gross margin per configuration |
| | SM—Retail price per configuration |
| | SM—Competitor price per configuration |
| | SM—Total units sold per configuration |
| Action Levers | A1 For product configurations with negative profitability that have no impact on other configurations and low sales volume, discontinue selling. |
| | A2 For product configurations with negative profitability and high sales volume, raise prices to achieve a 40 percent margin. |
| | A3 For product configurations with low profitability and medium-to-high sales volume, raise prices to achieve 40 percent margin. |
| | A4 For product configurations with low profitability and low sales volume, consider discontinuing. |

**Competitive & Market Information**

| | |
|---|---|
| Industry Information | N/A |
| Competitive Intelligence | N/A |
| Market Information | N/A |

## Monetization Framework Components

| | |
|---|---|
| Quality Data | We have a data warehouse to pull product sales and order information. We will need to set up processes to identify the configurations to be targeted, extract bill-of-material and production cost information from the ERP system, and consolidate into an analytic dataset. |
| Be Specific | We will target product configurations with gross margins less than 30 percent. |
| Be Holistic | We will monitor the overall client order to ensure that high-value orders are not hurt by the effort to reduce low-volume product configurations. |
| Actionable | We will either retire a product configuration or increase prices. |
| Grounded in Data Science | We will use data mining to analyze product configurations at the component level and market-basket analysis to identify a profitability number. |
| | The team will develop an impact number that will let us know how many other configurations this configuration impacts. |
| | The team will develop a velocity metric that will provide insight into sales volume for the configuration. |
| Monetary Value | Reduce operating costs, improve gross margin and reduce inventory costs, and improve inventory turns. |
| Confidence Factor or Probability | N/A |
| Decision Matrix | We will assemble a decision matrix. |
| Measurable | We will be able to measure impact through reduction in low-value production configurations. |
| Drives Innovation | The online option selection modifications will encourage clients to adopt new styles more quickly. |

The team now has a complete Monetization Strategy that they can use to communicate to leaders and stakeholders getting support for their plan of action and the changes to be implemented in business practices and processes.

## Decision Matrix

With our requirements completed, let's put together our Monetization Strategy Decision Matrix. We are assembling the matrix to answer our two decision questions:

D1 Should we discontinue low-profit or unprofitable configurations?

D2 Should we raise prices for these configurations?

To answer our decisions, we will add our success metrics along with the new metrics the Data Science team has developed in the Decision Matrix based on the four building blocks of a decision matrix: *acts, events, outcomes,* and *payoffs.*

In our case, the acts are the choice to raise prices or retire a product configuration. The events are the individual product configurations or the Configuration ID. The outcome is the Total Units Sold per Configuration metric. Finally, the payoff is the Gross Margin Profitability metric. Table 7.1 shows the Decision Matrix with a sample of the product configurations.

In our sample, we can see some clear candidates to retire and others we would want to raise the prices on. For any product

**Table 7.1   Decision Matrix Based on a Sample of Product Configurations**

| Configura-tion ID | Retail Price per Config-uration | Cost per Configuration | Gross Margin per Configuration | Competitor Price per Configuration | Total Units Sold per Configuration | Impact Number | Velocity Metric | Gross Margin Profitability |
|---|---|---|---|---|---|---|---|---|
| 53–00348 | $1,325.00 | $1,391.25 | −5% | $1,590.00 | 2322 | 1 | 1.03 | $(66.25) |
| 25–90011 | $999 | $919.08 | 8% | $975.00 | 405 | 3 | 1.01 | $79.92 |
| 48–00001 | $750 | $825.00 | −10% | Discontinued | 50 | 0 | 0.99 | $(75.00) |
| 32–22132 | $950 | $1,016.50 | −7% | $1,140.00 | 1300 | 0 | 0.98 | $(66.50) |
| 11–48719 | $1,299 | $1,337.97 | −3% | $1,399.00 | 2073 | 4 | 1.05 | $(38.97) |
| 14–09914 | $1,050 | $1,165.50 | −11% | $1,350.00 | 300 | 12 | 0.95 | $(115.50) |
| 25–90012 | $875 | $857.50 | 2% | $1,000.00 | 485 | 0 | 0.80 | $17.50 |
| 24–00010 | $900 | $945.00 | −5% | $1,080.00 | 22 | 1 | 0.99 | $(45.00) |
| 17–45231 | $1,000 | $1,090.00 | −9% | $1,000.00 | 901 | 7 | 1.00 | $(90.00) |

configuration with an impact number of 0 and low velocity and units sold, we would want to retire immediately. For any product configuration that has a high-to-medium volume and a velocity metric over 1.0, and is priced under the competitor price, we would want to raise prices immediately.

From our work, we can take immediate actions with the decision matrix on several of the configurations. For other configurations that are not so black-and-white, we would need to perform additional analysis.

# SECTION IV

# AGILE ANALYTICS

# CHAPTER 8

# Decision Theory: *Making It Rational*

While Data Science helps you turn information into actionable insights, Decision Theory helps you structure the decision process to guide a person to the correct decision. Decision Theory, along with Behavioral Economics, is focused on understanding the components of the decision process to explain why we make the choices we do. It provides a systematic way to consider tradeoffs among attributes that helps us make better decisions.

According to Martin Peterson, Decision Theory is "more concerned with rational decisions, rather than the right ones ... it seems impossible to foresee, even in principle, which act is right until the decision has already been made. It seems much more reasonable to claim that it is always possible to foresee whether a decision is rational."

As we go through the concepts in this chapter you will see how everyone utilizes some degree of decision theory and behavioral economics in their everyday lives as we make tradeoffs around decisions, most of which have elements of uncertainty.

A real-world example of applying decision theory comes from the security technology world. Often when evaluating security threats, there is a great deal of uncertainty about the type of threat and the right type of countermeasures to deploy. Normally a software engineer codes what they believe to be the best course of action when writing the code. However, this approach is changing. By leveraging decision theory, we can develop probable and reasonable options to help guide the decision to choose countermeasures to deploy that have the highest likelihood of success given the range of uncertainty at the time of the incident, thereby greatly increasing the chances for success.

In Decision Theory, there are two kinds of analysis, *descriptive* and *normative*. Descriptive analysis is what people *actually do*, how they actually make decisions. Normative theories seek to answer what people *ought to do*. Since most of the decisions we make are based on what people ought to do, we will focus our efforts here on the normative techniques and principles.

We layer in techniques from behavioral economics, which apply psychological insights into human behavior with economic analysis to explain decision making. Examples of behavioral economics include *cognitive biases* and *choice architecture*.

We are going to cover several practical techniques you can consider as additional Lego pieces when you build your analytical solution to monetize data. These techniques include: Decision Matrix, Probability, Prospect Theory, Choice Architecture, and Cognitive Bias.

## Decision Matrix

One of the most important tools we use throughout the Analytical Cycle is the Decision Matrix. A decision matrix reflects the outcome and values of various decision scenarios in a grid format. The decision matrix is a great tool to use when looking at a large group of decision factors to assess each factor's significance. This format enables the manager to quickly analyze relationships between the decision factors to determine the optimal choice.

*Acts, events, outcomes,* and *payoffs* are the four building blocks of decision theory. Acts are the actions or decisions that a person may take. Events are the occurrences taking place, usually with a level of uncertainty. Outcomes are the results of the occurrences, and payoffs are the benefits the decision maker receives from the occurrences. The benefits within the matrix can be numerical or descriptive in nature.

For example, we are trying to decide if we should drive for no cost or take the car service Uber for $11 to a show. At this particular venue, the parking is free but there are often delays that may make us late for our show. The two decisions we have to choose between are to drive ourselves or take Uber; these would be the acts. The parking delays are the events that cause a level of uncertainty. The payoffs in this scenario are the $11 spent on Uber versus driving ourselves for $0. An additional payoff is to be on time for the show. Here is our decision matrix:

|  | **Parking Delays** | **No Parking Delays** |
|---|---|---|
| Uber car service | On-time arrival/$11 | On-time arrival/$11 |
| Drive self | Late for show/$0 | On-time arrival/$0 |

From this decision matrix, we can see that paying the $11 would reduce our uncertainty of making the show on time. The question is whether $11 is worth reducing the uncertainty.

To make a good decision matrix, there are a few principles that we would recommend:

- **Actionable**—Among the core components of a decision matrix are the acts or decisions that we outline for the user. You need to make sure that decisions you are considering are actionable for the organization, particularly if you are in a large matrix organization. If the actions you outline are too difficult to implement, the analytical solution will probably not get off the ground.
- **Rationalize Attributes**—How many attributes or metrics do you need to show in your decision matrix to help someone make a decision? This may be one of the toughest questions to answer. While a natural tendency is to consider as much information as possible, we need to ask ourselves which metrics really drive the decision and focus on these.
- **Payoff**—You must determine a monetary value or some other utility derived from making the decision, like an on-time arrival to the show. This is the incentive to make the decision. In most of our work, we find adding a monetary value to the decision helps the analyst weigh the economic benefits versus the risks, leading to better results.
- **Publish Your Math**—Trust in the techniques deployed will be important as users want to know if your calculation for a particular metric matches their understanding. The simplest way to avoid any misunderstanding is to be transparent.
- **Publish Your Sources of Data**—Along with the calculation for a particular metric, the source of the data is another area to

create visibility around. By letting users know the source of the data for your analytical solution, they can have a better understanding of your results.

- **Probability**—Adding a confidence factor to an act or decision helps an executive weigh the risk of uncertainty against the payoff. We will discuss this topic in detail due to its high importance.

## Probability

The use of a probability or confidence factor can play a big role in a decision. It may be one of the most impactful Lego pieces you can use in building your solution. Probability is the likelihood of an event occurring; the higher the probability the more likely the event will happen. If you know that your next business decision has a 95 percent probability of being successful, it gives you greater confidence in making the decision over one that has only a 20 percent probability.

To show the impact that probability can have on your decisions, let's look at an article by V. Kumar, Rajkumar Venkates, and Werner Reinart, "Knowing What to Sell, When, and to Whom." They outline several techniques to leverage probability along with the pros and cons. Describing a method they developed called the Customer Probability Cube that generated significant returns for one of their clients, they write, "At the B2B firm, the new methodology increased profits by an average of $1,600 per customer, representing an improvement in ROI of 160%. Given the sample size of over 20,000 customers, the increase in profits amounted to about $32 million for the sample group alone." This is a great example of the power of probability and its influence on making the right decisions.

While there are several ways to represent probability, we employ a probability score or a descriptive measure. A probability score is an assigned numerical number attributed to an outcome, such as 95 percent. A descriptive measure may be the use of High, Medium, Low, or a relative score of 1 to 5 where 1 is difficult to achieve and 5 is easy to achieve.

Let's look at an example of a relative score of probability. In this fictional example, we are the Edison Credit Card company that sells our credit cards via online channels with no physical presence (see Table 8.1). Our marketing department has developed a decision

Table 8.1    Edison Credit Card Probability Matrix

| Segment | Emails to Send | Click-Through | Expected Click-Through Rate | Expected Conversion Rate | Total Expected Revenue | Cost per Email | ROI |
|---------|---------|---------|---------|---------|---------|---------|---------|
| Northeast | 500,000 | 23,000 | 4.60% | 3.20% | $84,640 | $0.12 | 141% |
| Southeast | 500,000 | 31,000 | 6.20% | 3.50% | $37,966 | $0.05 | 152% |
| Midwest | 500,000 | 19,000 | 3.80% | 2.40% | $46,512 | $0.05 | 186% |
| West | 500,000 | 25,600 | 5.12% | 1.20% | $44,544 | $0.06 | 148% |
| Canada | 500,000 | 24,000 | 4.80% | 4.00% | $102,720 | $0.15 | 137% |

matrix with the acts, events, outcomes, and payoffs. From this decision matrix, we would probably focus efforts on the Midwest and the Southeast given their ROI.

To help determine the best decision, working with our data scientist, we create a confidence factor for each of the segmented email campaigns on a scale of 1 to 5, where 5 is the easiest to achieve and 1 is the hardest. The ability to achieve takes into account current market penetration, overall saturation of the market with competing credit card companies, number of potential buyers that fit the credit card companies' target offer, or other factors. We update the decision matrix with the newly added Ability to Achieve metric, as seen in Table 8.2.

The updated matrix tells a different story than Table 8.1, which only leveraged ROI metrics. From this analysis we still determine that the Midwest is the best choice, but this time instead of the Southeast,

Table 8.2    Probability Matrix with Ability to Achieve Metric

| Segment | Emails to Send | Expected Click-Through Rate | Expected Conversions to Purchase | Expected Conversion Rate | Total Expected Revenue | Cost per Email | ROI | Ability to Achieve |
|---------|---------|---------|---------|---------|---------|---------|---------|---------|
| Northeast | 500,000 | 4.60% | 736 | 3.20% | $84,640 | $0.12 | 141% | 4 |
| Southeast | 500,000 | 6.20% | 463 | 3.50% | $37,966 | $0.05 | 152% | 2 |
| Midwest | 500,000 | 3.80% | 456 | 2.40% | $46,512 | $0.05 | 186% | 5 |
| West | 500,000 | 5.12% | 307 | 1.20% | $44,544 | $0.06 | 148% | 3 |
| Canada | 500,000 | 4.80% | 960 | 4.00% | $102,720 | $0.15 | 137% | 3 |

we determine the Northeast would be the second-best choice. These two segments have the highest probability to achieve the expected outcome. The West and Canada have a neutral ability to achieve the expected outcome while we have less confidence in our ability to achieve the expected ROI in the Southeast. Notice that Canada is by far the most profitable segment and has a high ROI, but the probability metric makes us question how much money to allocate to this segment.

The prior example has a relative descriptive factor to describe probability. Let's look at an example of using a probability score. In Table 8.3, we work with our data scientist to build a propensity model that scores at a customer level to determine who is most likely to accept our offer. The score provides a probability to accept the offer based on demographic and financial credit information. We also have limited marketing dollars and want to apply them against the highest likelihood for success. In this case, we choose everyone above 65 percent.

Developing a probability factor for your decision matrix takes time and resources, but it can be a large factor in the success of your analytical solutions and monetization strategies.

**Table 8.3    A Propensity Model**

| Email | Name | Propensity to Purchase |
| --- | --- | --- |
| bcho@gmail.com | Beddy Cho | 22% |
| suz@gill.com | Suzannah Gill | 88% |
| jwells@yahoo.com | Jen Wells | 75% |
| wzimbi@outlook.com | Wanda Zimbinski | 64% |
| dianaw@yahoo.com | Diana Wells | 87% |
| ada@gmail.com | Ada Wells | 35% |
| awells@outlook.com | Ayden Wells | 34% |
| theomontague@outlook.com | Theo Montague | 39% |
| beine@gmail.com | David Beine | 56% |
| mysuit@mab.com | Michael Mantegna | 65% |
| smallhands@gmail.com | Greg Sitkiwitz | 82% |
| mriad@yahoo.com | Magd Riad | 44% |
| hussmoo@apple.com | Hussian Moosajee | 25% |
| matty@google.com | Matt Mason | 64% |

## Prospect Theory

Developed by Daniel Kahneman and Amos Tversky in 1979, prospect theory describes how people make decisions around economic risk. The theory puts forth that people do not interpret risk rationally in economic terms. Daniel Kahneman elaborates on several elements that comprise prospect theory in his book, *Thinking, Fast and Slow*. We cover three of these components: *certainty effect, loss aversion,* and *diminishing sensitivity*.

- **Certainty Effect**—People have a strong preference for certainty and are willing to forgo opportunities in order to achieve it. For example, a person may choose a 100 percent chance of winning $100 versus a 90 percent of winning $150. The certainty effect reinforces our advice to include a probability or confidence factor in your Decision Architecture, helping to lead an executive to a better decision.
- **Loss Aversion**—All things being equal, people will give higher weight to a perceived loss than the equivalent gain, even if the final outcome is the same. To elaborate, the utility gains from receiving $100 should be equal between one situation in which you are given $100 and another in which you are given $200, but then lose $100. In both scenarios the end results are $100, but the perceived loss of $100 in the second scenario is viewed less favorably than just being given $100 outright.

   While it may be tempting to show both the costs and benefits of a particular decision, our internal biases may influence our judgment if the costs are too high. The cost associated with a decision may be perceived as a loss. Loss aversion tells us that when we frame a decision matrix, be careful in displaying the outcomes that have gains and losses in order to avoid triggering loss-aversion bias.
- **Diminishing Sensitivity**—People tend to focus on relative differences rather than absolute differences. For example, the subjective perception is that the difference between $100,000 and $95,000 is much smaller than between $1,000 and $6,000. Both are $5,000, but we weigh the difference in the second scenario higher.

When composing your decision matrix, the payoff amounts and how they are depicted could steer someone in the wrong direction. Add confidence factors and velocity metrics as needed to help overcome diminishing sensitivity.

## Choice Architecture

Choice architecture helps improve decision making by presenting the options in a carefully structured process. This can be accomplished in a number of different ways, from the number of choices to the default choice provided to managers.

A great example of choice architecture is the Save More Tomorrow Plan, in which individuals are opted into employee retirement savings plans. In their article, "Leaders as Decision Architects," John Beshers and Francesca Gino elaborate on the findings behind a default option with the retirement savings plan:

> [O]n average only half the workers at companies with opt-in systems join their plan by the time they've been employed at the firm for one year. Automatic enrollment generates participation rates of 90% or higher.

Listed here are three components of choice architecture that may help you with your monetization strategy:

1. **Defaults**—Consumers and users are more likely to choose a default option when one is provided. Defaults can help a person navigate to the correct choice. This phenomenon may be due to a number of reasons, one of which is that individuals interpret the architect of the solution as an authority and accept the presented option. Whatever the reason, consider setting defaults to steer an information user to a successful decision.
2. **Reducing Choice Overload**—When someone has too many choices it reduces their motivation to make a choice, which is called choice overload. For example, in her jam study, Sheena Iyengar offered a selection of two different booths for tasting jams. One booth had 24 options and the other had 6. Sixty percent of the customers were drawn to the booth with 24 options of jam while only 40 percent were drawn to the

booth with 6 options. The findings on purchases is where this gets interesting; 30 percent of the people who sampled from the smaller assortment decided to purchase while only 3 percent of the larger booth made a purchase.

It is better to present only a few choices or, in our case, decisions, to enable a better outcome. We can limit the number of decisions presented to a manager by providing a signal such as an alert or probability to help them quickly focus on issues that require attention rather than having to consider all options.

3. **Avoiding Attribute Overload**—When a product has too many attributes, it makes it difficult for consumers to evaluate options. For example, if a box of cereal has 20 different attributes that are displayed in the marketing message to the consumer, the customer will have a difficult time understanding how this cereal compares to other cereals in order to make an informed choice.

This holds true when designing your monetization strategy. If you put in too many metrics for a person to evaluate in order to make a decision, you may cause analysis paralysis. We recommend prioritizing the metrics to just those that drive action to enable better decisions.

To read more on this subject, we recommend the book *Nudge: Improving Decisions About Health, Wealth, and Happiness* by Richard Thaler and Cass Sunstein.

## Cognitive Bias

Cognitive bias is where an individual holds a view of a situation or object that is based on their subjective experiences, which may not be completely consistent with objective reality. Cognitive bias can play a big role in how we make decisions, which presents one of the most difficult challenges when composing your monetization strategy. This type of bias can impact many of the process steps within our methodology, interviews, working sessions, metrics, actions, decisions, and so on.

We are not suggesting that our learned experiences are not extremely helpful in guiding us to make effective decisions. However, these experiences should inform our decisions, not cloud them. We can often let prior experiences influence decisions to our detriment.

There is an entire field of study on this topic, so let's not go too deep, but consider that biases exist as you design your solution. Look to confirm a bias with facts or challenge the bias before making it a part of your analytical solution.

Here are some of the top cognitive biases we see when building our solutions:

**Confirmation Bias**—Confirmation bias is the inclination to look for information regarding a particular topic that confirms existing opinions, beliefs, and thoughts. If you are conducting an interview or working session, you may have to spend time priming the team with brainstorming activities related to thinking outside the box or keeping an open mind to assist with overcoming confirmation bias.

**Recency Bias**—This bias refers to the propensity to weigh the most recent information heavier and as more important than older data. This can often result in an information user not drilling into an issue to look deeper for causality while accepting surface-level information only.

**Anchoring Bias**—Opposite of recency bias, anchoring bias can be described as the inclination to anchor too heavily on the first piece of information you hear while putting less importance on subsequent data points. This is an important bias to recognize when working in sessions. For example, the order that the information is presented in will be important to determine the right Success Metrics and not just the first metrics that are considered.

**Overconfidence**—This bias can cause a person to overlook the facts of a situation that challenges their current understanding. This is probably most commonly found in experts who have been in a particular field for a long time. Experts may be overconfident in their understanding of the information, leading them to false conclusions that do not fully take into account changes in technology or market conditions.

**Bandwagon Effect**—The bandwagon effect occurs when a person adopts a belief or perspective because others have adopted a similar belief. This can be seen in workshops or group events as individuals with seniority can dictate the beliefs or decisions of the team. The bandwagon effect is one of the reasons we prefer to start with independent interviews to construct the decision architecture before team-based working sessions.

**Clustering Illusion**—The propensity to glean insights from random events is called the clustering illusion. We can often associate random events together due to proximity of the events. Our responsibility is to challenge this bias and prove it through data science. Data science can help us uncover relationships in the data to validate whether the clustering is real.

**Outcome Bias**—When a decision is based on the outcome of a prior event with little regard for how that event developed, outcome bias occurs. This can be especially true when trying to correlate marketplace activities with internal corporate strategies and initiatives, such as a big uptick in orders associated with a branding strategy. There may be some correlation between the two events, but you should be careful to consider other probable causes for the increase in orders such as a recent improvement in the economy.

**Salience Bias**—The propensity to focus on metrics that we are comfortable with versus a newer metric that we may not completely understand is known as salience bias. User training is vitally important to fight salience bias to ensure people adopt all available tools.

**Zero-Risk Bias**—People prefer certainty, even to their own detriment. Zero-risk bias is the inclination for reducing or removing a small risk to zero versus reducing another risk that may have a bigger impact. This can manifest itself in a decision to reduce risk in one manager's area at the expense of increased risk for the larger organization.

**Empathy Bias**—The propensity to underestimate the influence of one's feelings in the decision-making process. For example, a sales manager may have a winning personality, leading you to unknowingly overestimate that manager's actual performance.

**Ostrich Effect**—This bias is centered on a person's ability to ignore dangerous or bad data. To combat this bias, threshold signals make bad data difficult to ignore and can help an information user pay more attention to the issue.

Biases exist and it is our job to understand when they occur and architect a solution to minimize them. It is important to make sure that when you are driving out the decisions that fuel the Decision Architecture you apply the right amount of challenge to minimize the impact of cognitive bias on the outcome.

We covered a lot of ground in this chapter and provided you with many tools, or Lego pieces, that you can now utilize as you build your solutions. From Probability and Decision Matrixes to Choice Architecture and Cognitive Bias, working to create the right conditions for a quality decision is a multidisciplinary approach. The techniques in this chapter should help you structure the decision process to guide a person to the correct decision.

# 9

# Data Science: *Making It Smart*

**D**ata science is becoming more prominent in everyday analytical exercises, especially around big data. A good example of this is in the car industry. Your local car dealership may be paying for anonymized search data to understand what cars you might want to purchase. In Jacob LaRiviere's article, "Where Predictive Analytics Is Having the Biggest Impact," he writes about a car dealership leveraging big data and data science to optimize inventory.

> [B]ig data solution leverages the previously unused data point that people do a considerable amount of social inquiry and research online before buying a car. The increased prediction accuracy, in turn, makes it possible to achieve large increases in operational efficiency—having the right inventory in the right locations.

By applying data science, we derive greater insight from the information that can be used to guide someone to potentially overlooked opportunities and issues. In the case of the car dealership, they extract web search data for each dealership location to understand what cars are in higher demand in those locations, thereby adjusting stock levels due to anticipated demand.

To empower your analytics, you need to use data science techniques. Data science helps you turn information into insights that are actionable by employing techniques from many fields, including statistics, operations research, information science, and computer science. There are numerous data science techniques, including visualization, predictive modeling, forecasting, data mining, pattern recognition, artificial intelligence, and machine learning. Each of these techniques relies on data, including structured and unstructured data, with a focus in today's world on big data.

For now, let's look at each technique as a tool, or Lego piece, we can use when assembling an analytical solution. We focus on techniques that any practitioner can use to drive business value, often with the help of a data scientist. We will provide an overview of the techniques to give you context for how best to utilize each of these to create your monetization strategy. Several of the techniques have deep disciplines, but a general understanding is all you need to get started.

In this chapter we will cover:

- Metrics
- Thresholds
- Trends and Forecasting
- Correlation Analysis
- Segmentation
- Cluster Analysis
- Velocity
- Predictive and Explanatory Models
- Machine Learning

## Metrics

Let's start with a basic technique for any analysis, the metric. A *metric* is some unit of measurement that enables a manager to process information. The metric can be something as simple as gross sales or as complicated as the beta of a stock. You may hear the terms *measure* and *metric* thrown around in the same sentence as most people use them interchangeably. We are not too picky about the use of the two terms, but we do feel compelled to point out the difference.

A measure is a size, amount, or degree expressed in a numeric value. For example, a company's Earnings is a single number for how much the company earned in a particular time period. A metric is defined as a combination of two or more measures. Let's take an example of a common metric of valuation for a company, the price-to-earnings (P/E) ratio. The P/E ratio is calculated by taking two measures, stock price divided by the company's earnings, to assemble a quick reference point to the valuation of the company.

Companies are perceived to be inexpensive if they have low P/E ratios, and overpriced if they have high P/E ratios. You can ask someone to perform the math on their own, or provide a metric that provides relative scale for quick evaluation.

When calculating metrics, it is important to define and differentiate between four categories of metrics: *key performance indicators* (KPIs), *success metrics, diagnostic metrics,* and *operational metrics.* The distinction is important to enable the information user's ability to derive relevancy from the analysis. If we overburden the analysis with too many metrics, we may unwittingly cause analysis paralysis and confusion.

A great example of this comes to us from behavioral economics and choice architecture. Behavioral economics leverages a method of economic analysis with psychological insights to explain decision making. Alain Samson, PhD, defines it thus: "Behavioral economics uses psychological experimentation to develop theories about human decision making." A part of behavioral economics is Choice Architecture, first defined by Richard Thaler and Cass Sunstein in their 2008 book, *Nudge: Improving Decisions About Health, Wealth, and Happiness.* An example of choice architecture can be found at Google's cafeteria, where management implemented choice architecture to help employees adopt healthy eating habits. They posted a sign informing employees that people who choose larger plates tend to overeat. Due to this simple change, they saw an increase of 50 percent in small plate usage.

While Google still provided two options, a smaller or larger plate, they helped people make the better choice. In our solutions, we can implement choice architecture through the metrics we choose in our solutions. It will directly impact the usability of the analytical solution and type of choices and decisions it empowers.

There is also the "so-what?" factor if you provide too many metrics. The metric may be interesting, but if it is not used or does not drive an action, we question whether to deploy it in our solution.

Let's take a look at our four categories of metrics:

1. **KPI**—A key performance indicator can be thought of as an organizational metric that is used to determine progress on goals at all levels in the organization. These should be limited to five to seven top KPIs that align to the business's objectives and goals. An example might include Revenue, Units Sold, or Net Profit.

2. **Success Metrics**—We leverage success metrics to drive our decisions in our monetization strategy. As we discussed in the Decision Analysis chapter (Chapter 4), our success metrics are those that a managers can utilize to inform themselves about what decision to make. We usually uncover the success metrics at the end of a process of determining the questions, decisions, actions, and metrics that a manager makes on a particular topic.

3. **Diagnostic Metrics**—Diagnostic metrics are specific metrics for a particular subject area, department, or capability. These metrics help us further diagnose an issue or opportunity. In addition to success metrics, they should be linked to a particular decision and drive action, but not always.

4. **Operational Metrics**—These are the most basic metrics used to monitor or analyze the performance of a business process. They form the foundation for diagnostic and success metrics but are typically too narrow to rise to the top in an analytical solution.

Let's use the Edison Credit Card Company, which issues credit cards through the Internet, direct mail, and affiliate marketing, as a fictional example. We are charged with building an analytical solution for the company and need to bucket the following 10 metrics into our paradigm of four metric types.

1. Acquisition Cost per Customer
2. Email Marketing Click-Through Rate
3. Database Server Utilization
4. Customer Attrition Rate
5. Average Revenue per Customer
6. Affiliate Marketing/Finance Website Channel/Number of Referrals
7. Average Direct Mail Response Rate
8. Direct Mail/College Campaign/Response Rate
9. Average Interest Rate
10. Charge Off Percentage to Revenue

There are some clear winners for each of the buckets and there are several metrics that may be fungible depending on the analytical need. Clearly metric number 3, Database Server Utilization, is in the operational category. For the KPI bucket, numbers 1, 4, 5, and 9 all qualify as high-level metrics that drive the organization's performance. Metric numbers 6 and 8 are best suited for a specific diagnostic and therefore go into the diagnostic metrics bucket. For success metrics, metrics numbered 2, 6, and 10 are strong candidates.

Again, the purpose is to determine what metrics truly drive insights and actions relevant to the stated hypothesis and business objectives. A lot of analysts and data scientists can get lost in creating metrics that are not used or actionable. Horticulturists are fond of saying that a weed is simply a misplaced plant. We can view metrics in a similar manner. Placing the right metric with the right analytical solution is the goal.

## Thresholds

Once our metrics are defined, we add additional relevance to assist the manager with the ability to quickly decide if there is an opportunity or issue. We think of this as a threshold or a boundary range that is triggered when the metric falls outside of this range. It is the signal to the information user that further diagnostics may be needed or it is time to take action.

An example of how a threshold can be a signal for further investigation can be found at Intercontinental Hotel Group (IHG), where they have built a set of diagnostic analytical solutions that allow a user to determine if individual hotels are leveraging forecasting strategies to optimize occupancy. Once a certain threshold is hit, a visual alert is triggered, signaling the need for reforecasting.

To implement a threshold, let's return to our fictional example of the Edison Credit Card Company. If we know that our average Customer Attrition Rate is 15 percent a year, we may determine that a 2 percent variance is okay. We know that if this metric rises to 18 percent in any given time period, we need to investigate immediately to understand why attrition seems to be rising and what is occurring with the business or marketplace in order to take action. Here are some questions the manager may ask to diagnose the issue:

- Has the market moved to a lower interest rate and our credit card product is no longer competitive?
- Did we charge off a large number of bad customers, causing a spike in attrition?
- Is there a particular credit card product that is causing the bulk of the attrition spike?

To determine an acceptable variance range, you may deploy a few techniques from various sources. The company's financial analyst may determine these are the limits in order for the company to reach its financial targets. The variance may be an industry norm against a competitive set that typically sees a range of customer attrition between 13 and 17 percent. Another option is an analysis from a data scientist determining that the standard deviation from historical attrition rates for the company varies by 2 percent within a given year.

Let's take a look at standard deviation for this example as it might be more the norm if no clear threshold amount is apparent in the data. Standard deviation is a metric to quantify variation in a dataset. If the standard deviation is low, it suggests that the dataset points are close to the mean. A high standard deviation indicates that the variation in the dataset is dispersed over a wider range.

One standard deviation in the dataset will encompass roughly 68 percent of the distribution, which might be an initial tolerance level when you begin to determine the needed threshold for a metric. If a metric value falls out of the 68 percent expected range, we know that there might be an issue or opportunity. In this case, the standard deviation has been calculated as 1.129 percent based on a 15 percent average attrition rate. If the attrition rate rises above 16.129 percent, an alert will trigger, notifying the analyst that there may be an issue requiring further investigation. Given that attrition is undesirable, you are primarily concerned when the rate exceeds the upper bound of our threshold.

## Trends and Forecasting

Trends are a series of data points for a particular metric to show performance over time. In the diagnostic process, an analyst wants to quickly surmise if the issue is a onetime anomaly or a systemic concern that warrants further diagnosis. Forecasting is the ability to use historical data to determine the most likely outcome or outcomes in the future. Both trend analysis and forecasting can be used by the manager to dig deeper into a metric to determine if a pattern exists that can be leveraged to take advantage of an opportunity.

Weather forecasts powered by Monte Carlo simulations are an excellent example of forecasts. In today's world, storm trackers don't rely on a single forecast; they utilize many potential scenarios to understand the probability that a storm will take a particular path. Monte Carlo simulations select many data points for a given situation and produce a range of potential outcomes. For Hurricane Sandy over 50 different scenarios were run with over 10 million randomized atmospheric variables to determine the possible landing point, enabling a 20-hour window to alert residents to evacuate.

To further build on our fictional example, let's take the Edison Credit Card Company and look at how trend and forecasting may be employed. Customer Attrition Rate is a key metric measuring the churn of customers on a monthly basis. Taking one month as a data point for a decision may mislead the analysis. If a manager receives a reading that the current month of July has an attrition rate of 18.8 percent and the average is 15 percent, they have good reason to be nervous.

However, the manager will probably want to know if the issue is systemic or just an anomaly. At this point, a trend is a good tool that can provide more context to the metrics. In Figure 9.1, we see a five-month prior history along with a forecast for the next few months, August through October. With this new perspective, the manager is more likely to be at ease with the onetime anomaly.

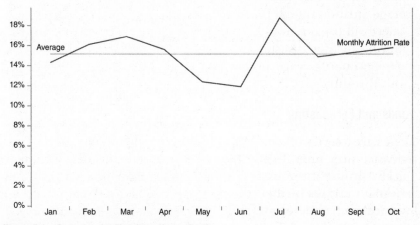

Figure 9.1　Customer Attrition Rate (Annualized)

## Correlation Analysis

Another key technique to assist you with determining the relevance of a metric is correlation analysis. A correlation is an association between two or more metrics where a linear dependency or relationship exists, but correlation does not necessarily mean causality. An actionable relationship is the key determinant for our purposes.

What does this mean? Correlation is determining *what* things happened together. Causality is trying to determine *why* something happened. A great example comes from an article by David Ritter, "When to Act on a Correlation, and When Not To." He contemplates the importance of correlation and causality when determining whether to take action based on risk and confidence in the relationship. In this example, the NYC Health department monitors the city for violations and has deployed sewer sensors to collect readings.

> These sensors detect the amount of grease flowing into the sewer system at various locations throughout the city. If the data collected shows a concentration of grease at an unexpected location—perhaps due to an unlicensed restaurant—officials will send a car out to determine the source.

This is a good example where casualty may be hard to determine, but with correlations and confidence in the meaning of the data, action for further investigation was taken. By sending out an investigative unit they may be able to determine the cause.

To find correlations that exist in the data, it is helpful to interview subject matter experts (SMEs) to gain an understanding of learned business rules and correlations that are institutional knowledge. These learnings are often the starting point for deeper analysis. We should take care to validate the insight gained from an SME, as organizational wisdom can be dated, inaccurate, or influenced by a cognitive bias. However, these are great starting points to investigate further through data science.

Another approach is to begin with a data scientist digging into a dataset to look for relationships. One approach is the Pearson's Correlation Coefficient (or simply correlation coefficient). It is obtained by dividing the covariance of the two variables by the product of their standard deviations. Let's briefly review the covariance and correlation coefficient:

- Covariance, a measure of how two variables are linearly related, is calculated by taking the average of the product of deviations (differences) of the two variables from their own averages:

$$\sigma_{xy} = \frac{1}{N} \sum_{i=1}^{N} (x_i - \mu_x)(y_i - \mu_y)$$

- Correlation coefficient ($\rho_{X,Y}$) is a scaled, unitless version of covariance. It is obtained by dividing the covariance of two variables by the product of their respective standard deviations, and can range from –1 to 1:
  - A correlation of –1 indicates the two variables are perfectly negatively associated (a unit increase in one variable is associated with a unit decrease in the other).
  - A correlation of 1 indicates the two variables are perfectly positively associated (a unit increase in one variable is associated with a unit increase in the other).
  - A correlation of 0 indicates there exists no linear association between the two variables.
- In Figure 9.2, (a) illustrates strong positive correlation, (b) strong negative, and (c) no linear correlation. In (d), the correlation coefficient is also 0, indicating no linear correlation— but clearly a curvilinear relationship exists ($y = -x2$).

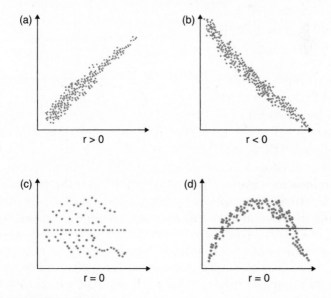

**Figure 9.2　Correlation Examples**

## Segmentation

Dividing organizations' customers, markets, and/or channels into groupings of similar characteristics or behavior is known as segmentation. The purpose of segmenting a population of data can be for a variety of reasons. One reason may be to further refine and target marketing activities to drive up relevance of a message. Another might be to segment customers in categories to determine profitability and potential. The basic premise of segmentation is by grouping your customer into the right segments you can target a specific message that would drive a lift in sales due to higher relevance of your message.

An analytic dataset typically has many characteristics useful for segmentation. For example, the attributes in a demographic segmentation may include: *geography, age, income, education,* and *ethnicity.* If an organization does not already have customer, market, or channel segments, this method can be of great use to find areas to monetize underserved segments. If an organization already leverages segmentation, there may be additional opportunities to further carve out sub-segments to drive additional revenue lift, assuming these sub-segments are commercially feasible.

Segmentation can also include letting customers self-select into a segment based on purchasing behavior. In Gretchen Gavett's article, "What You Need to Know About Segmentation," she writes about how her company, Quidol, markets their early pregnancy test:

> [The company] created two different products to appeal to two segments …: the "hopefuls" and the "fearfuls." The actual test products were almost identical, but the two products were given different names and package designs, were placed in different aisles of a drugstore, and were priced differently.

There was a $3 price difference in the two products, even though they were the same core product. The cheaper version, or "fearfuls," was marketed in a mauve background with no baby on the box, located near the condoms. The "hopefuls," the more expensive version, was marketed in a pink box with a smiling baby, located near the ovulation-testing kits. Based on the life experience of the individual purchasing the pregnancy test, they can opt into the segment that best fits them.

Let's take a look at our fictional example, the Edison Credit Card Company, to further refine this concept. From Edison's metrics that we reviewed earlier in the chapter, we infer they already have Customer and Channel segments. From the Affiliate Marketing Number of Referrals for the Finance Website metric we deduce they have channel segments and that one of the channels is Financial Websites. From the Direct Mail/College Campaign/Response Rate metric, we determine they have customer segments and have one targeted to college students.

After a few questions, we determine that they do not segment their customers based on a particular geography. After analyzing the company's campaign management and sales data, we identify five geographical segments with the following click-through and conversion data points (see Table 9.1).

Table 9.1    Marketing Effectiveness Decision Matrix

| Segment | Emails Sent | Click-Through | Click-Through Rate | Conversions to Purchase | Conversion Rate |
|---|---|---|---|---|---|
| Northeast | 352,488 | 16,214 | 4.60% | 519 | 3.20% |
| Southeast | 232,101 | 14,390 | 6.20% | 463 | 3.50% |
| Midwest | 177,033 | 6,727 | 3.80% | 161 | 2.40% |
| West | 483,282 | 24,744 | 5.12% | 297 | 1.20% |
| Canada | 58,972 | 2,831 | 4.80% | 113 | 4.00% |

From this analysis, we decide to focus more of our efforts on the Northeast and Southeast regions. We look for affiliates in these areas to partner with to drive more referrals. In addition, we place higher priority on our marketing activities and spend in these regions. This exercise shows that by segmenting the data, we find opportunities for additional revenue the company can drive.

Many segmentation exercises have more than one dimension. For example, in Figure 9.3 we create four segments that have Income, Household Size, and Age as segment dimensions to create their segmentation strategy. Multidimensional segmentation models are more complex to develop and comprehend, but the principles behind them are the same. Their purpose is to answer the questions, "How do we group our customers to best target sales and marketing activities to them?"

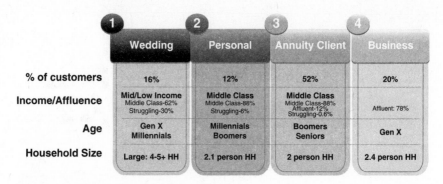

| | ① Wedding | ② Personal | ③ Annuity Client | ④ Business |
|---|---|---|---|---|
| **% of customers** | 16% | 12% | 52% | 20% |
| **Income/Affluence** | Mid/Low Income<br>Middle Class-62%<br>Struggling-30% | Middle Class<br>Middle Class-88%<br>Struggling-6% | Middle Class<br>Middle Class-88%<br>Affluent-12%<br>Struggling-0.6% | Affluent: 78% |
| **Age** | Gen X<br>Millennials | Millennials<br>Boomers | Boomers<br>Seniors | Gen X |
| **Household Size** | Large: 4-5+ HH | 2.1 person HH | 2 person HH | 2.4 person HH |

Figure 9.3    Multidimensional Segmentation Model

## Cluster Analysis

Cluster analysis is the grouping of like data points that are "similar" across enough characteristics to form a cluster and significantly "different" from other data points with respect to the same characteristics. Clustering is similar to segmentation, but is machine-learned and more mathematically intensive than segmentation.

For example, you may have a clustered approach around the propensity to purchase or likelihood to purchase a companion product. Marketers often use demographic characteristics of shoppers or locations to form clusters to better understand the different desires, needs, and behaviors of consumers in a marketable way (see Figure 9.4).

These data-driven clusters can be profiled with behavioral or transactional data and used to form market *segments* against which to action. In this case, we use segments and clusters almost interchangeably, with segments being clusters that are "brought to life" and utilized for marketing.

An example of this can be found at Thomson Reuters Corporation when it made a dramatic transformation into a global information services firm from a paper-based publishing company. In order to turn the corner, the company created segments aligned to the users of their financial products; these included institutional equity advisers, fixed-income advisers, and investment bankers. Next, they leveraged clustering techniques to drive strategic direction within these segments. In Richard J. Harrington and

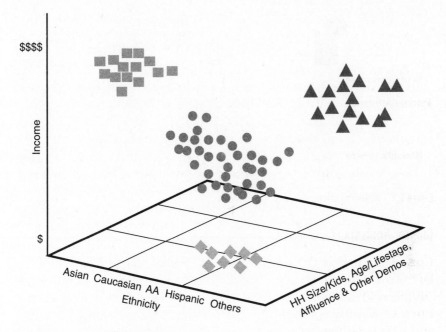

**Figure 9.4    Cluster Analysis Example**

Anthony K. Tjan's article, "Transforming Strategy One Customer at a Time," they write about the clustering approach:

> Within the investment management group, we identified three clusters of customers—users who had only basic needs, users who wanted advanced functionality, and high-end users who needed the best real-time information.... The implication was that there should be three versions of the offering that Thomson Financial was trying to develop for investment managers: one for each cluster. That insight into how preferences differed was absolutely critical to us when we reset our product development priorities. It also led us to do differential pricing—to charge more for additional highly valued features. And it made clear to us that we needed to move faster in the real-time data cluster; previously, Thomson had mostly prioritized serving the basic and advanced clusters. Ultimately, we developed value propositions for each of the three clusters.

This approach to clustering helped Thomson Reuters Corporation survive and thrive in the digital transformation that has occurred in the publishing and information industry.

An example of using visual display of information to understand underserved segments can be found at Sean Gourley's company, Quid, where they use semantic-clustering analysis to spot white spaces in competition for possible opportunities. They recently identified an opportunity to link gaming and biopharma together, producing a new market for advertising. "Such maps expose surprising relationships between and across sectors and, even more tantalizing, the white spaces among them—which can offer firms strategic opportunities to connect companies operating in different markets, to take existing products into new sectors, or to innovate with products and services no one has even dreamed up yet."

Cluster analysis comprises several data-mining techniques. A cluster cannot be universally defined because it is based on natural groupings of characteristics in the data that form a cluster depending on the technique being used. Two of the most common clustering techniques we discuss here are *hierarchical* and *k-means* clustering algorithms.

Before we can assign clusters, we determine which of the data points (units/stores, shoppers, consumers, hotels, etc.) are most similar. There are many mathematical ways to do this. For a simple example, we illustrate using stores and their associated shopper demographics (see Figure 9.5).

Stores 1 and 3 are most similar, or closest, to each other based on shopper area demographics. We use a mathematical "distance" formula to determine similarity and can see this easily in the example data.

But what happens when we have many more stores, and many more characteristics? A statistical clustering algorithm can take into account many more data attributes (i.e., shopper demographics), for thousands of stores, and iteratively determines which stores are

Which two stores are most similar?

| Store | Median HH Income |
|-------|-----------------|
| Store 1 | 27k |
| Store 2 | 32k |
| Store 3 | 64k |

...Now?

| Store | Median HH Income | % Caucasian |
|-------|-----------------|-------------|
| Store 1 | 27k | 62% |
| Store 2 | 32k | 87% |
| Store 3 | 64k | 68% |

...Now?

| Store | Median HH Income | % Caucasian | Median Age |
|-------|-----------------|-------------|------------|
| Store 1 | 27k | 62% | 55 |
| Store 2 | 32k | 87% | 36 |
| Store 3 | 64k | 68% | 60 |

**Figure 9.5** **Hierarchical Clustering**

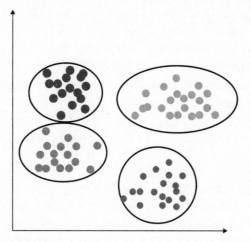

**Figure 9.6    K-Means Clustering**

most alike within groups (clusters) and most different from other groups (Figure 9.6).

Once a method is chosen for calculating the distance or similarity between two units, there are many options for building the clusters.

- **K-Means clustering** is a nonhierarchical, iterative clustering method that uses "seeds" to initiate the clusters, then iteratively assigns additional units to the same cluster based on similarity to the mathematical centroid of the cluster. The number of clusters ($k$) must be specified, and the user can use business rules or data-driven optimization methods to select the number. Cluster iterations are independent of each other and data points can be assigned and reassigned in each iteration.
- **Hierarchical** clustering is different from k-means in that there is no seed to initiate clusters, and each iteration is highly dependent on the others. Once a unit is assigned to a cluster, it cannot switch to another—although clusters may be combined or split, depending on the method. There are two main types:
  1. **Agglomerative**—A bottom-up clustering, where each data point starts in its own cluster and clusters are merged until there is a single cluster containing all data points. The user selects the number of clusters that yields the best results, often observing a dendrogram (tree diagram) of the clustering hierarchy.

2. **Divisive**—A top-down clustering, exactly the opposite of agglomerative. We start with a single cluster of all data points, and split based on similarity measures until each data point is in its own cluster, again observing diagnostic statistics or a dendrogram to choose the best number of clusters.

There are several great resources available that go more in depth into these techniques, including:

- *Statistical Consulting*, 2002 edition, by Javier Cabrera and Andrew McDougall
- *Data Science for Business: What You Need to Know about Data Mining and Data-Analytic Thinking* by Foster Provost and Tom Fawcett
- *Business Statistics: Communicating with Numbers*, 2nd edition, by Sanjiv Jaggia and Alison Kelly

## Velocity

Another important data science technique is *velocity*, which determines the rate of change and direction for a particular metric. It helps to understand if a metric is on an uptrend or downtrend. Velocity is similar to trends and forecasting where the business manager is solving for whether an issue is systemic or a onetime anomaly. Velocity is different in that it helps determine the rate of change and direction (up or down) for a metric.

Let's use the Edison Credit Card Company example from our segmentation discussion. We add a Conversion Rate Velocity metric to help us understand the direction for a particular segment. To explain how this works, if our conversion rate is 3 percent and our velocity is 1.0, we expect our conversion rate to maintain at 3 percent. However, if the velocity is 1.1, we expect the 3 percent conversion rate to go upward, possibly to 3.1 or 3.2 percent. If the velocity is 0.9, then we expect the conversion rate to start ticking downward, possibly to 2.8 or 2.9 percent.

Let's take a look at the updated Decision Matrix with Conversion Rate Velocity added.

In Table 9.2, we see that the both Southeast and the West regions are on the downtrend. Canada is expected to remain flat and the

Table 9.2    Decision Matrix with Conversion Rate Velocity Metric

| Segment | Emails Sent | Click-Through | Click-Through Rate | Conversions to Purchase | Conversion Rate | Conversion Rate Velocity |
|---|---|---|---|---|---|---|
| Northeast | 352,488 | 16,214 | 4.60% | 519 | 3.20% | 1.10 |
| Southeast | 232,101 | 14,390 | 6.20% | 463 | 3.50% | 0.95 |
| Midwest | 177,033 | 6,727 | 3.80% | 161 | 2.40% | 1.15 |
| West | 483,282 | 24,744 | 5.12% | 297 | 1.20% | 0.87 |
| Canada | 58,972 | 2,831 | 4.80% | 113 | 4.00% | 1.00 |

Northeast and Midwest are both on the uptrend. Does the Velocity metric change our investment decision?

In some cases, velocity may be very important; in others, velocity may be interesting, but historical values may change so often that it does not have much meaning for the analytical solution. It is in large part your job as the decision architect to work with the data scientist to determine what Lego pieces fit within the analytical solution you are creating.

## Predictive and Explanatory Models

We use statistical models to try to predict or explain a certain behavior by assigning a probability to an outcome. For example, in an acquisition, cross-sell, or upsell model, propensity to purchase may be a score associated with each potential customer based on certain input parameters. The manager may use this score to group the highest likely candidates and apply marketing dollars to that set. Conversely, in a churn or attrition model, the same methods may be used to predict the loss of a customer or subscriber and target the most at-risk groups based on propensity score deciles.

The above examples model a binary outcome (a sale happens or it doesn't). When the outcome is not binary (e.g., realized revenue, rooms booked, inventory sold, mobile data usage, counts of an event, multinomial outcomes, etc.), we use general or generalized modeling techniques such as linear regression, Poisson modeling, and a multitude of others.

Whether the purpose of a model is predictive or explanatory depends on the business question. The approaches between the two types are generally similar, but the application is not. A predictive model is often used for forecasting outcomes in the future, or guessing whether a certain behavior will happen. Sometimes, this is less important than understanding, or *explaining*, which characteristics of the business, customer, or environment are *driving* these outcomes—in which case the model becomes more explanatory.

Model accuracy requirements are more relaxed in the case of an explanatory model, as we try to understand directionally what is happening in order to drive change within the business. Predictive models, typically, must be highly accurate to be useful.

A good example of leveraging predictive models along with big data comes from the International Maritime Bureau (IMB), which uses these techniques to catch pirates. For the 2012 year, they were able to drop the reported incidents of pirate attacks for the first half of the year by 54 percent, some of which they attribute to two main factors related to their analytical solution. First, they brought in big data in a flexible analytical environment so that the data can be near real time. This data included interviews with pirates in custody, news stories about piracy incidents, data from mobile phones, email traffic, and social media posts from the pirates themselves. Once advanced analytics was applied to this dataset, Visualization was the next factor. Using geospatial mapping, they were able to visualize pictures to identify, track, and intercept the pirates and their organized networks.

## Machine Learning

Machine learning is the next frontier in Data Science and is getting a lot of attention as companies look to incorporate self-learning models to tackle tough business problems. Machine learning is a type of artificial intelligence that provides computers with the capabilities to learn on their own without being explicitly programmed. One important difference in machine learning is that it is focused on prediction, not causality.

Machine learning has high applicability to areas where you are trying to predict an outcome. One example of this is from Eric Horvitz and the team at Microsoft Research, who developed a machine learning model that can predict, with a high level of accuracy, whether a patient with congestive heart failure who is released from the hospital will be readmitted within 30 days. Through machine learning and hundreds of thousands of data points involving 300,000 patients, the machine is able to learn the profiles of those patients most likely to be readmitted. This is leading to patient-specific discharge programs aimed at keeping the patients in stable, safe regimes.

Other examples of how companies are deploying machine learning include personalized recommendations for customers, anticipating attrition of employees, credit scoring of loan applicants, and asset utilization for fleet maintenance. In their article, "How Companies Are Using Machine Learning to Get Faster and More Efficient," authors James Wilson, Sharad Sachdev, and Allan Alter provide several examples of how companies are increasing performance of certain tasks by 10 times the normal rate. One example cited,

> Clarifai, based in New York City, uses machine learning to find people, objects, or scenes in videos in far less time than a person can. In one demonstration, a 3.5-minute clip was analyzed in just 10 seconds. The technology can pick out kinds of people—mountain climbers, for instance—to help advertisers more efficiently match ads to the videos. It can also be used to help editors and curators find new ways to organize video collections and edit footage. This kind of auto-editing assistant can dramatically change the day-to-day tasks of workers in media, advertising, and film.

Through the various techniques discussed in this chapter, you should now have a basic understanding of Data Science and its ability to improve your analytical solution. These techniques play an important role in using your data to develop your decision architecture and monetization strategies.

# 10

# Data Development: *Making It Organized*

Data is the lifeblood of any analytical exercise and usually one of the bigger challenges. Sourcing, organizing, and stitching together data is typically where a large amount of time is spent in building an analytical solution. During these steps of pulling together the datasets, the quality of the data will be key. If the data is missing, incorrect, or inconsistent, the results of the analysis will be partial, or worse, incorrect. Once the data is compiled, determining the right analytical structure is important for performance, integrity, and scalability. Application of business rules and transformation of fields are also concepts that need to be addressed in order to make various datasets suitable for analysis. In this chapter we will cover several of the basic data concepts important to analytics—quality, type, organization, and transformation.

## Data Quality

The quality of the data may be the most important factor in determining the ability to produce usable insights from a dataset. The source of the data is often a vital indicator of the quality of the data. Is the data from an enterprise resource planning (ERP) system or a legacy system prone to human error? Does the data entry system allow free-form text or is it mostly lists the user selects from? Is the data structured or unstructured? All of these questions play a key role in determining the quality of the dataset and its reliability.

The core tenets of data quality include: *completeness, consistency, duplication, conformity, accuracy, integrity, timeliness, availability,* and *history.* Let's cover each of these concepts using the datasets in Tables 10.1 and 10.2 as examples.

## Completeness

The completeness of the data refers to any missing or partial data in the dataset. This can be due to a number of factors, including source systems that allow for free-form text. Another common source of incomplete data is non-mandatory fields in source systems that should require the information to be filled out.

In Table 10.1, we see that email addresses are inconsistent and phone information is sparse. We can also see that some of the address information and transactional keys are incomplete. The incomplete data for Customer ID presents a challenge later in this chapter. This type of missing information is referred to in the context of completeness of the data.

## Consistency

Data consistency requires that the values of the data must be consistent throughout the dataset. Any data must be valid according to defined rules. For example, a Social Security number is defined as a nine-digit number. This should be consistent throughout the various databases.

Consistency is not always as cut-and-dried as a Social Security number. For example, a metric definition for Average Transaction may be different in two parts of the organization. One department may view Average Transaction as the quantity of items purchased in an average transaction or its basket size; for instance, the average basket size is 2.7 items. Another department may view Average Transaction as the average dollar amount in a purchase, for instance, $83.69.

While technically both definitions may be correct, it is easy to see how the vagueness of the metric definition may produce two different interpretations.

## Duplication

Data duplication refers to multiple records in a database that are exact or partial duplicates of each other. For example, two records of the same customer might exist in the same dataset. The problem

**Table 10.1  Customer Record**

| Customer ID | First Name | Last Name | Email | Mobile Phone | Home Address | City | State |
|---|---|---|---|---|---|---|---|
| 598234 | Jerry | Twain | Jerry.Twain@gmail.com | 404-927-5555 | 131 Buckhead Street | Atlanta | GA |
| 598235 | Tricia | Hemingway | | | 455 Finley | Havana | La Havana |
| 598236 | George | King | | 212-499-5555 | 949 Broadway, Apt 6 | New York | NY |
| 598237 | Jenny | Dickens | Jenny.Dickens@gmail.com | 415-809-5555 | | | |
| 598238 | Jane | Orwell | Jane.Orwell@gmail.com | | 333 Main Street | Boston | Massachusetts |
| 598239 | Olivia | Faulkner | Olivia.Faulkner@gmail.com | | 5001 Denny Way | Seattle | Washington |
| 598240 | Grant | Woolf | Grant.Woolf@gmail.com | 310-290-5555 | 322 Hoover St | Los Angeles | CA |
| 598241 | Gale | Rowling | Gale.Rowling@gmail.com | | 2950 Landis St | San Diego | CA |
| 598242 | Tommy | Austen | Tommy.Austen@gmail.com | 310-922-5555 | 323 Hoover St | Los Angeles | California |
| 598240 | Jerry | Twain | Jerry.Twain@gmail.com | 404-927-5555 | 3434 Marietta Blvd | Atlanta | GA |

**Table 10.2    Transaction History**

| Transaction ID | Customer ID | Product Description | Quantity | Price | Total Amount |
|---|---|---|---|---|---|
| 45077–01 | 598241 | Nine West Blazer | 1 | $213.00 | $213.00 |
| 45077–02 | 598239 | Calvin Klein Dress | 1 | $158.00 | $158.00 |
| 45077–03 | 598239 | Kate Spade Shoes | 1 | $312.00 | $312.00 |
| 45077–04 | 598235 | Ralph Lauren Polo Shirt | 1 | $56.00 | $56.00 |
| | | Tommy Hilfiger Tank Top | 1 | $34.00 | $34.00 |
| 45077–06 | 598235 | INC Socks | 3 | $5.50 | $16.50 |
| 45077–07 | 598235 | Ray Ban Sunglasses | 1 | $110.00 | $110.00 |
| 45077–08 | 598242 | Nike Shorts | 1 | $42.00 | $42.00 |
| 45077–09 | 598242 | Nike Dryfit Shirt—White | 1 | $32.00 | $32.00 |
| 45077–10 | 598242 | Nike Dryfit Shirt—Blue | 1 | $35.00 | $35.00 |
| 45077–11 | 598241 | INC Blouse | 2 | $46.00 | $46.00 |
| 45077–12 | 598241 | Charter Club Blouse | 1 | $35.00 | $35.00 |
| 45077–13 | | Bass Loafers | 1 | $225.00 | $225.00 |
| 45077–14 | 598234 | Nautica Sweater | 1 | $77.00 | $77.00 |
| 45077–15 | 598234 | Perry Ellis Collared Shirt | 1 | $69.00 | $69.00 |

with duplicate data is that the data consumer is unsure which one is correct. Duplication of data can occur often in a database for a number of reasons, such as the architecture of the data storage system, a source system that allows for multiple entries, and bad joins when connecting data.

For example, in the Customer Record dataset in Table 10.1, we observe two records for the same customer, Jerry Twain. We observe this might be the same person due to the mobile number being the same. Otherwise we might treat this as two different individuals. Since we now have two records for the same person, which one is the correct version? It appears that Jerry moved at one point, but we do not know which address is the correct address, 131 Buckhead Street or 3434 Marietta Blvd.

### Conformity

Conformity refers to how well the data adheres to standards. For example, if we were to refer to a country code for China as CHN, but in other parts of the data the name of the country is spelled out as China, this makes sorting, grouping, and comparing the data difficult.

In Table 10.1, we see that the standards for state are not consistent in the dataset. A few of the records refer to California as CA while other records spell out the full name. If we attempt to do any type of aggregation or sorting based on state, we will end up with inaccurate and nonconforming results.

### Accuracy

When data is inaccurate it is difficult for people to trust it. For data to be accurate, it must be consistent, nonduplicate, and complete. If there is a formula issue or incorrect descriptive elements such as address, Zip code, or phone number, the user of the information will not know what records are correct and which are inaccurate.

In Table 10.2, we see a lot of missing data along with some mathematical issues where it appears that the point-of-sale system did not record a transaction correctly. In transaction 45077–11 we see that Gale purchased two INC Blouses, but was only charged for one. This is a lost revenue opportunity as well as a calculation issue that makes one doubt the accuracy of the Total Amount field.

### Integrity

The integrity of data refers to the accuracy and consistency of the data over its lifecycle, ensuring that when the data moves from system to system it maintains a level of quality and standardization. This is typically performed by keys that are unique to that record that enable it to connect to other tables or datasets. There are two main types of data integrity: *entity integrity* and *referential integrity*. Let's explore both.

Entity integrity is concerned with the use of a primary key, which is a unique value for that record that cannot be assigned to any other record. Referential integrity refers to the need for a primary key in one table to exist in another table in order to link the two tables together. The primary key is the principle tool for linking together datasets or tables within a database. All records must be populated with a unique primary key; null or duplicate values are not allowed.

For example, in Table 10.2, we see that not all records have a Transaction ID, which is the primary key for this table. This should never be allowed in a dataset as we do not have a reference value for the record and will not be able to guarantee that it is unique.

When combining datasets or tables with one another, a foreign key is often employed. A foreign key is a field in one table that uniquely identifies a record in another table or dataset. It helps connect one table with another while keeping the record values unique.

For example, when looking at the dataset in Table 10.2, we see that the Customer ID field has several missing Customer IDs. This is unfortunate as we no longer have a reference for these transactions to know who purchased what products.

### Timeliness, Availability, and History

Depending on the use of the data, the timeliness, availability, and history can be key factors. The timeliness of the data refers to how often the data is updated. If the dataset is updated only once a year, the data may become stale toward the end of the year, but may still be suitable for long-term trend analysis.

The availability of the data refers to how often it will be accessible for analysis. Is the data available for a onetime pull? Can it be pulled on demand, or is it generated according to a schedule? Depending on the type of analysis you want to perform, availability of the data can determine your ability to analyze the data. For example, our analysis needs daily updates to see the most recent purchases, but due to system availability we are only able to access the data on a monthly basis. This could severely impact the type of analysis and responses we are able to assemble.

Lastly, the history of the data refers to how much history is available. Is the volume of transactions so large that the system only keeps 60 days' worth of data, or is it an ERP system that has more than 10 years of data? Data science typically drives a need for more history rather than less. If there is not much history to pull from, it may be hard to forecast or predict future events.

## Dirty Data, Now What?

Now that we understand the importance of quality data, there are several tools available to assist with de-duplication of data or matching to solve for which record is the correct one. These tools also can transform the data based on business rules. For example, you might have a business rule that converts any fully spelled-out state into its abbreviation, such as California to CA.

These tools fall into the category of data cleansing or ETL tools. Typical tools include Data Stage, Pentaho, Jaspersoft, Informatica, Ab Initio, Talend, KETL, and many others.

## Data Types

### Metadata

Before we dive into the rich and various types of data we can encounter, let's take a minute to talk about metadata. Metadata is a set of information about data, or simply put, data about data. In order to understand a particular element in a record, we need to understand how to interpret the data element. Metadata provides the information that helps someone interpret a piece of information.

According to Ralph Kimball, there are two types of metadata: technical and business. Business metadata is the definition of the element, business purpose, and calculation. This definition is focused more on the business user to provide an understanding of what the intent of the data element is for business use.

### Example of Business Metadata

- Name of Field:        Customer ID
- Business Purpose:    Unique identity for each customer
- Calculation:             Sequentially assigned number based on when the customer either purchases a product or signs up for a loyalty program

Technical metadata comprises the technical components of a data element such as database location, granularity, indexes, data type, column name, and relationship between tables. Technical metadata is more relevant to the IT department's use of the data element.

### Example of Technical Metadata

- Data Type:      Integer
- Length:          9 digits long
- Primary Key:   Yes
- Location:        Customer Record

Metadata is an important resource for the business and IT organizations to govern and standardize across functional areas within a company. Existing and new elements should be tracked and cataloged. We talk more about metadata when we get further into our discussion of analytical data structure.

### The World of Data

Data comes in many shapes and sizes. Different types of data are better suited for different types of analysis. Financial information is well-suited for reporting, trending, and forecasting, operational data is well-suited for statistical analysis, and marketing data for descriptive analytics. Let's review a few of the key data types you are likely to encounter.

### Structured versus Unstructured Data

The degree of organization of the data dictates whether it is structured versus unstructured. Structured data is easily organized into a table in a database with columns, rows, and well-defined data types. Structured data is typically found in relational databases, OLAP datasets, and structured datasets.

Unstructured data lacks column-and-row organization and typically comprises text objects such as a blog, social media posts, or email messages. Techniques such as text mining are used to create organization from this type of information. Digital images are another form of unstructured data that can be analyzed for patterns, as found in diagnostic imaging.

### Operational versus Analytical Data

Operational processes typically create rich flows of data in a company. Operational databases are structured and optimized for quick insert into and retrieval of single records from a database. For example, a high-volume point-of-sale system is optimized to get data into the database quickly so that the purchase transaction can be processed promptly without causing the customer to wait. Operational databases are highly relational in nature with many thin and long tables. These table structures are designed to be highly efficient and are not easily accessed for analytics.

Analytical data structures are optimized to retrieve large volumes of data needed for analysis of trends and patterns. They typically require fewer joins to other tables and may have repeating values in them. These structures often have pre-aggregated information to allow for quick access to summarized information. Examples include data warehouses, OLAP cubes, and reporting data structures.

### Data Objects

Analytical data is stored and accessed in data objects such as flat files, dimensional models, columnar databases, and OLAP cube structures. Each of these types of objects lend themselves to a particular type of analysis or performance.

Flat files are big long files with many columns and rows. They usually have repeating values in the dataset to allow for quick calculations, summarizations, and filtering of information. They perform well for dashboard reporting and statistical analysis.

Dimensional models are relational data structures that are optimized for reporting systems. They typically have facts and dimensions that are organized to model the business function. The fact tables are organized to be long and thin with few repeating values. Facts are the quantitative measures in a business such as sales amount or unit quantity. Dimensions are wide with lots of columns and have repeating values. They are typically descriptive in nature, such as customer name, address, or product type.

OLAP cube objects are pre-aggregated datasets allowing the user the ability to slice-and-dice a large dimensional dataset quickly. The OLAP cube object is commonly used for financial information, allowing the user to view detail and aggregated information seamlessly.

Columnar databases are growing in popularity, especially for large datasets, including big data technologies. Both relational and columnar database use traditional database languages to access data, like SQL, and both service well for visualization tools. However, by storing data in column versus rows, which is a relational database, the query can access the data it needs faster by scanning just the columns versus having to scan a large set of rows.

## Data Organization

Now that we have an understanding of the nature of data that we encounter, we turn to discussing the processes we need to implement to make the data useful to our analytical purposes.

## Data Movement

The data that we would like to bring together for an analytic project is typically found in different places in many shapes and forms. If we are fortunate, most of it is housed in a well-maintained data warehouse where the data has been extracted from operational sources, cleansed, standardized, and quality checked. This process is typically referred to as ETL, an acronym for *extract, transform,* and *load.*

## Granularity

Identifying the granularity of our data is one of the first efforts we undertake to understand the data prior to analyzing it. The concept of granularity refers to the degree of distinguishable elements a field value may contain. A high-granularity field will contain many unique elements whereas a low-granularity field will contain few. For example, in a table with three years of history, an Order Year field is typically low granularity with only three possible elements, 2013, 2014, and 2015. In the same table, an Order Time field with precision to the minute will be much lower granularity with up to 1,576,800 possible values in the three-year span.

This lowest level of dimensional field values or combination of field values that result in a single record is referred to as the grain of the data. It may be represented by a single field, the primary key, or a combination of key fields, referred to as a composite primary key. Most fact tables typically have a time dimension grain such as year, month, day, hour, or second.

Granularity limits what can be analyzed and what can be joined. For example, we have a Customer Sales table that aggregates monthly sales at a customer segment level, such as High, Medium, or Low value. With this table, we are unable to speak to the range of monthly revenue per customer within a customer segment because we have lost visibility to individual customers and are only able to identify them as a group.

Aggregated tables, while useful for delivering performance and simplicity of analysis, in many cases lead to frustration when diagnostic paths are blocked. It is difficult to predict in advance which data paths are required in each and every use case. As a result, the preferred solution is to attempt to stay as close as possible to the grain of the source data to the degree data storage space and processing power permit. Aggregated tables are useful as side tables to meet query response performance requirements for downstream reporting dashboards when detailed drill paths are not necessary.

### Structuring for Analytics

If we have access to an analytical data mart or a schema on our corporate database, we typically structure our data in three layers, as illustrated in Figure 10.1. We discuss each layer in more detail later but let's first review the structure at a high level. The bottom of the structure typically contains the least analytically complex data; it is usually associated with source operating systems or data warehouses. As we progress upward through the analytic and reporting layers, the transformations become increasingly complex and the tables more consolidated although the granularity of the data many not decrease. That is, at the analytic and reporting table layers, we typically pre-join fact and dimension tables in order to improve performance for reporting and analysis tools but avoid aggregating unless absolutely necessary. From an analytic perspective it is generally preferable to retain the highest degree of granularity your database resources and storage space will permit.

### The Base Layer

The base layer comprises the tables into which we load the data we extract from available data sources—operational systems, data

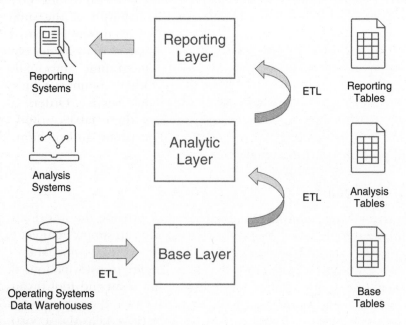

Reporting Layer

Reporting Systems

ETL    Reporting Tables

Analytic Layer

Analysis Systems

ETL    Analysis Tables

Base Layer

Operating Systems Data Warehouses

ETL

Base Tables

Figure 10.1    Analytical Data Structure

warehouse, flat files, or external data sources such as cloud services. The goal of the base layer is to get the data from the various sources into one place. In order to maintain data integrity, auditing and quality checking processes should be put in place when moving data from source systems to our analytical structure. In addition, it is best to retain consistency with source field names, data types, and table structure at the base layer.

We might choose to employ some simple transformations at this level to de-normalize fact tables coming from the data warehouse. This means that we may pre-join our fact tables to some of the most common dimensional tables to replace foreign key values with human-understandable descriptive values. For example, we might replace numerical product ID 1234 with its descriptive element of "Blue Socks." As mentioned earlier, de-normalization is less efficient from a data storage perspective, but it greatly facilitates the ability to comprehend the data.

### The Analytic Layer

We refer to the second layer as the analytic layer, comprising the tables built from the base layer. These tables transform the data from the base layers into structures that support our analysis. Typical tables at this layer include measures enriched with a wide variety of dimensional attributes to analyze the behavior of the subject of analysis. There is usually some form of a customer table that collects attributes of the customer behavior, product or service types, descriptive geographic information, demographic information, analytical model scores, and so forth. Other common tables at this layer include Product, Billing, Customer Service, Orders, and Shipments tables to name a few. Each of these tables would be enriched as needed with dimensional attribute information to support the downstream analytics.

### The Reporting Layer

In many cases, tables in the analytic layer provide the information sufficient to deliver the analysis needed. We can simply connect our analytic or data visualization tool directly to build our analysis. In other cases, the analysis may call for complex transformations that place a heavy performance burden on the front-end tool through which users access our analysis. In these cases, there is one more table type we need to develop in what we refer to as the reporting layer. Typical table types found at this level wrestle with issues of granularity such as fact-to-fact joins, hierarchical joins, cross-record comparisons, rolling 12-month averages, and year-to-date metrics.

### Challenges

One of the biggest challenges when developing an analytic data mart is to determine which transformations or calculations to have the reporting tool perform and which ones to build into the analytic data mart ETL processes. Generally speaking, calculations performed at the reporting tool layer offer the greatest flexibility to provide dynamic analysis; however, there can be significant performance issues depending on the resources available. It is important to engage end-users in these decisions to determine the degree to which they are willing to trade off flexibility versus performance. Some users may place a high value on returning results quickly, whereas other users require dynamic ability to modify elements of the analysis more easily and are willing to wait a bit longer for results to return.

Regardless of whether we have access to an analytic data mart, a schema, or the internal data store, we inevitably produce data objects that fit into one of these categories. At the start of the analytic project, we plan adequate time to thoroughly understand the character of our data and determine the types of data objects we need to support our analytics.

## Data Transformation

In addition to organizing our data for analytics, another critical process we need to undertake is transforming our source to support the analytics we plan to conduct. Source data rarely comes directly in the form needed for analysis. Once we have ensured the correct extraction of data, we apply several levels of transformations to ready the data for analysis. Let's discuss the most basic types of transformations we encounter—ETL, analytic and reporting business rules, and metric transformation.

### ETL Business Rules Transformations

As we discussed earlier, ETL transformations typically apply transformations to the data to ensure conformity with corporate standards, such as standardizing country codes and state names. Other transformations are typically handled at the ETL level and include removing extra spaces at the beginning or ending of field values, conversion to standard data types such as currency and time zone, and standardization of field names.

### Analytic and Reporting Business Rules Transformations

In addition to data type and field transformations, we also transform our data to comply with business rules associated with our topic of analysis. It is important that we thoroughly understand the business rules governing our analysis prior to embarking on our analytic journey to ensure that we set out properly equipped.

For example, we may be analyzing the performance of a marketing campaign with a test and control group of customers. The test group received a marketing email promoting a program, whereas the control group did not. We want to know if the test group was more likely to purchase the product as a result of the marketing campaign versus the control group. Customers received the email throughout the month of March and we have a monthly sales report of product purchases by customer from March through May. The agreed-upon business rules that we will want in our data transformations include attributing purchases by test group customers within 60 days of the receiving the email, implying that they have been influenced by the campaign.

We need to examine the stipulated analytics and reporting business rules early in the process to ensure that we have the data we need to perform the metric transformations required by the project.

### Metric Transformations

The data measures that come directly from our data sources will typically be straightforward counts or measures of quantity, size, or volume. In order to discern patterns, trends, or relationships, we apply mathematical transformations to our base measures to develop metrics that enable insight into relationships, movement, and distribution. These transformations provide the power to our analysis. Defining, calculating, testing, and interpreting the transformations needed for the analysis can represent one of the most time-consuming aspects of the analysis. The analytic and reporting business rules of the project determine the mathematical transforms we apply to the measures and metrics of our project.

Common mathematical transformations we discuss are:

- Rate metrics
- Compound metrics
- Distribution metrics
- Rank or ordering metrics
- Velocity metrics
- Incremental or variance metrics
- Statistical transformations
- Algebraic transformations

### Rate Metrics

The most common type of transformation involves calculating rates such as quantity per unit of time or size per unit of product. Price or cost per unit are commonly found rate metrics, as is production quantity per day.

Cost per unit = (fixed costs + variable costs * total units produced)/
total units produced

### Distribution Metrics

Distribution metrics measure the relationship of the part-to-whole such as percent of total or cumulative percent. Service revenue as a percent of total revenue is one example.

Service % of revenue = revenue from services/
(revenue from services + revenue from product sales)

### Ratio or Index Metrics

Ratio or index metrics involve dividing one measure or metric by another, such as a price efficiency metric, which measures the relationship between an effective product price and a benchmark price. If the ratio is greater than 1, then the product is commanding a higher price in the market relative to the benchmark and conversely if it is lower than 1.

Price index = current price/average market price

## Compound Metrics

Whereas rate metrics typically divide one measure by another, compound metrics sum or multiply one metric by another. Compound metrics typically found in the business environment include number of man-hours for a project, which is calculated by the number of people assigned to a project multiplied by the hours per person to be spent on the project. FTE (full-time equivalent) is a related metric that sums the number of hours each person on a project or team spends on the project and then divides by a benchmark number of hours representative of a single full-time employee.

$$\text{FTEs} = (\text{sum of hours spent by employees})/ \text{benchmark hours per FTE}$$

## Velocity Metrics

Velocity metrics capture the rate of change or movement of a metric from one period to the next. These metrics are typically represented as period-over-period growth rates. Annual revenue growth would be a commonly found value. Compound annual growth rate (CAGR) is another velocity metric commonly found in financial reporting. We cover this topic in the Data Science chapter (Chapter 9) as well.

$$\text{CAGR} = (\text{starting value}/\text{ending value})^{(1/\text{number of periods between start and end})} - 1$$

## Incremental or Variance Metrics

Metrics that measure the difference between two measures are incremental metrics. Examples include variance of actuals to budget or the difference in sales between a group of customers offered a marketing promotion and a control group that did not receive the marketing offer or treatment. This type of incremental analysis is commonly referred to as lift analysis.

$$\text{Year-over-year variance rate} = (\text{value this year} - \text{value last year})/\text{value last year} - 1$$

## Statistical Transformations

With statistical transformations, we start to move into the area of data science and data mining. There are numerous transformations developed for statistical analysis. Statistical metrics most commonly found in the business world include mean, median, standard deviation, standard error, $z$-score, $r$-squared, $p$-value, and $t$-value.

$$Z\text{-score} = (\text{value of a data point} - \text{the mean of the dataset})/$$
$$\text{standard deviation of the dataset}$$

### Algebraic Transformations

Algebraic transformation uses more advanced forms of algebra or calculus, such as exponents, square roots, and logarithmic transformations. Net Present Value (NPV) is a typical algebraic transformation found in the business world. NPV represents the current value of a stream of future expected cash flows, taking into consideration the time value of money.

$$\text{NPV} = \sum_{k=0}^{n} \frac{Ck}{(1 + r)^k}$$

## Summary

In this section we have covered one of the more difficult but important aspects of analytics, that is, ensuring that the data is of good quality, that we have the appropriate data structure for our analysis, that it is properly organized, and that we have applied the mathematical transformations needed to expose underlying trends and patterns of behavior. This aspect of the project can be the most tedious and it is tempting to cut corners and skip steps in order to get on with the more enjoyable aspects of designing charts and visualizations. However, we can be sure that missteps or ignored steps in this stage of the project will be regretted further downstream.

# CHAPTER 11

# Guided Analytics: *Making It Relevant*

## So, What?

Imagine you are a newly hired analyst for the Edison Motors (EM) car company. Your first week on the job, your manager tasks you with producing a Vehicle Safety and Quality Dashboard to track two of the company's KPIs—Safety and Quality. Directing you to the customer complaints database, your manager tells you the executives want to know how many customer complaints are received, what are they about, where are they from, how they compare to our competition, whether any were hazardous, and so on. She also tells you that it would be nice if the dashboard could help spot patterns and trends and provide early warning alerts to growing quality or safety issues.

You get the dataset, explore the data, clean it up, and within a week you have a dashboard that you think is pretty good (see Figure 11.1).

You show it to your manager, whose response is underwhelming to say the least.

> Well, I can see you have the major points covered—where, what, hazard, trend, competition. But it doesn't really tell me anything the execs don't already know. California, Texas, and Florida have the most complaints, but they are also our biggest markets, so that would be expected. I see a jump in complaints in 2014 and 2015 and the complaint component chart indicates the jump was due to air bag and electrical complaints, but we already know that due to the two recalls we had. It doesn't look like we have a large percentage of serious hazard complaints, but then, if we did, we would be out of business.

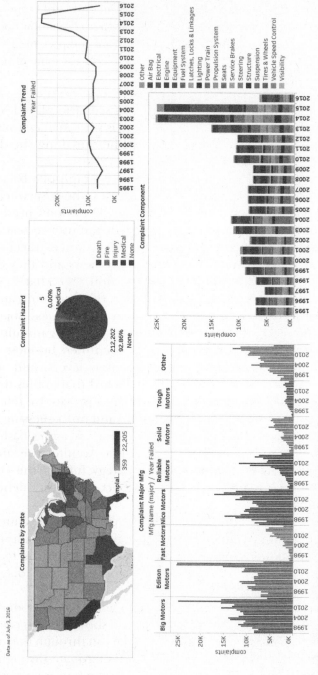

**Figure 11.1    Edison Motors Customer Complaints Dashboard**

I would like to know how many death, fire, and injury complaints we have had but I can't read that from the chart. I can see
that our competitors have complaint issues as well but how does
it compare to us relative to size and compliant component? This
is a good start, but see what you can do to address some of the
questions I raised.

Your boss is being kind. This is a common scenario played out day
after day in many organizations. The truth is your manager nailed it
when she said the dashboard doesn't tell her anything she doesn't
already know.

Too many dashboards, charts, and reports simply play back information that is readily apparent. In many cases, they overwhelm the
user with lots of data but little information. They don't present the
information in a manner to make it easy for the user to read. They
place the burden on the user to process the data and extract insights.
In short, they simply help the user read the news and they do not
answer questions. Rather they beg the question, "So, what?"

One of the key premises of this book is that too often analytics
and reporting occur in silos, isolated from key business objectives,
disconnected from decisions. If, instead, your organization has
developed a Decision Architecture with identified business objectives, question analysis, key decisions, action levers, and success
metrics, then your job of building a dashboard that guides the user
through the analysis to the *so-what?* question, a process we refer to as
Guided Analytics, becomes straightforward and not a guessing game.
The Category Tree lends itself naturally to a cascading dashboard
layout. The Action Levers of the Decision Architecture and the
Business Levers of the Monetization Strategy inform the content
of the dashboards and diagnostics. The Success Metrics define the
KPIs to monitor.

Even as we begin with a well-thought-out Decision Architecture,
the iterative nature of Guided Analytics development results in new
insights from exploration of the data that may lead us to revise
and extend some of our underlying hypotheses and diagnostic
evaluations.

In this chapter we use our imaginary scenario to introduce fundamental principles of Guided Analytics and show how you can apply
them to a typical analytical solution. We take you through the journey
of crafting Guided Analytics that help users navigate through complex and interconnected data. We also show you how to present data
visually that is pleasing to view and easy to comprehend. We show you

how, by building your dashboards on a firm foundation of visual analytics and user experience principles, you can relieve the users of the burden of processing information, letting them focus their attention on the story the data would love to tell them.

## Guided Analytics

Guided Analytics is both art and science. Decision Architecture and Monetization Strategy provide the structure and analytic goal. Data science and data development contribute the insights, and design of the user interface and user experience bring art to the table. However, even before marrying science to art, if we want our analytics to have impact, we must bring out the Voice of the Data to support the solutions. The Voice of the Data is actually the harmony of two voices:

1. The Voice of the Customer
2. The Voice of the Business

In the following sections we follow the Voice of the Data through a journey that gives life to the voices of our customers and business processes, telling us what our customers want through their actions, informing our strategies, and showing us which levers have the most impact.

### The Voice of the Data

Presentation of analytics has come a long way in understanding that business analytics is more than presenting tables full of data. Rather it tells stories that speak to business managers, stories that get users excited about the opportunities, fearful about the threats, and ready to conquer the competition.

Business analytics is well suited to tell a story because all data has a voice, be it the voice of the customer, the voice of the process, or the voice of the business. You may be familiar with surveys, referred to as Voice of the Customer surveys, that ask customers what they think about a product or company. While these surveys are useful and can provide pertinent information to gain a deeper understanding of what our customers think about our company's products and services, they suffer from several limitations. It is impossible to be able to ask customers all the questions we would like to ask; the more we ask, the fewer customers we find willing to answer. So we typically rely on statistical methods to try to achieve an approximation of customer views accepting limitations on what we can know.

There is another Voice of the Customer that is overlooked or drowned out in our business reporting practices. That is the record of each and every business transaction the customer leaves with us when they buy our products or services, when they call our customer care centers, when they return products, when they stop doing business with us.

Before the advent of analytic databases with increasingly powerful CPUs, cheaper data storage, easy-to-use data-mining programs, and data visualization tools, customer granular data was expensive to keep, difficult to analyze, and hard to comprehend. Accordingly, customer performance metrics have typically been reported as aggregated averages for the whole group or at best some predefined segment, such as average revenue per consumer user versus average revenue per business user. With advances in analytic processes and technologies, we no longer have to settle for aggregates and averages. Such figures are a good place to start but they are not the end.

Let's return to our Customer Complaints dashboard project for Edison Motors. The name itself indicates that there is a powerful voice of the customer in the data—they are voicing their dissatisfaction with our products. But there is also a voice of the business in the data as well. By examining when, where, and what our customers are complaining about, we can uncover flaws in car design that may not be suited for certain terrains, or quality issues in our production processes or problems in our customer care processes.

Marrying the data with other sources that we have about the market and competitors, we may discover that customers hold us to a higher or lesser standard of performance than our competitors. Examining patterns in the data can tell us if there are seasonal patterns at play. And knowing something about the types of customers may give us insights into shifting patterns of behavior. In turn these insights can inform the Actions and Business Levers we select when developing our Decision Architecture and Monetization Strategy.

### The Voice of the Customer

Let's take a look at who is complaining (Figure 11.2) based on whether they are the original owners of the vehicle and compare it to the mileage on the vehicle at the time of the complaint. We also want to know if average mileage (Figure 11.3) is increasing for both ownership cohorts, Original Owner and Not Original Owner, at the same rate.

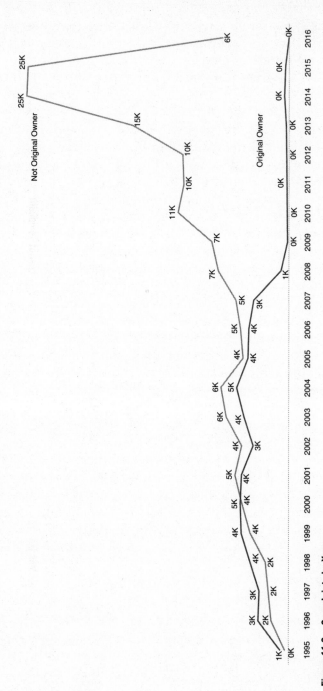

**Figure 11.2  Complaints by Year**

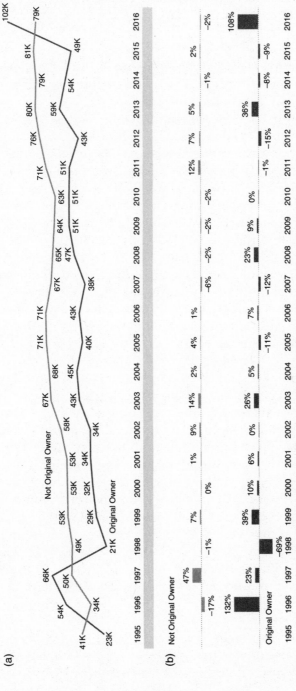

**Figure 11.3   (a) Average Mileage by Year of Complaint; (b) Annual Mileage Rate of Change by Year of Complaint**

187

The charts are telling us some interesting information. As shown in Figure 11.2, prior to 2007, original owners complained about as much as used car owners. After 2007, complaints from original owners declined dramatically whereas complaints from used car owners increased sharply. We also notice in Figure 11.3a that average mileage is increasing both for original and used car owners, but at a higher rate for original owners (Figure 11.3b).

We decide to check on the length of time the customer has owned the car at the time of complaint (see Figure 11.4).

Making a note to examine the anomalies in 2002 and 2013 later, we observe that while both cohorts exhibit increasing trends, original car owners appear to be holding onto their vehicles longer at a higher rate than used car owners, with a noticeable notch increase in 2007 with the commencement of the Great Recession.

We wonder if there is a relationship between vehicle mileage, ownership period, and complaints. We run through a few charts to check and note similar decay curves of complaints relative to vehicle ownership period (Figure 11.5). We also observe that used car owners tend to complain more in the first few years of ownership whereas original car owners tend to hold out longer, but both drop off after a period of usage (Figure 11.6).

There are many other paths we could travel down, but we believe you get the point and realize you have a story to tell your boss about the pattern of customer complaints, which is as follows.

Vehicle owners tend to file complaints more in the early period of their ownership when they are less familiar with the vehicle and issues may need to be ironed out with the new car. Over time, the problems have been addressed or the owner accepts the condition as normal. Following the beginning of the economic crisis of 2007, original car owners started holding onto their cars longer, resulting in a greater percentage of older or more problematic cars available in the used car market. There appears to be a relationship between the average mileage of the vehicle and the number of complaints that declines with the increased mileage of the car. By studying this probability pattern and monitoring the age of the fleet of our cars in the market, we might be able to anticipate and better prepare for waves of customer complaints.

This story can help guide the Decision Architecture team developing action levers that involve customer satisfaction, product development, or customer service business levers.

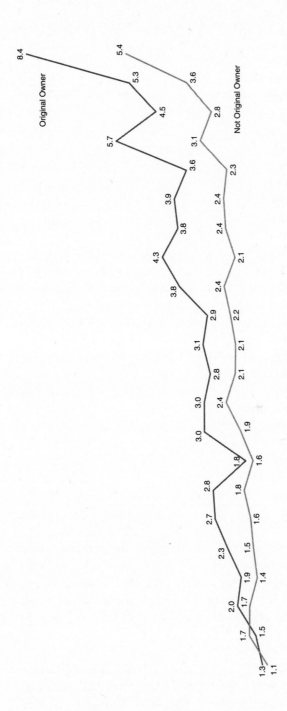

**Figure 11.4 Average Length of Ownership by Year of Complaint**

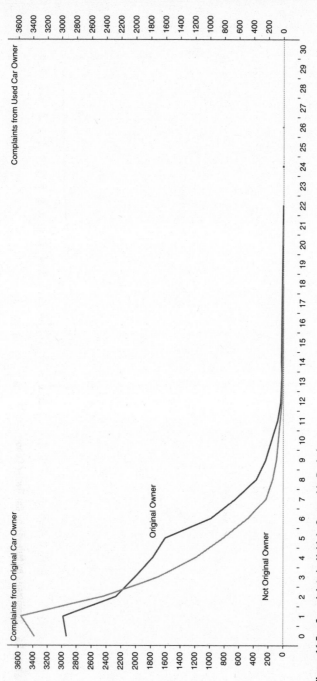

**Figure 11.5  Complaints by Vehicle Ownership Period**

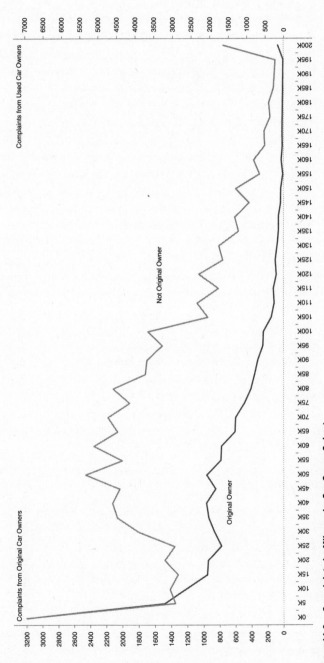

**Figure 11.6 Complaints by Mileage by Car Owner Cohort**

191

## Customer Signatures

While each customer is unique, business marketing thrives on the fact that segments of likeminded customers with similar attributes can be identified. Many segmentation models group customers based on static (or relatively static) characteristics of the customer, such as gender, interests, lifestyle, demographics, cultural heritage, and so on. While such segmentation schemes are useful when you can identify your customers, in many businesses it is not possible to know who your customer is.

Advances in digital marketing technologies are helping to overcome this blindness, but in many cases we simply are not able to know who is really behind the clicks or purchases. What really matters is how our customers interact with our products and services. It is in this interaction that the voice of the customer in our data can speak volumes. Using our Decision Architecture to identify and apply data-mining techniques, we can identify customer patterns of behavior at key decision points in our marketing programs. We think of these patterns as customer signatures. Each customer has a unique signature, but with advances in data mining we can identify common patterns of behavior that permit us to segment our customers based on communities of interest.

If we are a communications company, for example, we might identify a cluster of customers who, on a regular basis, have a significant percentage of text messaging late at night within the vicinity of a local college. Applying other factors, we can reasonably determine we have identified a segment of college students and can tailor our direct marketing efforts to this cluster.

## The Voice of the Business

In the same way that our customers speak to us through our data, our business processes also have a voice. When we are able to look inside the data and behind the averages, we can see patterns and outliers that all tell us useful information about how our business is performing in the market.

Let's take a closer look at the complaint trends since 1995. Looking at a sparkline chart of complaints by major component category sorted by greatest to least complaints, we observe a range of patterns, many of which display a steady signal of noise (Figure 11.7). But the pattern for the power train catches our attention.

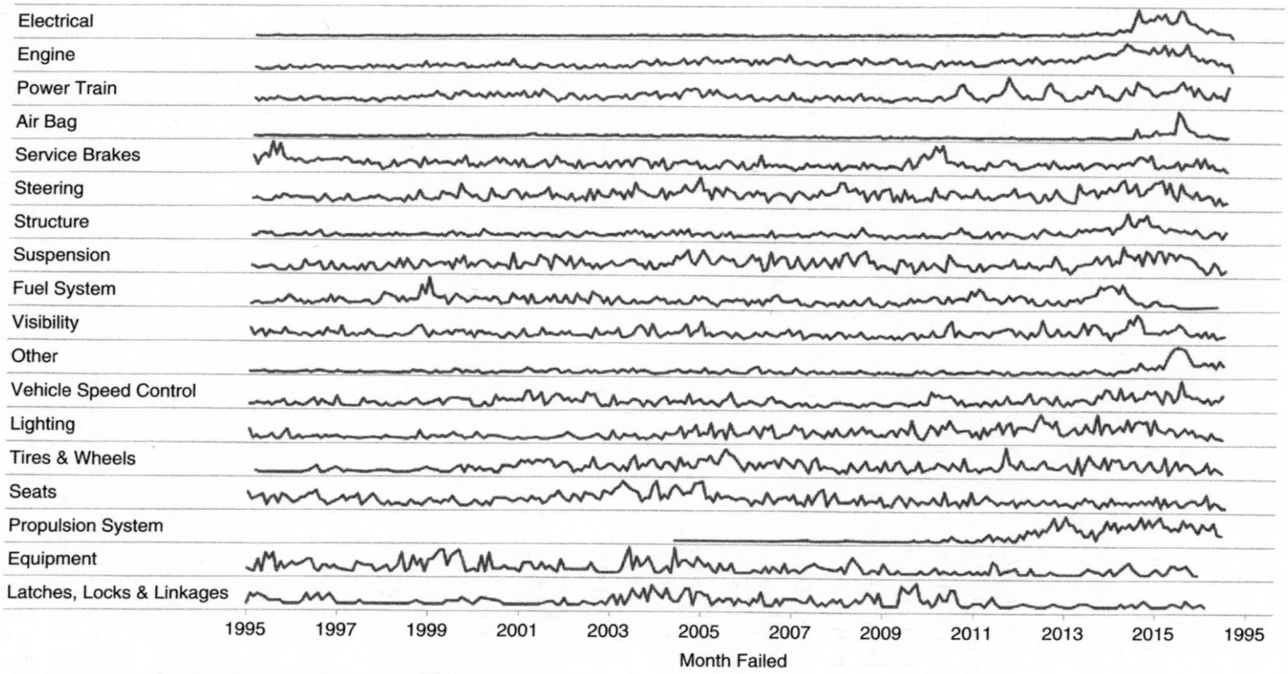

**Figure 11.7 Monthly Complaints by Vehicle Component**

### Sparkline Charts

Sparkline charts are small trend charts, usually lines or bars, that communicate only the general movement of the metric. Sparkline charts are designed to condense trend information to its essence, that is, displaying the direction of movement and the degree of variation.

Since 2010, there appears to be an annual spike mid-to-late summer (see Figure 11.8). With further analysis you determine the pattern is concentrated in a sedan model in the summer. The Voice of the Business is suggesting there are design or production issues leading to heat-related problems, giving rise to a spike in complaints each summer.

You see an opportunity to use control charts to create an alert tool. When the data crosses the *upper control limit* (UCL) you have a signal that is significant and you have visibility into the Voice of the Business to determine if it is an issue that is recurring, growing, or getting better, as illustrated in Figure 11.9.

But the charts are rather complicated with a lot of data. Thinking about your boss's feedback, you realize it is difficult for a reader to comprehend at a glance. More work is needed to present the charts in a manner quick to comprehend and easy to navigate. User interface (UI) and user experience (UX) play an important role in developing Guided Analytics that are quick to read and easy to use.

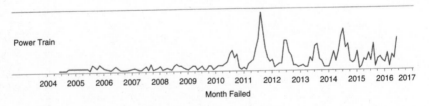

**Figure 11.8   Monthly Power Train Complaints by Sedan Model**

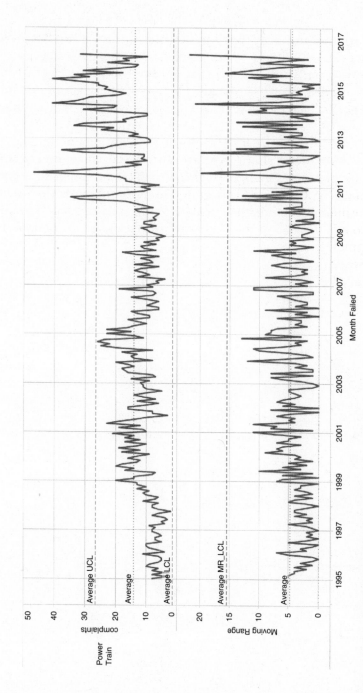

**Figure 11.9   Sedan Model Power Train Control Chart**

## Summary

We have covered the basic function of Guided Analytics and the role it plays in our methodology for Decision Architecture. We have introduced you to the voices of the customer and business that speak through your data. Many rich stories about customer experience and business performance can be found in the data once you learn how to listen.

In the next chapter we take you through the principles of UI that help you create better charts to tell your story so that your audience can get the point at a glance. In the subsequent chapter, we cover the essentials of UX to aid you in designing dashboards that work for your audience rather than making your audience work to get your point.

# 12

# User Interface (UI): *Making It Clear*

## Introduction to UI

The concept of the *user interface* (UI) originated in the field of industrial design and refers to the space where the user interacts with the machine. UI easily extends to the field of computer systems and analytic tools. The term *dashboard*, typically referring to a control panel in an automobile, is widely used in a business reporting context to indicate the UI for visual charts and reports that managers use to monitor the performance of their business.

Unfortunately, the success of the dashboard concept may have become its own enemy. Report designers often take the concept too literally and present results in the form of gauges, dials, and other objects suitable to the analog of the mechanical world of a car control panel but completely irrelevant in the digital information world.

The borrowed concept of a control panel dashboard not only interferes with developing efficient presentation of visual information, it also limits understanding of richness in display of visual analytics. A car dashboard is primarily a passive display of key control metrics—fuel level, engine temperature, speed; an information dashboard provides the opportunity to interact with the information—to slice and dice, to journey through the analysis to follow results to root cause with a few mouse-clicks.

When our car dashboard signals a problem, most of us get out of our car and open the hood, then stand by the side of the road scratching our head until a mechanic can be summoned to tell us what went wrong.

With Guided Analytics the analyst can build expert knowledge into the visual charts and information flow to enable the manager to find out what is going wrong when a poor performance signal activates, or even better, how performance can be improved.

In this chapter, we take you through the techniques to build good UI into your analytical solutions and introduce the fundamental principles that make these techniques effective.

## The Visual Palette

Let's work on unleashing the powerful insights in our control chart (see Figure 11.9) from the previous chapter that are getting drowned out by poor UI. As we make over the chart, we introduce fundamental concepts of UI that can guide you in building clear and impactful charts.

Similar to a painter who faces a blank canvas when beginning a new work, analysts face a similar two-dimensional area of white space when setting out to create charts, tables, and dashboards. Incorporating essential principles of visual design makes the difference between a dashboard that presents a smorgasbord of graphs and data and a well-designed presentation of information guiding the user to important elements quickly and efficiently.

We think of the space, objects, and attributes that we use to build a visual object as our *visual palette*. Four elements of visual design form the foundation of our visual palette:

- Color
- Form
- Size
- Placement

We apply design principles from a number of seemingly unrelated fields of research to these elements, including the fields of psychology, design, and photography among others to help us understand how we process information visually and how we can use these principles to make our work more powerful. Applying these principles to the visual presentation of our analytic results greatly improves impact and effectiveness. We introduce these concepts as we work through building a Guided Analytics dashboard.

Key design principles we cover include:

**Data–Ink Ratio**, an information efficiency concept first intro-
　duced by information visualization pioneer Edward Tufte
**Pre-attentive processing**, a visual perception concept from the
　field of vision research
**Gestalt principles of pattern perception** from the field of
　psychology
**Z-pattern of scanning**, an information reading concept from the
　field of typography
**Rule of thirds**, a visual ordering concept from the field of
　photography

## Less Is More

As analysts, we rarely encounter a data point we don't love. However,
there is discipline taught in writing and editing to cut and cut again
that applies very well to Guided Analytics. Let's apply that principle
to our control chart from the previous chapter and see what we can
do to remove distracting elements.

First, we observe that we have two graphs (Figure 12.1) that
communicate similar information but in different contexts. While
the lower moving range chart highlights the statistical signals more
clearly, the upper control chart does a better job of presenting
context and trend. So let's remove the lower chart from our dashboard view (Figure 12.2). But we don't need to fear losing useful
information; we can make it available in a detail sheet for those who
want to know more.

The labels on Figure 12.2 control chart "reference lines" also
get in the way and distract attention. Users who have had Lean/Six
Sigma training will already know the meaning of the lines. Those
without such training can intuitively determine that the lines represent some upper, lower, and middle limit. We can place a discrete
footnote or tooltip on the dashboard to provide more specific
explanatory information.

We also have labels that aren't adding new information to the
chart (Figure 12.3). The axis title "complaints" is hard to read
vertically and repeated needlessly when we look at more than one
component, so we place it at the top of the axis. In addition, the

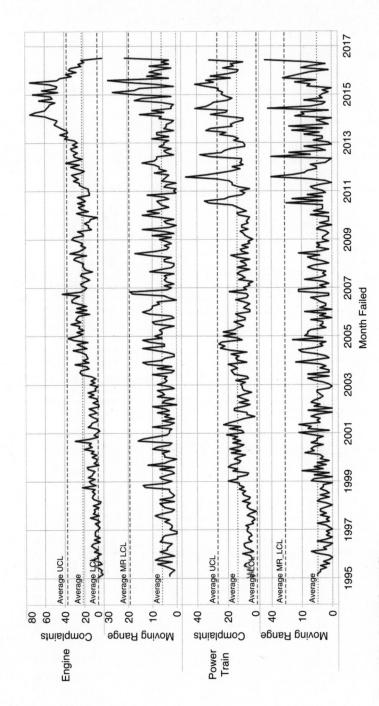

**Figure 12.1 Original Control Chart**

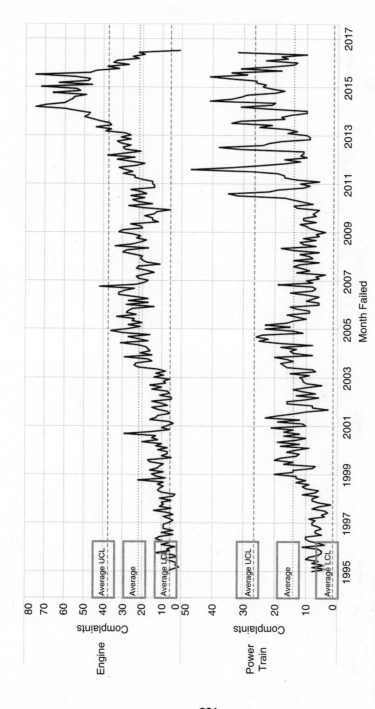

**Figure 12.2   Simplified Control Chart**

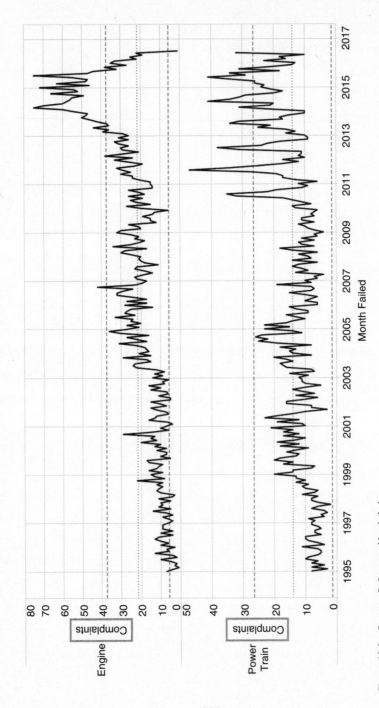

Figure 12.3   Remove Reference Line Labels

lines are the valuable part of the chart encoding the information we want to present but they are also a bit overwhelming. If your chart is in color, primary colors such as black, blue, red, and green pack a lot of punch and therefore should be used sparingly, principally when we want to attract attention. If everything is shouting "Look at me!," it is difficult to focus on any one thing in particular. Size also communicates information when one thing is bigger than another, so let's try reducing the width of the lines and choose a less impactful color (Figure 12.4). That will give us room later in the process to use color to call attention to interesting parts the story.

The horizontal gridlines are useful for identifying a specific value on the line, but we are more concerned about highlighting patterns and signals and not communicating an exact number. Since the chart may be displayed on a screen, perhaps even as small as a cellphone, few users will actually take a ruler to the screen to determine the value of a specific point. We can use the popup window feature in our visual tool to communicate the value when they hover.

Due to the potential for seasonality, the vertical gridlines for the years aid in the interpretation of the chart, helping the user to clearly see annual segments, so they can stay as shown in Figure 12.5, our made-over chart.

### Data–Ink Ratio

Why do we perceive this chart to be so much easier to grasp at a glance? We employ the power of the data–ink ratio, a concept introduced by Edward Tufte in his seminal work, *The Visual Display of Quantitative Information*. Tufte defines data–ink as "the non-erasable core of a graphic" and the data–ink ratio as the "proportion of a graphic's ink devoted to the non-redundant display of data-information." Tufte's point is that a good visual graphic maximizes the data–ink ratio so that as much of the graphic's ink is devoted to communicating useful information as possible. Stephen Few later extended the concept to include the data–pixel ratio when applied to computer dashboards.

### Less Is More—Until It Isn't

Gridlines are easy candidates for removal when working to increase the data–ink ratio, but our example illustrates a situation where

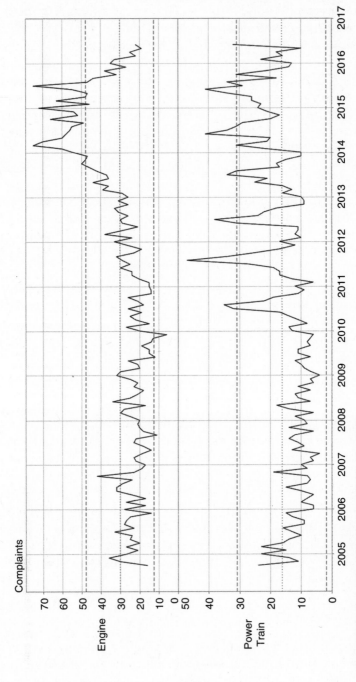

**Figure 12.4  Reposition Axis Labels and Modify Line Width**

204

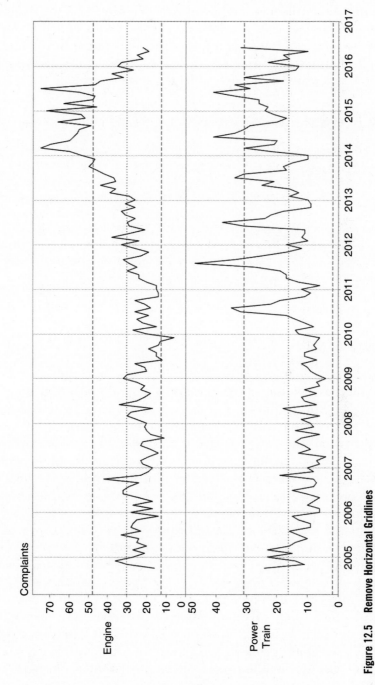

Figure 12.5   Remove Horizontal Gridlines

careful thought must be applied to determine if the chart element is communicating information. In this case (Figure 12.6), the vertical gridlines guide the user in assessing annual cycles and therefore contribute to communicating information, illustrating the counter-principle famously articulated by Albert Einstein, "Everything should be made as simple as possible, but not simpler."

---

### Essential Resources about Information Visualization

The principles underlying good visual design are a rich subject for research and, fortunately, there are many good resources to consult. Four books stand out and are widely consulted by practitioners in the field: *The Visual Display of Quantitative Information* by Edward Tufte, *Information Visualization: Perception for Design,* by Colin Ware, *Information Dashboard Design* by Stephen Few, and *Universal Principles of Design* by William Lidwell, Kritina Holden, and Jill Butler (see Bibliography). The discussion in this chapter draws from these works among others to help us grasp the fundamental principles we need to be able to produce visual designs that are both effective and aesthetic.

---

### With Just One Look

Our made-over chart is definitely easier on the eyes but it doesn't pop. If there is a message here, it is doing a good job of hiding.

Now we turn to how we can use visual principles to guide our users to focus on the story the data wants to tell. Color is the most powerful visual tool we have at our disposal. As such, it is often misused, drawing attention to points that have no business being center stage or assaulting our senses with a cacophony of poorly chosen, overpowering colors, shouting at us, causing our visual perception to shut down. When used purposefully and sparingly, well-regulated and carefully chosen color can work for us to make our point. We should always approach color with fear and respect.

Figure 12.7 illustrates how color can be used sparingly to deliver impact.

By adding a small circle shape to indicate a data point and coloring it differently when it is out of range, we allow our users to quickly focus on periods when there is a potential problem. They can easily tell if it is a persistent problem or a repeating problem. They can tell if the problem was building, as in the engine problems in 2014, or

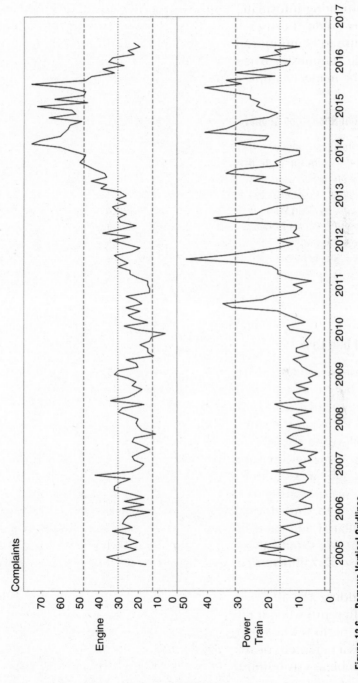

**Figure 12.6 Remove Vertical Gridlines**

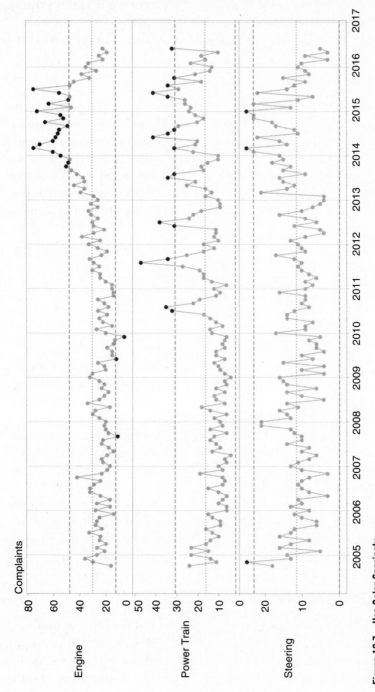

**Figure 12.7  Use Color Sparingly**

if they suddenly occurred, as with the power train issues starting in 2010. And all we did was add a splash of color.

Let's discuss briefly why color used in this manner works for us.

### Pre-attentive Processing

Color is one of the most powerful of the visual properties that are processed pre-attentively. As the term implies, these features are processed by our visual memory before we consciously comprehend the object. Pre-attentive processing occurs in the first few fractions of a second that we observe an object, allowing us to quickly assess an object visually. Even before our mind grasps that we are looking at an orange ball, we have already processed that we are seeing something orange and round.

The features of an object that are pre-attentively processed are

- Color
- Form
- Spatial placement
- Motion

In Figure 1 of Figure 12.8, you can quickly grasp that there are two differently colored objects even though the form is different. It requires more time to determine that there are 3 circles, 2 diamonds, and 4 squares.

Figures 2 and 3 of Figure 12.8 illustrate that while we can distinguish size and placement pre-attentively, the impact of these features pales in comparison to color even when viewed in shades of gray or full color.

However, effective pre-attentive processing requires a difference between the target and the non-targets and that the non-targets should be similar. Figure 4 within Figure 12.8 illustrates that when all features are different, nothing in particular stands out.

## Gestalt Principles of Pattern Perception

The other powerful set of principles of visual perception that we can put to work for us are the Gestalt principles of pattern perception. These principles, first introduced in 1923, have become the bedrock for principles of visual design. There are numerous resources

**Figure 1 Color**

Pre-attentive processing lets you quickly see that there is one dark shaded circle and one dark shaded diamond in the set below. You require more time to determine the number of diamonds, squares, and circles in the set.

**Figure 2 Size**

We can distinguish that the dark shaded circle is larger than the other objects but not as easily as to note that the color is different.

**Figure 3 Placement**

Aligning the objects by size helps to process the image.

**Figure 4**

Nothing is immediately distinguishable among the three objects because all elements that are pre-attentively processed are different.

Figure 12.8    Pre-attentive Processing

available to explore these concepts further, including Colin Ware's and Stephen Few's books referenced earlier.

You may be familiar with the statement, "The whole is greater than the sum of the parts." Kurt Koffka, the noted Gestalt psychologist, makes a key counterpoint:

> It has been said: The whole is more than the sum of its parts. It is more correct to say that the whole is something else other than the sum of its parts, because summing is a meaningless procedure, whereas the whole–part relationship is meaningful.

Koffka's point is that Gestalt principles of perception are not based on addition; rather the perceived whole has an identity independent of the parts perceived individually. This idea has important implications for visual analysis in that a business insight drawn from studying a carefully constructed sequence of charts can arise independent of any of the components.

Figures 12.9, 12.10, and 12.11 provide a brief summary of the primary Gestalt principles of pattern perception that lead to the visual perception of a group of objects as a visual whole. In addition, the Gestalt psychologists also identified the Law of Good Gestalt, also known as the law of *Pragnanz*, a German word relating to simplicity

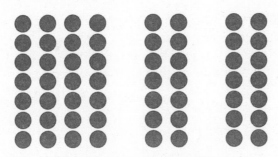

Objects that are in close proximity to
each other are perceived as related

**Figure 12.9    Proximity**

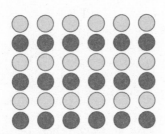

Objects that are similar to each
other are perceived as related

**Figure 12.10    Similarity**

Objects can be perceived as whole even when
gaps are present in the outline or form

**Figure 12.11    Closure**

and conciseness. This law expresses the idea that elements of an object will be perceived holistically if they form patterns that are regular, simple, and orderly. This overarching principle is important to keep in mind when designing charts based on complex data or analysis.

## Putting It All Together

Let's revisit our original dashboard (Figure 11.1) to do a makeover applying what we have learned about the visual principles of perception.

### Color

While it may be less apparent in a grayscale version, too many colors are being used. Let's use a standard color palette based on light gray for background elements and a darker shade of color for elements we wish to pull to the foreground to call attention. In an environment where the dashboard will be presented in color you could choose orange or blue for the foreground color. In cases where the dashboard may be presented in grayscale, a darker shade of gray will work nicely.

Showing total complaints by competitor doesn't really communicate useful information since larger manufacturers will have more complaints simply due to their size. We can index by market share

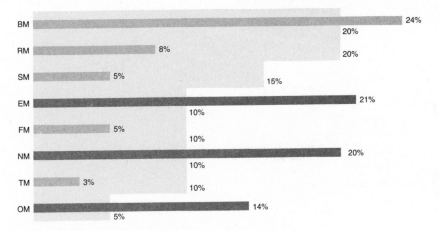

**Figure 12.12    Complaints by Competitor**

and highlight manufacturers that have a share of complaints greater than their share of the market (Figure 12.12).

The only place where color is adding new information is the map where it indicates more or fewer complaints. Our analysis has already given us the insight that seasonal patterns of weather or temperature could play a role in performance. However, the seasons are always changing and many states have wide temperature variations between hot and cold so the volume complaints relative to the temperature change in some cases could be due to correlation, not causation.

Users of this dashboard are mainly interested in complaints that stand out and have a strong relationship to regional location. After creating an index to adjust for market share and applying results from data mining for significance, we can create an alert to highlight the states with complaints greater than what would normally be expected (Figure 12.13).

We replace the original complaint trend with our new control charts and decide to add some menu controls to zoom in by date and filter by manufacturer, model, and component (Figure 12.14).

Looking at the distribution of complaints, there is simply too much fragmentation to produce a meaningful chart suitable for a dashboard. Let's create a word cloud highlighting complaint

Figure 12.13    States with Greater-than-Expected Complaints

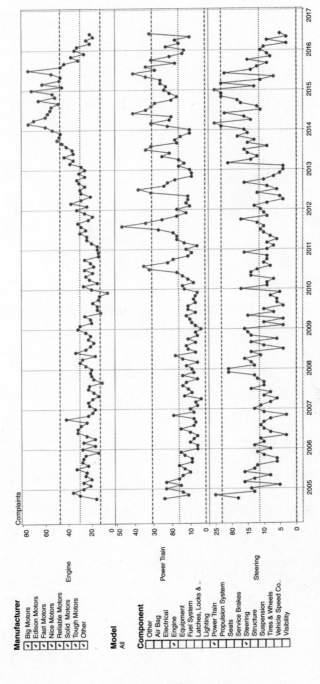

**Figure 12.14   Menu Controls**

215

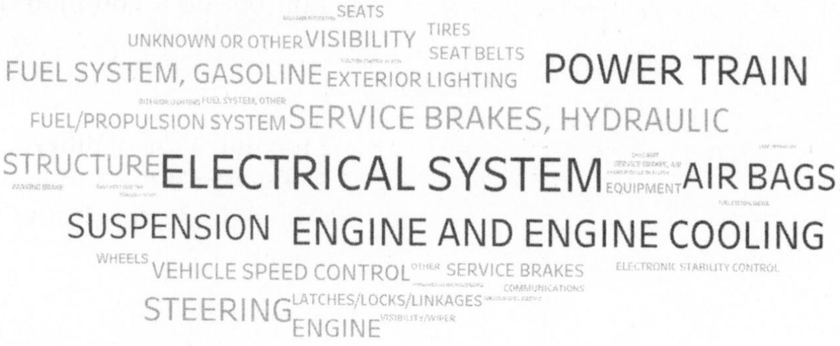

**Figure 12.15    Word Cloud**

components that we can use to filter the dashboard and navigate to a more detailed view (Figure 12.15).

### Elements of the Visual Palette

Let's revisit the changes we made in the context of the four elements of the visual palette.

### Color

We used color to draw attention to the aspects of the analysis that we want our users to focus on.

### Form

We also addressed issues of *form*, which is the principle that determines the shapes we will use to present our analysis, for example, determining when it is best to use line or bar charts to present certain types of information. We converted a highly fragmented bar chart to a word cloud that effectively draws attention to the primary components causing issues and can serve as a launch-pad to more detail on demand.

Here the adage from architectural design, "form follows function," becomes relevant. Comparison and distribution analysis are best represented by bar charts. Time series and change analysis are better represented with line charts. Key results and KPIs work well with simple text charts. Word clouds are not very effective for communicating quantitative information but do a good job of capturing attention.

## Size

Size communicates quantity effectively but too much use of different sizes to communicate information can become confusing and hard to interpret. Similar to our use of color, we employed size selectively in places where we wanted to emphasize a point.

## Placement

Having reworked our chart elements, we turn our attention to where we will place the objects on the dashboard. Placement of objects in visual space is as critical to effective communication as the objects individually.

Let's talk about a few design principles used in advertising and newspaper design layouts, photography, and film. You may find it curious that we are bringing in principles from fields that on the surface do not seem related to analytics. The discipline of visual and guided analytics is highly multidisciplinary because it engages our sense of sight and visual perception as well as our sense of logic and analysis. Guided Analytics is a holistic practice that draws from the whole person, the right and left brain.

The first principle is *Z-pattern of scanning*, a principle based on observations about how we read. Since we write from left to right, we similarly read from left to right across the top of the page; once having reached the end of the line, we scan back from right to left to the next few lines down and then back from left to right, tracing a Z-shaped pattern. If the page we are viewing is more image based than text based, the Z-shaped pattern is an even easier process to use to comprehend the material before us. Therefore, the most valuable places on a dashboard are the Z pivot points in the upper left at the beginning of the pattern, the upper-right corner, the middle of the diagonal, the lower-left corner, and the lower-right corner at the end of the pattern. These five points are golden points that have important consequences for decisions about where to place information on the dashboard.

Because the reader starts in the upper left, introductory and scoping information should be placed here. This helps the reader to establish a context for the following information. The upper right is a stopping point before moving down the action-packed diagonal of the *Z*, so supporting information is better placed here. Information such as dates and logos are good candidates. Such information helps to orient the reader before moving on to consuming the main story the analysis is trying to tell, the focal point of the dashboard. The most impactful information, therefore, should be placed in the center section of the dashboard. The bottom of the *Z*, essentially the finish line of the reader's scan, is the place for closure, conclusions, supporting information, and calls to action.

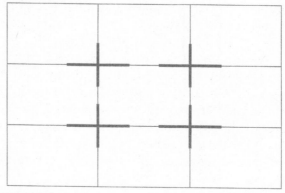

**Figure 12.16    Rule of Thirds**

Another important principle used in film and photography is the *rule of thirds*. This concept divides the visual area into a 3 × 3 matrix (Figure 12.16). Strategies are developed for placing visual objects in the thirds, the top or bottom third, the left or right third, as well as the center third. Objectives to create visual interest and emphasis determine where visual objects are placed on the grid.

### Good Gestalt—Less Is More

Figure 12.17 is our made-over dashboard incorporating the principles we have just reviewed. While these principles from the literary and visual arts play an important role in our work in visual analytics, discretion when to adhere and when to deviate is an important skill based on education and experience.

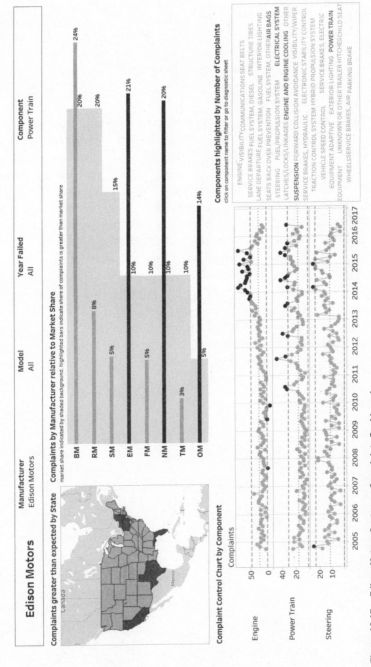

**Figure 12.17  Edison Motors Customer Complaints Dashboard**

## Summary

Comparing the made-over dashboard to our starting point, the power of the Good Gestalt is driven home. We improve the dashboard by reduction rather than addition. Color is one of the most powerful principles of visual perception and we use it to great advantage not by using a lot of it, but by using it selectively to draw attention and create focus.

Through understanding key principles of visual perception, we are able to place our analytic objects such that they align with the typical flow a reader will follow to absorb the information.

But the job is not finished. We also must create an effortless experience for our users, an experience that guides them through the complex analytic process we labored through in a way that shares the gain but not the pain. We are firm believers in the view that "analytics is a journey" and the value is not in the destination, but rather in the steps taken to get there. If we don't guide our users through the logical processes used to arrive at conclusions or insights, they will lack confidence in the solution that leads them to make the right business decision.

In the next chapter, we discuss how to build a user experience to guide our audience through the analytics in an effortless manner to help them build understanding and confidence in the information.

# 13

# User Experience (UX): *Making It Work*

The concept of "path of least resistance" is a principle borrowed from physics that can be applied to industrial and visual design. This principle captures the observation that the easiest method to complete a task is the method most likely to be used. It also underlies the concept of shortcuts. How many of us prefer to use the hard way to reach a goal when an easy way is readily available?

In this chapter, we go over the third aspect of Guided Analytics, that is, the techniques we use to guide the user through the analytic train of thought. We want to minimize the mental effort the user spends trying to process the visual information and maximize the opportunity for the user to comprehend the key insights. We introduce concepts from a wide range of fields, including psychology, industrial engineering, object-oriented design, and linguistics, that will aid us in developing dashboards that drive insights and action rather than ones that make the user work to understand the information.

Key principles we cover include:

- Performance load
- Flow
- Modularity
- Propositional density

## Performance Load

Performance load in our context is a concept introduced by Lidwell, Holden, and Butler in *Universal Principles of Design* to capture the idea that "the greater the effort to accomplish a task, the less likely the task will be accomplished successfully." The authors describe performance load as comprised of *cognitive* and *kinematic load.*

### Cognitive Load

The effort required to comprehend a dashboard, read the charts and text, and understand the conclusion is a form of cognitive load, that is, the mental effort required to comprehend the information presented. Cognitive load was first introduced by John Sweller in 1988 and has since led to significant research and insight into the principles impacting the ease or difficulty of perceiving graphical objects.

Reviewing our made-over dashboard (Figure 12.19), we have objects with varying degrees of cognitive load. Our complaints control chart and fair-share analysis are relatively high in cognitive load, calling on the reader to process complex relationships and patterns, whereas the map-and-word cloud charts are relatively low in cognitive load. Taking advantage of what we have learned about the Z-pattern of reading, we pair a lower cognitive load object with a higher one on the top and bottom lines of the Z. We give balance to the overall presentation and allow the cognitive effort the reader expends to grow, peak, and decline as they traverse the chart.

### Working Memory

Colin Ware, in his must-read book for information visualization practitioners, *Information Visualization: Perception for Design,* provides an excellent introduction to the memory systems that are used when processing visual information. Ware provides a comprehensive review of the current understanding of the components of our memory system and how they work. Two fundamental principles introduced by Ware in particular, *visual working memory* and *attention,* help us to learn how to design dashboards that reduce cognitive load and make it easier for our audience to grasp our key points.

Visual working memory is a critical concept for our purposes and is a component of *working memory,* the system the brain uses to access and process newly received and retained information in order to act on it. Visual working memory processes information we see, whereas its counterpart, *verbal working memory,* processes information we hear. *Long-term memory* is our store of retained information, knowledge, and experiences. Some information may be retained for life; other information may be discarded from lack of use.

Research indicates that working memory in general and visual working memory in particular can only store information for a brief period of time with a limited capacity for a small number of objects. These findings are important to our work. This fundamental limitation could be one reason for the popularity of the "rule of 3" writing principle, which suggests that a statement can be more memorable and effective if it contains three items of interest. Marketing copywriters have lived by the rule of 3 since it was introduced by advertising pioneer E. St. Elmo Lewis in the early 1900s. Brian Clark, an online marketing expert, has attributed the rule of 3 to the popularity of the quantity *three* in classic fairytales—such as *The Three Little Pigs, Three Billy Goats Gruff,* or *Goldilocks and the Three Bears.* It is likely the original storytellers had to rely solely on the working memory capacity of their illiterate audiences to captivate and entertain them. The rule of 3 is powerful and we can use it to our benefit as we reveal information that leads to insights.

As analysts, our goal is to help users transfer insights gained from dashboards residing in working memory to long-term memory stores that can be used when making business decisions. If an insight is profound and enduring, we want to develop paths of least resistance to guide users to transfer this information from flashes of insights lighting up working memory into learnings stored in long-term memory.

### Attention

Attention is a closely related aspect of our memory system required for users to effectively process the information in working memory. Most people today have heard of the rise in attention-deficit disorder or the concerns of short attention spans that our digital world might be fostering. We are all well aware that attention can be easily disrupted. While an important goal is to keep our users' attention, a more important goal is to focus their attention on the key bits of information that drive the analysis and lead to insights. As such, we also need to think about how to use design principles to draw the user's attention without being disruptive to the smooth flow of thought or giving rise to an unpleasant user experience.

## Kinematic Load

We've already discussed the principle of cognitive load. Another related principle, less obviously relevant to our work, is the partner concept, kinematic load, described by Lidwell, Holden, and Butler as the degree of physical activity or motion that is required to complete an effort. In our context, high kinematic load results from having to traverse the screen to access a set of filters on the right side and another set of filters on the left side. This example requires a higher degree of physical movement than if the filters were grouped together in one section of the dashboard.

Taken together, cognitive load and kinematic load comprise performance load, which is the mental and physical activities users have to engage in order to interact with our dashboards. The greater the performance load, the less likely the dashboard is to be used.

Our goal as analysts and communicators is to minimize performance load while at the same time presenting the information necessary to drive good business decisions that grow revenue or reduce costs. We should work hard to make our dashboards simple and easy to use but once again we refer to Einstein's famous dictum, "Everything should be made as simple as possible, but not simpler."

## Choice Overload

The difficulty of predicting precisely who may be viewing our analytic story and their scope of interest presents challenges to making our dashboards simple and compact. Is the user looking to understand the forest or the trees? Do they want to see the top line or the bottom line? It is tempting to place as many filters as our users desire, allowing them a large variety of analytical capabilities. We may think we are helping them out by placing any combination of the attributes they might want to drill through, but we may be making their task more difficult by inadvertently creating choice overload.

Barry Schwartz, in his 2004 book, *The Paradox of Choice: Why More Is Less*, popularized the concept of "the paradox of choice." Related experiments at supermarkets in 2000 by Iyengar and Lepper described in their article, *When Choice Is Demotivating: Can One Desire Too Much of a Good Thing?*, imply that consumers buy more when faced with fewer varieties. Yet at the same time, how can we explain the success of "long-tail" businesses such as Netflix as described by

Chris Anderson in his popular 2008 book, *The Long Tail: Why the Future of Business Is Selling Less of More.* We also touch on this topic in our chapter on Decision Theory (Chapter 8) when we discus Choice Architecture.

Clearly both concepts touch chords of reality and have important implications to the value and usability of our work. Presenting too many choices risks cognitive overload with users overwhelmed by the number of choices to be made, thus leading to the perception of our dashboard as too complex. Presenting too few choices narrows the analytic value to our audience, leaving them with unanswered questions and the inevitable request for more detail.

## Go with the Flow

This is a hinge point where Decision Analysis integrates with Guided Analytics. Rather than throwing the best charts we can concoct onto a dashboard with as many options as we can squeeze in, we take a different approach and lay out a progressive reveal of analysis and insights. This approach helps you to manage the complexity of the information by following the natural path of analysis for the business problem as determined by our decision analysis. Using our methodology, the Category Tree is the guided experience that will provide a user with a natural path for analysis.

Our approach to decision analysis relies on time-tested methods of breaking complex questions into decisions that are housed in a Category Tree. Recent research in complexity analysis, advances in data-mining techniques, and data visualization platforms are giving us analytic tools to get inside the complex structure of business decisions without forcing us to lay them flat on a linear scale or process.

In addition to following the flow of the analytic thought process outlined by the decision architecture, there is another important concept of flow that can serve our purposes. *Lean Thinking* by James Womack and Daniel T. Jones popularized the concept of "flow" in manufacturing, which was developed by Toyota in its world-famous Toyota Production System, also referred to as just-in-time manufacturing. Flow indicates the smooth flow of materials and work through a production process without the undesirable wastes of *time spent waiting, useless motion, overproduction,* or *accumulation of parts or materials.* The fundamental concepts of flow also apply to our analytic tasks as well.

Corresponding wastes in the analytic process are time spent waiting for queries to return information or render visualizations, useless mouse-clicks from poorly designed menu systems, and presentation of too much information at once. Wait time is particularly undesirable because the user's train of thought is interrupted, information stored in working memory is jeopardized, and attention span is at risk. If a dashboard takes too long to return results or requires too much time to comprehend in our fast-paced business world, the user has already moved on to the next burning issue they need to think about.

Our job is to design Guided Analytics that present the right information at the right time in the right amount. Poorly designed and overloaded dashboards presenting too much complex information at one time increase cognitive and kinematic load, leading to disuse and lack of interest.

In order to meet the challenge of presenting complex information in a digestible manner, we turn our attention to several key techniques to use—progressive reveal, detail on demand, and modularity.

### Progressive Reveal and Decision Architecture

Progressive reveal takes the user through the analytic journey one step at a time or one level at a time. The information is presented to the user through an ordered process that can follow several different patterns, such as building from the component inputs up to a concluding insight or conversely presenting the main point and then allowing the user to step through the underlying logic. Progressive reveal can allow the user to drill down from a higher level of aggregation to a lower level in a hierarchy or examine corresponding components on the same level, a process commonly referred to as *slice-and-dice*.

Progressive reveal contributes to a productive user experience because it lets the user step through the analysis in a manner similar to the analyst who created the information, giving the user the opportunity to gather the same learnings and insights along the analytic journey as the original author. We are fond of commenting that the value of analytics is not in the answer but in the journey to the answer, a concept similar to the adage that it is more valuable to teach a person to fish rather than hand them the fish. Similarly, presentation of insights in a manner that allows the user to step through the logic and component parts lets the user build an understanding of how the drivers of the problem interact.

Business problems are complex because business is a network of interacting systems each with its own set of inputs, drivers, and outputs that interact with each other. The technique of progressive reveal allows us to get into the deductive process of the analysis and examine intermediate influences that would otherwise be subsumed in the end result. The Question Analysis process will help you take the user on this journey as you progress through the questions with them.

Decision Architecture is the critical structure that captures the logical flow and guides the analytic process. It lets us look at top-level KPIs and gives us the map to dig into root causes when the metric flashes a problem. These questions and metrics hang on our Category Tree that outlines our navigation path. In our case study at the end of the book we illustrate how Guided Analytics works in the context of Decision Architecture.

### Data on Demand—Connecting Data to Decisions

The technique that enables progressive reveal is the ability to present detail on demand. Recent advances in technology have opened up access to volumes of data at greater levels of detail than would have been possible not so long ago. The economics of storing data at its most granular level is now at a price point creating parity for businesses large and small.

Data storage has become incredibly cheap. CPU processing power and parallel processing can now be implemented on wafer-thin chips. These advances mean that we no longer have to aggregate our data in order to consume it, thereby opening up the world of big data.

While high-level summarization of key metrics is essential to understanding overall performance, once data is aggregated and disconnected from the lower-level data, valuable detailed information is lost and this can disrupt the ability to follow an analysis to lower levels. Similarly, advances in database technology and analytic algorithms are giving us the tools we need to process the increasing levels of detail data now available without relying solely on aggregations and averages.

The ability to store and process vast quantities of data has resulted in a data tsunami that risks overwhelming managers with information overload that can lead to analysis paralysis. That is where the power of the new breed of analytic tools coupled with a well-thought-out Decision Architecture and Monetization Strategy keeps us from drowning in data. It allows us to channel our data into flows that support our decisions to take actions that drive business strategies.

Analytic databases allow us to structure and store our data at its most granular level and yet retrieve a few records or millions of records within seconds. Data visualization tools allow us to access our data directly and transform it from byte to chart with just a few clicks. This combined power of large volumes of data just a click away enables us to design Guided Analytics that present key insights as the default, but open up access to underlying detail.

In our case study at the end of the book, we show how a business manager can estimate the value of opportunities to grow revenue through engagement and retention strategies and click his way through to specific customers to target in order to execute the strategy.

## Modularity

Our Decision Architecture, through the use of Category Trees, also supports another important design technique—modularity—that we can use to enhance the ability to consume large volumes of data. It is important to understand the levels of the decision architecture, modules, or chunks of analysis that can be built and called out through the guided analytic process when needed. We often group this information into specific areas of analysis that the user is interested in, such as performance, orders, sales, or marketing. Modularity prevents us from getting locked into a single sequential path that the user must walk through even if it is contrary to their current thought process.

The components of our analysis have a building-block approach, similar to the Lego pieces we use to think about our Decision Architecture. We give our users the flexibility to study and build the logic flow that follows their train of thought as they are working through the analysis rather than forcing them to comply with a predetermined train of thought. Modularity is a key technique that allows us to plug-and-play analytic components to let the voice of the customer or the voice of the business speak out in harmony.

When building modules, interfaces between the different modules should be standardized to facilitate smooth movement, ease of transition, and quick comprehension. Consistent fonts, color schemes, orientation principles, and menu functions should be applied between dashboards and within objects on dashboards. Inexperienced dashboard designers may attempt to add novelty by changing presentation elements within different sections of their dashboard in order to be less boring. This only achieves disorientation and frustration as users must reorient to new visual environments as they navigate the analysis.

## Propositional Density

Propositional density, described by Lidwell, Holden, and Butler in *Universal Principles of Design*, is one final concept that we use to enhance our ability to design visual elements that pack a punch. Propositional density captures the idea that words or images can carry more meaning than meets the eye.

In business and reporting, a common example is the use of the color red for negative numbers such as profit or variances to plan. Red is also associated with the color of blood and the process of bleeding, which is seldom a good thing. As such a P&L with a lot of visible red figures not only communicates that the company is losing money but also carries along with it the idea that the situation is not healthy, perhaps even dire.

Propositional density is an important tool for visual arts designers when designing logos. The YouTube logo, for example, encloses the word *Tube* in a box shaped to resemble an older-style television screen, communicating that YouTube is a service where you can put yourself on TV without having to say it in so many words.

Similarly, when we design our analytic visualizations we also want to take advantage of the power of propositional density to communicate deeper meaning when possible. One common technique when working with the data of a company is to use the color palette of the company to encode elements of "good" versus "bad." Red and green are almost universally recognized as signifying bad and good respectively, but in addition to carrying the baggage of being visually inaccessible to the roughly 8 percent of males that are red-green color blind, too much use of red and green in a visualization risks triggering association with Christmas, an example of unwanted propositional density.

Working with the color palette of the company to identify one color to signal good elements and another to signify bad helps to evoke harmony with the company logo and other communications carrying a sense of belonging, personalizing the visualization to the corporate culture. Up or down arrows, checkmarks, open boxes, stars, and other shapes, when used sparingly, can help to pack multiple layers of meaning into a single visual element.

Good use of propositional density can significantly increase the communicative power of the visual element without adding additional pixels or objects, thereby increasing the data–ink ratio of our work. However, as a counterpoint, we need to be careful to not overdo it, evoking too many deeper meanings, which may cloud, confuse, or harm our primary message.

### Pies and Donuts, Are They Good for You?

Most experts in data visualization do not recommend the use of pie charts, citing the poor ability of these types of charts to communicate comparative information. The more effective alternative in almost all cases would be a simple bar chart that communicates comparison through length rather than through area as in a pie chart. Most people are good at comparing lengths, easily determining when one bar is longer than the other, and are poor at comparing areas or slices of a pie.

However, despite their shortcomings, pie charts and their close cousin, donut charts, are ubiquitous, frequently encountered in business presentations, news articles, and visual media. They have been around since 1801 when it is believed the first pie chart was introduced by William Playfair, an early pioneer in the visual presentation of information. If these charts are such poor performers, why have they stayed on the stage for so long with no signs of exiting?

One explanation could attribute their longevity to *path lock-in*, a principle introduced by Brian Arthur in *Increasing Returns and Path Dependence in the Economy*. Path lock-in is the principle governing the success of VHS videotapes over Betamax videotapes in the early days of videotaping technology even though many considered Betamax to be a better technology. VHS is believed to have become the winning technology because the critical mass of VHS users grew faster than Betamax. The positive market response encouraged equipment manufacturers to standardize on VHS until it became the remaining technology in the market.

Similarly, it could be that with early and long widespread use, people are familiar with pie charts and know how to interpret them, so they prevail due in part to a form of path lock-in.

It could also be that propositional density is another factor contributing to the prevalence and ongoing use of pie and donut charts. In addition to functioning as a visual chart element, pie charts have a real-life counterpart that bar charts do not. Real-life pies are generally viewed in a positive light as something desirable and tasty, a core member of the comfort food group. As such, the concept of a slice of pie can carry additional deep levels of meaning. It may be that pies and donuts are capable of evoking positive, comfort food associations, adding propositional density to charts unconsciously, which can explain their ongoing popularity.

## Simplicity on the Other Side of Complexity

Early in our careers, we were introduced to the concept of "simplicity on the other side of complexity." It is a concept that has stuck with us through many career twists and turns and continues to guide us in our goals. The concept was articulated by U.S. Supreme Court Justice Oliver Wendell Holmes, Jr.

> The only simplicity for which I would give a straw is that which is on the other side of the complex—not that which never has divined it.

The idea is that when we first encounter a problem or an issue, we tend to see it in simple binary terms, up or down, yes or no. As we learn more about the topic, we begin to grasp the complexity, the myriad component parts, and the competing dynamics and begin to realize that the issue is not as simple as we thought. Hard work, skill, and training help us to get beyond the simplicity and grasp the richness of the problem we are facing. In many cases, we stop there, proud of the effort, the deep insights, and the rich data we have accumulated in our journey through complexity. However, Justice Holmes challenges us to press on, to synthesize the insights and data, to pull out the essentials that represent the key points upon which the direction of the issue rests.

## Summary

In this and the preceding chapters, we have sought to equip you with tools to help you and your users navigate the analytic journey through the mountains of data in order to build your monetization strategies and analytical solutions. We cover techniques you can use to make your work accessible to users without overwhelming them with too much information, too early, and at the wrong time.

In Section V we discuss deployment principles, processes, and organization ideas that are essential to successful deployment and adoption within your organizational environment, large or small.

# SECTION V

# ENABLEMENT

# CHAPTER 14

## Agile Approach: *Getting Agile*

Aconsistent theme of our discussion is that the processes we advocate do not follow a linear, one-way flow of execution. Rather a more agile, iterative cyclical approach is required to be effective. As Figure 14.1 indicates, iterative processes with feedback loops and agile development cycles are embedded across the flow of the primary phases of the project. In this chapter we introduce the agile nature of the processes we use to develop analytics in our Decision Architecture methodology.

### Agile Development

First a word about Agile Development. In 2001, a group of software developers formed the Agile Alliance and published a "Manifesto for Agile Software Development." The Agile Alliance enumerated core principles that emphasize a people-centric, pragmatic, collaborative, and iterative approach to software development projects.

While the Agile Manifesto was written in the context of software development, there are many parallels to development of analytical solutions as both subject areas consist of complex, interconnected, dependent processes to deliver a working product. Business analytics and business software are driven by the same purpose, which is supporting the needs of the business to deliver better products and services to satisfy customer needs.

Business priorities and objectives change frequently in tandem with changes in the customer market, making it difficult to pin down concrete requirements that persist for a long development cycle.

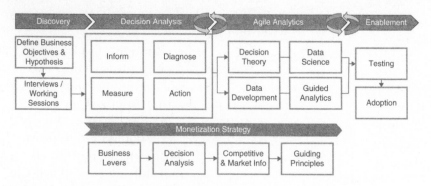

Figure 14.1   Decision Architecture Methodology

This does not imply the converse—a state of chaos, where business requirements are constantly changing and nothing can be managed through standard processes.

We tend to work on market-facing projects and those that have been the most successful have embodied to a significant degree the core principles described by the Agile Alliance simply because markets tend to be fluid and dynamic. In this chapter we describe how these principles apply to an analytics project.

## Riding the Wave

The business questions that managers struggle with on a daily basis do not always persist for lengthy periods of time. Some business questions are driven by competitor price and promotion moves in a particular market space, product quality issues that need to be addressed rapidly to stay alive in the market, changing customer tastes, rapidly evolving technology that is constantly moving the goal post, and so forth. Other business questions are time tested and have longer cycle times, such as optimizing production processes, managing commodity product sales, anticipating seasonal trends, and demographic-driven demand. Customer demand for health care driven by an aging population is one example that can be planned for well in advance. When thinking about health-care needs for an aging population, for example, every potential customer for our addressable market has already been born.

Analytical projects addressing challenges and opportunities arising from long-term trends can and should be managed through a structured development process. Business decisions and investments needed to take advantage of these opportunities can be substantial and transformative, requiring careful thought and thorough review.

Other trends, such as technology adoption, fashion cycles, and pricing moves, have much shorter cycle times. These trends often break fast and furious, requiring quick response and decisive action. In these cases, an agile-like decision method as we have developed in our Decision Architecture methodology is the most effective response. Hands-on, information-on-demand tools provide managers the dynamic information environment they need to quickly assess a business opportunity and decide a course of action.

## Agile Analytics

In the framework presented at the beginning of this chapter, we identify the iterative nature of the development process through cyclical arrows. We do not believe we can overstate the importance of an iterative approach to analytic project development. Let's discuss how we adapt agile software development principles to our Decision Analysis and Agile Analytics phases, addressing the two primary components that drive a project—process and people.

These principles describe a process that is fluid, dynamic, adaptive, where *change* is not a dirty word.

### People—Collaborate

- Form working teams of business managers and developers.
- Give the working team the latitude and trust them to get the job done.
- Let the teams self-organize with minimal governance.

### Processes—Iterate Early, Iterate Often

- Deliver actionable analytics early, frequently, and build on them.
- Establish a steady pace of development that is sustainable.
- Strive for continuous improvement, embracing changing requirements when they improve the product.

#### A Team Sport

We often remark that Analytics is a team sport. The idea of the brilliant data scientist locked away in a quiet room unlocking the secrets of the business with sophisticated analysis that only geniuses can understand simply does not work in the business world. Business problems are messy, data is never clean enough, and customers are not always rational. Scientific analytic principles developed to tame well-behaved atoms and molecules rarely provide clear answers when applied to populations whose first mantra is "break all the rules."

Having said that, analytics provides insightful pictures into patterns of behavior that are used to predict trends and response. Additionally, analytics in the business environment must be coupled with hard-to-quantify soft knowledge, that is, expert, intuitive knowledge based on hands-on experience and direct interaction with the business process.

As such, close interaction between the business managers and the analytic developers is an essential ingredient to develop analytics that drive action. Because the process we describe embraces change and continuous improvement, frequent communication among the principal parties in the project is necessary to ensure the project stays focused on the goal and does not meander off course.

### The Cassandra Effect

If the analytics are developed apart from the participation of the managers with the responsibility to use them, they may have difficulty adopting the analytical solution due to lack of trust in the methods used. This is often called the Cassandra effect. Cassandra was the daughter of King Priam and Queen Hecuba of Troy. Greek legend has it that Cassandra had the gift of prophecy or foresight to see the future but also the curse that no one would believe her. According to legend she foresaw the tragedy of Troy but was powerless to change the course of action because she was not believed. Analysts who develop predictions and forecasts in isolation from the managers whose necks are on the line to deliver the results risk the same fate with their insights and information disregarded even when they point to the correct course of action.

### Analysis Paralysis

We have all run up against the bane of modern business with access to so much rich data—analysis paralysis. As we discuss in Decision

Theory and Guided Analytics, when presented with too much information or too many choices, the manager can become overwhelmed, not sure of which way to turn. This does not mean that we supply incomplete or limited information that risks steering the manager in the wrong direction; rather we present analysis results that shed light on the key levers that a manager needs to address the situation at hand. The good-enough principle is crucial in the early stages of an analytics project to ensure we are addressing the right priorities and are focused on decisions that matter. Other supplemental analysis providing nuance and detail can follow later.

How do we know which levers are key and which are supplemental? A well-constructed Decision Analysis and Monetization Strategy can provide the map to identify critical leverage points to address early and those that can be developed over time.

### What Do You Want? What Do You Have?

Using the data of the business to tap into new revenue opportunities or unlock trapped productivity is the essence of our proposition that internal business data is the best asset for monetization that businesses have. The nature of a data monetization project is that the opportunity is not well understood, hidden in the trends and patterns of the data, and lost in the averages.

In large organizations, IT is typically the steward of the business data, responsible for data quality and security and most familiar with what data is available. IT processes rely on structure and discipline to ensure they can protect and deliver quality data to the organization. Marketing and Finance are typical consumers of the data for analytics. When a marketing analyst embarks on a Monetization Strategy project, one of the first stops will be to IT with a data request. The IT manager will ask for data requirements, but oftentimes the analyst does not have great visibility into the data sources available and what is needed at the outset may be different from where the analytics will end.

A tug-of-war may ensue, with the analyst presenting requirements in broad terms, hoping to cast as wide a net as possible, whereas in reality she may only use a portion of the requested data. However, retrieving large quantities of complex data can be a time-consuming process for the IT manager, and if all clients follow similar strategies, IT can easily become overwhelmed with "data gopher" activities and fall behind delivering its core processes. The IT manager will attempt to narrow the scope; the analyst will fight to keep it broad.

If the IT manager and analyst are able to form an agile team where agreements are made to work with small batches in an iterative fashion, the analyst has the opportunity to learn the data needs as the analysis progresses and the IT manager spends less time pulling large amounts of unused data.

Many organizations, realizing the waste of valuable IT resources spent chasing data, have begun to make data sources more readily available to the business through on-demand business intelligence (BI) "sandboxes" in the data warehouse where users can run their own queries, or analytic data marts, which are separate databases storing the data to support analytics. This opens up much more visibility to the business manager but at the same time creates a responsibility to learn how to work with data more directly in a responsible manner.

### A Picture Tells a Thousand Words

As discussed in the chapter on Guided Analytics, visualization is powerful. Data visualization should be imbedded early in the process as part of the Decision Analysis phase; don't wait until you get knee-deep into the Agile Analytics phase to start visualization efforts. Visual presentation of information requires unique data modeling and structure, triggering serious rework if not included early in project.

### Not Every Child Is Beautiful

The products of analytic projects can become like children to the core team members who work together from inception to production. Just as no parent has an ugly child, project teams risk losing perspective about the value of their analysis. Many a team has spent countless hours, over many months, preparing a strategy presentation for the executive management only to be sent back to the drawing board because they had veered off course. Early and frequent results review meetings between team members and stakeholders help to ensure that the project stays on course. As new information and learnings become available, these can be shared with stakeholders at an early stage, as the insights gained may prompt the leaders to modify the direction.

### Meet Early, Meet Often

An agile process thrives on frequent communication among team members. We find regular, short stand-up meetings of the working team are necessary for team members to keep in sync yet preserve enough time to get work done. We will put in place weekly status meetings to drive broader communications and provide vehicles for issue and risk escalation. An agenda should be followed but should be flexible enough that the team can deal with expected issues. The time should be strictly limited to encourage members to be prompt and focused. Agenda items not covered are placed on the agenda for the following meeting.

Between meetings, members are encouraged to ask questions as they arise and resolve via email or chat. If the project is significant enough, a war room could be set aside where members can work side-by-side and address issues in real time.

## Summary

The nature of an analytic project is one of discovery. We begin with a hypothesis about a business issue and then embark on a journey of exploration and analysis, gaining new insights along the way and discarding others. We typically start with a simplistic view of our business issue and trudge through the valley of complexity, emerging on the far side of simplicity with a deeper understanding of the nature of the action levers available to us to manage the business.

In this chapter we have outlined foundational principles with respect to how people and processes can interact to ensure that the journey is productive, profitable, and enjoyable for all involved.

CHAPTER

# 15

# Enablement: *Gaining Adoption*

**A**n analytic project, no matter how brilliant, is worth nothing if it does not inform decisions and drive actions. In this chapter, we address techniques you can use to get your project adopted in your organization. We cover *testing* of the solution to validate it delivers as expected, *training* of target users to promote understanding and adoption, and phased *rollout* to build momentum and a solid user base.

## Testing

The type and degree of testing needed for your solution is dependent on the scale and level of automation. Will the solution be rolled out enterprise-wide or will it be deployed to a small user group? Will one or two developers be responsible for Data Development, the Analytical Structure, and Guided Analytics, or will a team of developers be involved?

Large and complex projects designed for enterprise deployment with a high degree of automation require a more formal and structured testing, training, and rollout process. Smaller, focused projects impacting a small group of users can adopt a more agile process. Let's review both scenarios.

### Enterprise Projects

Decision Architecture projects on an enterprise scale involve several departments working together in cross-functional teams with a number of roles. A team working on an enterprise-wide Decision Architecture project typically requires a wide scope of capabilities, comprising *facilitation, documentation, data architecture design, data analysis, data science and decision theory, analytics, UI/UX design,* and *dashboard development.* These capabilities require cross-functional and cross-departmental collaboration across a broad range of roles, such as project leader, decision architect, decision analyst, data scientist, data librarian, data analyst, data architect, data developer, guided analytics developer, UI/UX designer, project manager, and trainer. Chapter 16 discusses these organizational capabilities and roles in greater detail.

While some of the roles may be held by one person, generally speaking, the project team for large, enterprise solutions will be more complex than a small group of people working in a room together. For many large organizations, team members are likely to be located in different countries around the world. In these cases, coordination and testing every step of the way is essential to ensuring the end solution, once brought together, works as intended rather than becoming a jumbled mess.

Large decision architecture projects have a lot in common with software development projects. Accordingly, the testing processes are similar. During the development process, analytic, data, and guided analytic developers will use *unit-testing* processes to ensure the analysis provides correct results, the data is correct and repeatable, and the front-end tools comply with design and usability requirements.

Following completion of development testing, *user acceptance testing* (UAT) is the next testing process. In this step, developers and selected end users form a test group to ensure the final solution works as intended. Testers and users may be located in many different locations, so it is best to make use of an online issue-tracking tool or document to log issues found.

During the UAT testing phase, testers and developers collaborate as needed to meet the project schedule. Table 15.1 is an example format of an issue log we use in our projects when a system issue logging tool is not available. The issue log is essential to keep track of issues identified, root causes, solutions, and timing in order to maintain project schedules. A well-maintained issue log also serves as an institutional learning tool, as it can be shared with other teams working on similar projects to benefit from the issues raised and solutions developed.

**Table 15.1 Issue Log**

| Item No | Issue | Issue Description | Priority (HML) | Tester | Tester Comment | Issue Entered Date | Issue Resolution Date | Owner | Owner Comment |
|---|---|---|---|---|---|---|---|---|---|
| 1 | Alert for Revenue metric on Exec Dashboard | Alert is not triggering for revenue decreases above threshold | M | Sarah | Should change color when revenue decreases below 10% | 10/15/2016 | 10/20/2016 | Bill | Found and fixed issue with the display action |
| 2 | Null handling for displacement calculation | Current displacement metric is incorrect | M | Wenming | Need to add *zero-if-null* test to the formula | 10/15/2016 | 10/20/2016 | Amal | Modified the calculation as requested |
| 3 | Missing data for property ABC | When ABC is selected in the property pull-down menu, no data is displayed | H | Sarah | | 10/16/2016 | TBD | Sergio | Looking into ETL process; will update when problem is identified |

### Small-Scale Projects

Small- to medium-sized organizations or departmental solutions within a larger organization are likely to develop smaller scale Decision Architecture projects. The teams typically will be smaller and often colocated, making for ease of communication and collaboration. Essential roles found in even the smallest projects include data developer, decision/business analyst, and guided analytics developer. In small-scale projects the development team and user team often overlap so it is more difficult to draw a line between unit testing and UAT, but it is still a good idea to follow a structured process in order to keep the project moving.

We also recommend maintaining an issue log to document issues found and resolutions applied even in cases where the tester and the owner may be the same person. This preserves organizational learning and helps to develop best practices in order to not repeat mistakes on subsequent projects.

### Version Control

Early in the development cycle it is important to develop a standard nomenclature for release names, helping team members to maintain version control and avoid redundant work or rework. Release naming nomenclature ranges from the simple v1.0 to more complex multi-component names. Useful best practices identified by Princeton University Records Management can be found at records .princeton.edu/blogs/records-management-manual/file-naming-conventions-version-control and include agreeing on standards for the following:

- Filename vocabulary
- Punctuation symbols, capitals, hyphens, and spaces conventions
- Date formats
- Order of elements within the filename (i.e., filename-date-version)
- Version-numbering digits (i.e., 01 or 001) and levels

## Adoption

Once a project has completed UAT, it enters the Adoption process step comprising Training and Rollout. User adoption and coaching are important to ensuring the solution is utilized. How well the users adopt the solution and how often it is used will dictate the value derived by the organization.

### Training

Training is a critical step to ensuring user adoption. With busy schedules and many competing projects, users will not spend valuable time on a solution they do not understand or know how to use. Key training components include content, medium, and adoption.

> **Content**—Deciding on the right level of content and number of training programs is based on the amount of information you are asking the user to absorb. If there is a high amount of content or the content is complex, we recommend splitting the training into several parts with hands-on exercises to assist with the learning process.
>
> **Medium**—Several mediums can be leveraged, including in-class or online training in which participants are instructor-led through the various topics with real-world exercises to help drive home concepts. Another option is to automate the training through the recording of a webinar session where students can learn on their own schedules. Finally, a written manual that is paper- or PDF-based can be used for self-study. Finding the right medium will be based on your organizational culture, the level of complexity, and the familiarity of the student with the concepts.
>
> **Adoption**—The adoption rate of the end user can be a function of the amount and complexity of content, as well as the medium and progression of the individual along the learning curve. The progress of an end user through the learning curve should be monitored by coaches and managers to ensure the individual is leveraging the new analytical solution to drive the quality of their decisions higher.

There are several methods we deploy to create quick references to help managers tie the solution to actions in their daily work.

- **Dashboard Tool Tips**—If your solution becomes a dashboard, highlight tools tips for certain metrics that trigger once a threshold is crossed. The tool tip can provide a list of possible actions based on the metric.

- **Hyperlink**—In the solution, provide hyperlinks to systems that managers can use to take action based on the decision. For example, link to the CRM tool if the action is related to an email campaign.
- **Training Materials**—Another source of action is to develop training materials as a reference guide that the user can utilize going forward to look up actions they can take. These can also come in the form of cheat-sheets, which are abbreviated versions of training materials meant to be for a quick glance or reminder.
- **Strategic Workbook**—Another method is a strategic workbook, also called a runbook or playbook, that takes an analyst through the subject matter, the analytical tool, and the associated actions. It is broader than just training materials in that it encompasses industry background information, specifics around the particular discipline (e.g., market intelligence), review of each node in the Category Tree, and each of the Lego pieces available, and finally prescribes actions to take based on situations.

It is important to tie the actions with decisions allowing analyst and end user to see the correlation and develop a deeper understanding of the solution and how to make use of it.

### Rollout

While it may be tempting to go for the big-bang approach and throw your solution out there to get it going, we strongly recommend using a phased rollout approach. This approach lends itself well to the iterative development style we emphasize throughout this book. Depending on the time available and complexity of the project, we roll out the solution in up to three expanding user group phases: pilot, expanded pilot, and full user base.

### Pilot User Group

When we are ready to deploy a solution after successful completion of the testing process, we first identify a small group of Pilot users to use the solution in a production environment. Although by this point we have been through some degree of unit testing and UAT, we believe in the Agile principle to get the solution into the hands of real users as soon as possible to uncover application and usability issues that simply cannot be detected in a development environment. We also select one of the team members to act as the Project Champion during the rollout phase, serving as the primary point of interface for the user groups.

We seek out key influencers and heavy users of the analytic solution to form the Pilot group. During the Pilot Rollout phase, we continue to maintain an issue log as presented in Table 15.1 to capture issues raised by our Pilot group. In addition, we also maintain an enhancement log, shown in Table 15.2, as end-users often identify opportunities for improvement that were not scoped in the original requirements. Sometimes these enhancement opportunities are easy to address and can be resolved through a "dot-release," that is, we can include the enhancement in version 1.1. In other cases, the enhancements requested are more involved and may require an additional development cycle to implement a solution. In some cases, the request is simply not feasible or too far out of scope for the solution.

In all cases, we keep a record of the enhancement requests and the planned disposition to maintain a clear channel of communications with our Pilot user group. It is important that they see their input is taken seriously and acted upon in some capacity in order to encourage ongoing participation. Depending on user locations and the scope of the project, we may schedule conference calls to discuss feedback and proposed solutions. A highly engaged Pilot user group is an invaluable component to the development of the final solution in terms of usability and utility. Once invested in the success of the project, Pilot users often become unofficial champions during the broader adoption phase.

### Expanded Pilot Group

After a period of time, we are ready to move from the Pilot phase to the Expanded Pilot phase. By this time, we may have iterated through several versions and have an increasingly well-honed solution. The Expanded Pilot group will extend to a broader group of influencers and users likely to access the solution on a regular basis as part of their standard work. The process is similar to the one followed with the Pilot group, but with a larger group we might

**Table 15.2  Enhancement Log**

| Item No | Enhancement | Enhancement Description | Priority (HML) | Tester | Tester Comment | Issue Entered Date | Target Release | Est Level of Effort | Owner | Owner Comment |
|---|---|---|---|---|---|---|---|---|---|---|
| 1 | Forecast accuracy | Display forecast accuracy in the tooltip on the diagnostic dashboard | H | Tom | This will help users judge the likelihood of hitting the forecast targets | 11/20/2016 | V2 | M | Sergio | Will have to source forecast accuracy metrics and join into the analytic dataset |
| 2 | Add an Opportunity diagnostic dashboard | Add diagnostic metrics and analytics to assess the likelihood of the opportunity | M | Alicia | Would help users determine which opportunity they should prioritize | 11/21/2016 | V3 | H | Amal | Will need to define requirements, develop metrics, source data, and incorporate into the data model |
| 3 | Market names | Replace market names in the current tool with those used by the sales department for field reps | H | Crystal | Current market hierarchy is an older one used by the marketing department but not in sync with one just rolled out by sales to the field reps | 11/22/2016 | V1.5 | L | Sergio | We have identified a source for the new sales market hierarchy and can add to the solution to use in addition to the marketing department hierarchy |
| 4 | Property Management Report | Include metrics from the Property Management Report in order to be able to compare solutions | M | Crystal | While this analytic solution is helpful to determining actions in the marketplace, it would be helpful to be able to compare with performance metrics from the current Property Management Report | 11/22/2016 | N/A | N | Patty | This solution is not aimed at property management diagnostics; inclusion of property management metrics would increase the complexity of the ETL processes, impact front-end performance, and be redundant to existing reports |

choose to establish automated means to collect feedback, such as a project email or online comment site.

With the Expanded Pilot group, we are less likely to uncover new issues or enhancements if we had a thorough run with the Pilot group. Rather we are more focused on driving understanding of the intent of the solution and how to use it. Information gathered during this phase is passed on to the training team to incorporate into training materials.

Even though the process is still technically in Pilot, the solution is live, in production, and delivering value. Pilot users are able to make use of the information, actions, and strategies identified through the solution to enhance their daily work.

### Full User Rollout

Having worked with the Expanded Pilot group, the last process step is full rollout to the entire targeted user base. By this time, the solution is fully in production, maintained by the production team, and the development team has moved on to development of the next version or other projects.

In small-to-medium organizations or small groups within a large organization the Pilot, Expanded Pilot, and Full User Rollout steps may condense into one or two steps.

## Summary

Without user adoption, the efforts you put into your solution will not be realized. Make sure you establish the right level of training and coaching to fit the solution you are enabling. Check in often with the users during the rollout phase and after to receive feedback on additional requests or issues they are finding. Lastly, if possible, create a community around the solution to drive continued innovation and adoption.

# CHAPTER 16

# Analytical Organization: *Getting Organized*

As we mentioned at the beginning of the book, the explosion of information is accelerating and the next big explosion, the Internet of Things, is upon us. When our machines begin talking to each other the rate of information produced each year will go exponential. The CEO of Alphabet, Eric Schmidt, commented,

> Between the birth of the world and 2003, there were five exabytes of information created. [Today] we create five exabytes every two days.

Just in case you do not know the definition of an *exabyte*, which we did not, it is defined as "a unit of information equal to one quintillion bytes, or one billion gigabytes."

Organizations are capturing as much of this information as they can, trying to figure out what can be monetized and what can be discarded. Most organizations are collecting everything, assuming it will be useful eventually. This may be the right approach, but what can be done today to monetize the information you have collected?

To make sense of this amassed information, different roles are needed inside the organization to collect, codify, and monetize this abundance of information. We propose several new roles and a team structure to accomplish this challenge.

## Decision Architecture Team

Our recommendation is the creation of a cross-functional team focused on monetizing the company's information assets by

251

leveraging the Decision Architecture methodology we present in this book. This team should be organized across divisions, sharing best practices, tools, and techniques.

Many organizations have started on the journey of implementing data governance as a centralized function that captures data standards, linage, and metadata. The purpose of the Data Governance group is to serve as a centralized governing body providing oversight of the company's data standards and quality. The question we ask most organizations is, why stop there? Wouldn't collecting your organization's major decisions and actions provide as much value if not more? We believe the next evolution is the collection of organizational wisdom through the gathering of decisions and actions. Once these are collected and processed, systems and analytical solutions can be created and embedded with this wisdom to drive better decisions.

To accomplish this, your organization needs to establish a Decision Architecture team as either a part of the data governance team or a completely new organization. The Decision Architecture team will have several roles with a varied set of disciplines. The individuals within this team can be part of a centralized team or matrixed in. We will review these options in the next section. For now, let's focus on the structure, capabilities, and governance of the team.

### Project Based versus Business Functional

One of the first decisions to make is to decide if the team should be purely project focused or business functional in nature. This is a tough decision and may differ by organization and maturity of the analytical capabilities of the company.

A project-focused team is easier to enable within a company. The work load is dependent on a backlog of projects from various departments, and even the smallest of projects can get the team started. The team can work in a matrixed environment with team members rolling back to their respective groups once the project is completed. Or the team can work part time on these projects if there is not enough demand for a full workload.

There are a few drawbacks to a project-based approach. If the team is project driven, the larger groups with bigger budgets receive the majority of the focus. In addition, it is hard to scale best practices, tools, and techniques across the organization since the focus is on the current project at hand. Lastly, the nature of project work creates a finite timeframe, implying the group may not be around after the project is completed, limiting investment in needed infrastructure. If your organization starts with a project-based approach, it will probably want to move to a business functional model once the project work is self-sustaining.

A business functional model is a centralized team with various members aligned to specific departments within an organization. There may be a decision architect assigned to each department, such as Finance, Marketing, IT, Sales, and so forth. This focused approach can help the decision architect become more familiar with the department's business, data, decisions, and challenges. They will also be able to build strong relationships within the department they serve, facilitating faster project completion with a higher degree of relevance. This focus will enable them to bring in best practices and monetization strategies from peers and other departments to help their area mature faster. Lastly, the architect will stay around long after the project is completed to see the results of prior initiatives and take these learnings with them to the next project.

The downside of this model is that it takes longer to implement and achieve success. Patience is needed on behalf of the business as the team builds the infrastructure necessary to support this function. In addition, this type of approach may become bureaucratic through sheer weight and size; projects that go across departments may take longer and require additional resources.

Both of these approaches have benefits and drawbacks. You should assess your organization's politics, culture, analytical capability, maturity, and quality of data to determine the right approach.

### Capabilities

There are many capabilities that the Decision Architecture team is able to provide in building analytical solutions. The overall focus and goal of the team is to help the organization monetize its data and make better-quality decisions. They are able to meet this goal by the use of the techniques, methods, and processes we have outlined in this book. Let's review several of them:

> **Decision Architecture**—The core capability of the team is the production of the Decision Analysis, Monetization Strategies, and Guided Analytics. This capability includes methods for

capturing information as well as codifying and distributing it to various stakeholder groups. For example, if a new monetization strategy is developed that drives a higher Asset ROI for a vehicle type centered on maintenance scheduling and predictive wear and tear, this solution along with the decisions and actions it enables may be useful to other departments within the organization. The Decision Architecture team is on point to propagate this solution to the various stakeholder departments to drive cost savings for the company.

**Facilitating Techniques**—The team needs methods for conducting interviews and working sessions to capture the elements of the Decision Architecture. This includes leveraging facilitation techniques such as icebreakers, root-cause analysis, cause-and-effect diagrams, brainstorming, and prioritization methods. In addition to the various techniques, the team needs a base understanding in conducting interviews and working sessions. These involve leveraging tools such as ground rules, issues and risks lists, and action plans.

**Inventory and Cataloging**—Collecting and codifying the elements of the Decision Architecture is another key capability focused on organizing and inventorying the various data elements, decisions, questions, metrics, and actions. This includes documenting the use of the Decision Architecture elements across the organization, the quality of these elements, and the effectiveness of their use. For example, after building the Decision Architecture for two departments, the team notices that the groups are making similar decisions for one of their diagnostics. This is a great opportunity to collaborate between the two groups to share the collective wisdom and approaches of both teams to drive synergy across the organization.

**Defining Metrics and Decisions**—Defining the various metrics and decisions throughout an organization is another key capability. This function may overlap with Data Governance somewhat. The major difference between the two groups is that the Data Governance team is focused on definitions and standards for business metrics whereas the Decision Architecture team is focused on decisions and actions derived from the metrics. Both have a focus on business metrics with different outcomes.

**Monetization Strategies**—Another key capability is Monetization Strategies, which are specific strategies for driving economic value from a company's data assets. These include analytics or diagnostics that can be utilized at a departmental or corporate-wide level. Examples include: Pricing, Valuation, Retention, Cross-Sell/Up-Sell, Revenue Opportunity, Cost Saving, and Asset Utilization. One of the team's core capabilities is to develop specific repeatable strategies to monetize the company's data.

**Data Science and Decision Theory**—Another key capability is the use of data science and decision theory techniques to help monetize company data or perform specific studies. These techniques include Thresholds for Metrics, Correlation Analysis, Segmentation, Clustering, Forecasting, Scenarios, Decision Matrix, Probability, Choice Architecture, and Optimization. For example, when trying to determine the probability of achieving a specific opportunity, the data scientist calculates the value of the opportunity and a corresponding ability to achieve. Not only is the metric usage repeatable, so is the design pattern that can be leveraged for similar metrics.

**Data Analysis**—Data analysis capabilities are a core capability of the team. Data analysis is the technique or method of inspecting, transforming, and analyzing data with the goal of using it to develop a quality decision that is actionable. Everyone on the Decision Architecture team should have a deep familiarity with data analysis and its concepts.

**Guided Analytics**—When the Decision Analysis is completed, development of a Guided Analytics solution is another responsibility of the Decision Architecture team. Development of guided analytical solutions helps users visually navigate through information and diagnostics to make quality decisions that drive actions. These tools are easily deployed, visually intuitive, and provide exception-based analysis to quickly identify issues and opportunities. These tools can be leveraged by executives, analysts, managers, and field workers. The level of automation can vary from an Excel-based tool to a fully automated system. Much of the work we do to build monetization strategies encompasses some type of Guided Analytics tool.

**Measurement**—Once an action is taken, measurement is a key capability of the team. Tools and techniques are needed to measure performance of specific monetization strategies and actions. In addition to measurement, the tools should provide feedback on success of the overall strategy, progress on tests, and learnings for continuous improvement.

Based on your company and the team's maturity, you may decide to add additional capabilities to their portfolio. These may include the addition of data science techniques, specific tools like SAS, R, Tableau, QlikView, Power BI, Data Architecture and Development, and Six Sigma methods. The team's evolution and capability will increase as they add value to the organization.

### Governance

Governing the Decision Architecture of an organization is important as adoption and enablement increase through the use of analytical solutions. We recommend that a company develop a *governing board* for Decision Architecture to oversee direction and strategy.

The governing board should be made up of a matrixed team of functional leaders with a stake in the success of the company's monetization strategies, decisions, and actions. This group is responsible for establishing the charter, ensuring consistency, prioritization, standards and policies, compliance and security, and communications of the Decision Architecture team. Below is a detailed description of the recommended governance board responsibilities:

- **Team Charter**—Establishing the charter for the team should be one of the first deliverables for the governing board. This includes ensuring the mission, objectives, and efforts of the team are aligned to corporate objectives. In addition, the team may want to build a roadmap, approved by the board, that lays out their agenda for a forthcoming period.
- **Standards and Policies**—As an organization develops its Decision Architecture and analytical solutions for various functional business capabilities, standards and policies should be established. Standards can be as simple as the list of decisions for a particular group or as complicated as the definition of the Success Metrics for a company. A policy is a

principle adopted for the organization to follow. In the case of Decision Architecture, an example of a policy might be to set rules for the types of diagnostics for certain roles within the organization. To further the example, if an organization has a store manager who is responsible for staffing of the store, the policy might dictate they need to use a specific *staffing diagnostic* as the primary analytical tool to make hiring decisions.

- **Decision Architecture**—Overall responsibility for the Decision Architecture of the company, including Decision Analysis, Monetization Strategies, and Agile Analytics, as well as endorsement of the tools and techniques utilized and governance of the analytical solutions.
- **Monetization Strategies**—Reviewing and maintaining the various strategies for monetizing the organization's data assets, and leveraging these strategies across departments to scale and improve the quality of decisions and actions. These strategies will constantly evolve as business and market conditions change.
- **Team Resources**—Administration of roles and responsibilities of the team aligned to the charter. Depending on the capabilities required of the team, the mix of team skillsets may vary. This includes the decision for which roles should be full time within the team and which should be matrixed. Lastly, resource leveling of the roles to ensure adequate staffing will be another responsibility.
- **Financial Resources and Prioritization**—Each of the work efforts under the Decision Architecture team should have a business case and alignment to the business objectives of the organization. Based on value to the company, the governing board should approve financial resources. If there are a large number of projects and competing resources, the governing board should also prioritize work efforts, which may influence both financial and team resources.
- **Risks and Issues**—Resolving major risks and issues as they arise for the team and removing roadblocks and providing timely resolution, enabling the team to deliver without impediments.
- **Compliance and Security**—As decisions and actions are cataloged, compliance with the overall standards and policies of

the organization is necessary to ensure that a specific action does not contradict a corporate or government policy. Lastly, securing the business architecture of the company to ensure competitive intelligence does not end up in the wrong hands.
- **Communications**—Providing communications to various stakeholders on the progress of the Decision Architecture team, issues and risks, policies and standards, and general updates.

### Collaboration

Another responsibility of the Decision Architecture team is collaboration with various stakeholders and groups within your organization. Understanding the various team's agendas, capabilities, and initiatives helps the Decision Architecture team plug into existing capabilities and initiatives. This will save the team time, remove competitive barriers, and increase the likelihood of collaboration.

A great example of collaboration comes from Space X's work with NASA. Space X wanted to make faster decisions to speed up its time to market for its customer NASA. Eric Winquist, in his article, "How Companies Can Learn to Make Faster Decisions," discusses the costs of delayed decisions:

> According to Forrester, for every hour a product team spends on heads-down work, they spend 48 minutes waiting on decisions. That equates to more than 3.5 hours of "wait time" in an average eight-hour work day. If a company cuts wait times in half, it can gain more than $370,000 annually in productive time across a 25-person team.

Fortunately for Space X, they were able to solve for this issue.

> SpaceX increased communication in order to speed up their process. Using collaborative technology, NASA now has direct visibility into each project and can identify which SpaceX engineers are working on a specific component. Importantly, they can also start a conversation with these engineers in order to make decisions in real-time. The collaboration system allowed SpaceX to cut its average wait time for defining product requirements by 50% and eliminated the costly weekly four-hour status meeting.

When establishing the Decision Architecture team, work to build an engagement model of how the team will work with other teams, both internal and external, to avoid delayed decisions, competing initiatives, and overall lack of communication.

### Training

Another responsibility of the Decision Architecture team is training the end users of the analytical solution, which we covered in the Enablement chapter (Chapter 15). User adoption and coaching is a key aspect to ensure the solution is utilized. How well the users adopt the solution and how often it is used will dictate the value derived by the organization. As a reminder, the key training components include content, medium, and adoption.

## Decision Architecture Roles

In order to execute on the capabilities outlined earlier in this chapter, we propose several roles for the Decision Architecture team. The roles can be matrixed into the team or they can be a direct report, depending on the work capacity, career path, and organizational structure of the company. The roles we recommend include a manager/leader, decision architect, data librarian, data/decision analyst, trainer, UI developer, dashboard developer, and data architect/developer. Let's review each:

**Manager/Leader**—The manager of the Decision Architecture team is responsible for the overall guidance of the team, participating in the governing board, career management for team members, success of the work efforts, and aligning value to the organization with these work efforts. A background in analytics, statistics, business intelligence, and data analysis is recommended.

**Decision Architect**—The Decision Architect is a new role for most companies. This role is a mix of business architect combined with a data analyst who understands analytics. The Decision Architect is responsible for engineering the analytical solution leveraging the various disciplines within the team. They are the main facilitator in the user interviews and working sessions, designing the architecture through

Question Analysis, Key Decisions, Success Metrics, and Action Levers. They apply these to Category Trees while utilizing Data Science and Decision Theory to articulate a monetization strategy for the analytical solution.

**Data Scientist**—The data scientist applies mathematical techniques to the data to turn it into actionable insights. The techniques include metric definition, correlation analysis, segmentation, profiling, clustering, forecasting, optimization, and opportunity analysis. These individuals should have a math degree and strong understanding of data and statistical techniques.

**Data Librarian**—The data librarian is a new role for most organizations, especially those with big data investments. Knowing where to find data in an organization is often based on tribal knowledge and requires a data detective. With more data entering an organization than ever before, and much of it unstructured within a big data environment, the cataloging and organizing of this data is vital to being able to fully utilize it. The data librarian is responsible for knowing where data exists, cataloging it, moving it, and stitching it together to enable analysis.

**Data/Decision Analyst**—The data/decision analyst understands how to source, transform, and manipulate data. They are able to deconstruct the Question Analysis into a set of information needs and align them to the decisions and actions. They work with the data librarian and data developer to source the information and bring it together into an analytical structure for the dashboard developer. In addition, they often work hand-in-hand with the data scientist to implement correlations, thresholds, opportunities, and other techniques.

**Trainer**—The trainer assembles training material and trains the user of the analytical solution. They teach, guide, and coach individuals up the learning curve until there is a level of proficiency for adoption and usage to drive value to the organization.

If the solution will have a certain level of automation, the following additional roles will be needed:

**UI/UX Designer**—The UI/UX designer produces intuitive designs that are easy for users of the analytical solution to interpret and adopt. The designs that the UI/UX designer

**Figure 16.1    Using UI to Communicate Efficiently**

produces allow you to quickly interpret information and guide you to an issue or opportunity that needs further investigation. Consistency across analytical solutions for the UI enables a shorter ramp-up time as the users do not have to relearn how to use the tool; they simply have to learn the data.

For example, the UI element in Figure 16.1 displays two pieces of information: ability to achieve an opportunity, and potential revenue lift. The UI element is telling a user that the potential lift for a particular action is 10 percent, but the ability to achieve it is low. It is this type of intuitive design that the UI/UX designer enables in the analytical solution.

**Data Architect/Developer**—The data architect/developer extracts information from the various source systems and develops the analytic structure to support analytics and reporting. This might entail extraction, transformation, and formatting of data into various analytical structures. Data quality is key and determines how much transformation is needed. This role works closely with the data librarian, data analyst, and data scientist.

**Guided Analytics Developer**—The Guided Analytics developer develops dashboards, visual analytics, and visual diagnostic tools to make the analytical solution accessible to end-users utilizing the Decision Architecture, the data architecture, and the UI design. They also enable any monetization strategies developed through data science and decision theory techniques. This role brings together the various disciplines to create the Guided Analytics experience for the user.

## Subject Matter Experts

One of the most important aspects of this process is to identify your subject matter experts (SMEs). These individuals are knowledge experts in a particular role, function, subject, process, or capability.

They know the business rules, history, lessons learned, and often the questions to ask to make effective decisions. You may need more than one SME depending on the breadth and depth of the subject matter you are covering.

Leveraging these individuals is useful during many touchpoints in the process. During the interview process, they are often a leading source of questions and decisions that we ask or make about the data. When creating the diagnostics elements, they are often the source of Success Metrics. When creating the Category Tree, they can validate the information flow and the use of the questions, decisions, and metrics for each of the nodes in the tree.

Once an SME trusts the data and the outcome of the decision process, they can help to ensure the relevancy of the information is on target with how the information user will leverage the tool. In addition, the Monetization Strategy will need their validation to gain broader adoption and their stamp of approval during the roll-out, which will often be a key measure of adoption.

One note of warning: be aware of any biases that may exist with the individual. We cover these in our Decision Theory chapter (Chapter 8). We all bring these with us; your job is to recognize them and make sure it does not affect the analytical solution.

## Analytical Organization Mindset

> *A person who never made a mistake never tried anything new.*
>
> **Albert Einstein**

> *You don't learn to walk by following the rules. You learn by doing and falling over.*
>
> **Richard Branson**

> *There is only one way to avoid criticism: Do nothing, Say nothing, and Be nothing.*
>
> **Aristotle**

As we conclude this section, we want to raise issues of changes in the organizational mindset needed to be successful. When an organization adopts a Decision Architecture framework, they begin to measure business decisions and actions to a larger extent than previously. With this measurement comes the need to develop a mindset that failure is okay. The measurement is there to guide the company on whether the actions are working or need to be changed. This culture where failure with adaptability is okay is typically referred to as "test-and-learn" or "fail early, fail often." As long as the organization is *learning* from actions that do not work, there is no failure.

This organizational ethos of test-and-learn is driven by hypotheses that are developed and tested in everyday actions. For example, if you are a product company that is developing new products, there is constant innovation occurring around new flavors, styles, technology, and package sizes to drive the next product wave of innovation for your company and industry.

This philosophy can be adopted by service companies as well. If you sell life insurance, your company can test new insurance services in particular markets to gauge the likelihood to buy and profitability. This level of innovation should not be a once-a-year activity; it should occur continuously. Great test-and-learn organizations are constantly testing new products and services in their various markets to see which ones might be the next big winner.

We recommend starting small, looking for quick wins, and evolving through iteration. The process of developing an analytical culture is a journey. If an organization starts on this journey without tangible results in the short term, the initiative will often fail under its own weight as the organizational energy to support it collapses or wanes with business cycles or shifting priorities.

# SECTION VI

# CASE STUDY

# Case Study: Michael Andrews Bespoke

In this case study we review the company, Michael Andrews Bespoke (MAB), sales strategy, and monetization opportunities using our Decision Architecture methodology to illustrate the application of these methods in an actual business context. MAB has a business objective to grow revenue by 10 percent and has hired you to create a monetization strategy that they can execute to achieve this goal.

We begin with the Discovery phase of our Decision Architecture methodology.

## Discovery

Michael Andrews Bespoke (MAB) is a New York City–based custom couturier founded with the goal of crafting fine tailoring for discriminating clients. They accomplish this through designing, customizing, and producing quality men's professional clothing using the best fabrics with the height of style. MAB's clients value quality and service. MAB's stylists are experts at meeting the uniquely high standards of each client, one at time.

### Growing Revenue

MAB's business is focused on a high-end niche segment with few of the price pressures typical of mass fashion markets. Delivering high-quality products with excellent service is table-stakes if the business is to survive. Clients of custom clothing place a high value on quality, design, and fashion and are willing to invest when they find a provider meeting their exacting needs. With a business model that is highly personal and differentiated, profitability is not the primary challenge as in most of fashion retail. Rather MAB's challenge is to attract prospects who value custom clothing, convert them into a full-package wardrobe experience, and retain them in a long-term client relationship.

### Client Acquisition

MAB's acquisition strategy involves attracting the attention of discerning clients through various channels such as search optimization, website, email campaigns, and advertising in targeted magazines. The best channel for attracting new clients is referrals from satisfied clients.

### Client Engagement

When a client new to custom clothing makes their first visit to MAB's well-appointed studio, a MAB stylist introduces the client to the custom clothing experience of hand-crafted and personally styled menswear. More than simply selling high-end men's clothing, MAB's stylists pride themselves on expert and honest style advice, offering opinions on everything from the best cut to the most flattering patterns and colors. Through this process, clients with means and appreciation for perfectly fitted clothing become committed to an investment in personal style and a quality wardrobe.

### Client Retention

MAB retains valuable clients through quality production and timely delivery of their products. MAB offers free alterations on garments for six months after delivery to ensure their clients are satisfied. From this level of personal interaction, clients view MAB as their partner in their clothing experience. Clients satisfied with the quality of MAB's service and products engage in a long-term relationship with MAB over years, maintaining their wardrobe, adding new styles, and replacing worn clothing.

In sum, MAB's business is driven by acquiring discerning clients, committing these clients to an investment in a personally styled wardrobe, and retaining them in a long-term partnership.

### Client Types

The heartbeat of MAB's business is its client base. MAB thrives on meeting the professional and personal needs of clients who value custom clothing and are seeking a partner to bring their style to life. Custom clothing clients are passionate about their wardrobe, viewing it as an essential tool of their livelihood and an expression of their personal self.

In thinking about the client base, MAB finds it helpful to evaluate the client types based on their wardrobe desires and needs. After discussion with Michael Andrews, the founder and namesake of MAB, we learn of two core needs leading a client to invest in a custom wardrobe. Based on these core needs, clients can be broken down into two primary persona types:

*The Wardrobe as a Professional Asset*
New York City is a rich market for clients who are expected to wear high-end suits every day to work, such as investment bankers and lawyers. While they appreciate quality and good service, these clients view their clothing as an extension of their work and consider the investment in a custom wardrobe as a cost of doing business. They trust MAB to deliver the right style that will set them apart within the norms of their industry.

*The Wardrobe as an Expression of Personal Style*
This client type loves clothes, can afford them, and wears suits to work even when not required because he wants to. He views his clothing as an extension of himself. This persona is seeking to build a complete custom wardrobe to speak to his personality. He buys slowly, concerned about fit and design. He likes being part of the design process and can be more discerning and value conscious. This type of client will budget specifically for his wardrobe investment.

Other, secondary client personas that MAB serves include:

*Purchasing for Special Events*
Another client type that MAB services are guys shopping for a special event, such as a wedding. They are willing to spend extra to ensure they look their best for the special day. Tuxedos are the primary clothing item these clients will purchase.

*Purchasing to Enhance Their Style*
MAB also attracts the guy who loves clothes and collects clothing experiences, following styles and fashions, changing

with the times. This client seeks out MAB to purchase a custom suit to add to his ensemble, often with exacting requirements because he is seeking to fill a specific niche in his wardrobe.

*Hard to Fit*

The final client type that MAB services is the hard-to-fit guy. Falling outside the norm of physical dimensions, unable to find ready-to-wear options that fit, often his only option is custom tailoring for the times when he needs to look his best.

### Client Life Cycle

The typical life cycle of a client's journey in the custom clothing experience follows three stages:

*Exploratory Stage*

At this stage, clients try out the custom clothing experience and/or the stylist they engage to service them. They may begin with a suit or jacket and pant order to see what works for them. If they have the financial means and are well-served, they engage in a longer-term relationship with MAB. Clients facing a special event or challenge or seeking to enhance their wardrobe may not move beyond the exploratory stage, but nonetheless are a valuable source of business for MAB.

*Commitment Stage*

If MAB is successful in providing a client the style, value, and service they require, they will engage in a relationship that can span years. Clients in the commitment stage investing in a custom wardrobe for the first time or overhauling an existing wardrobe will typically spend a considerable sum of money on a wardrobe comprising suits, sport coats, pants, and shirts.

*Maintenance Stage*

Having established their core wardrobe, a client will maintain it, replacing items over time as they wear out or styles change. The professional wardrobe client, viewing his wardrobe as an extension of himself, is more likely to maintain his wardrobe over an extended period of time due to the utility nature of his clothing needs. The personal wardrobe client's motivation for his wardrobe investment is personal and intrinsic; once satisfied, his volume of purchase activity may decrease.

## Business Analysis

Michael Andrews began the business in 2006 based on his personal passion for custom clothing, growing it to be a successful operation by 2009. Reaching his personal capacity to market and service the business, Michael brought on two stylists who helped him quadruple the business in just four years. As the client base evolved from the exploratory stage to the commitment stage, MAB needed to make a greater investment in stylist time and teamwork in order to service the more demanding needs of the client. With expansion of the stylist force to service the growing business, the original stylists, strong individual contributors, struggled and eventually left the business in 2013. Even with the departure of his two most experienced, top-grossing stylists, Michael was able to face the challenge of building his stylist team while maintaining strong revenue growth.

Three years later, in 2016, with the stylist team on solid footing, MAB annual revenue growth has continued on a strong trajectory, between 7 and 8 percent for the past three years. Michael's business problem is one many managers would love to have. He wants to develop a strategy to take a healthy company with good growth and make it better.

To understand key drivers of the business, we perform initial discovery to identify metrics we can use to evaluate MAB's business growth opportunity. When engaging in discovery, it is helpful to work from the top down, first examining overall performance and then successively drilling into underlying components.

In many of the charts we present, absolute values with respect to revenue have been removed to preserve the confidentiality of the data; however, the patterns and trends are not obscured.

## Business Performance

The first observation we can make is that while MAB has healthy revenue growth, total client orders have been declining since 2011.

### Spend and Order Volume

In 2010 Michael expanded his stylist force to service his growing client base. In 2011 and 2012, MAB's business focused on higher volume, lower spend clients. However, whether a client buys one or several suits, time spent servicing the client is approximately the same. When they repeat purchase, less time may be needed, but

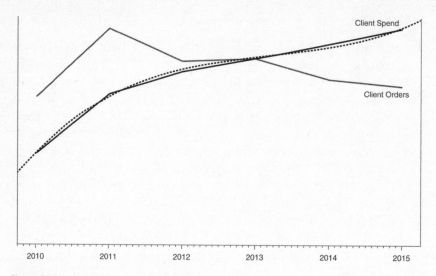

**Figure CS.1    Annual Client Spend and Orders**

many clients purchase only once or twice a year, so time efficiencies are not easily gained.

Figure CS.1 is a graph representing the growth in client spend versus the decline in client orders. The company is able to devote more of the stylist's time to servicing clients at a higher spend level, thereby resulting in larger purchase orders and growing revenue.

### Business Capacity

We know from a capacity analysis that the order servicing capacity is approximately 190 orders per month, considering normal hours of operation and preserving ample studio space for each client to have a comfortable experience. During peak season, MAB may work extended hours to accommodate the bursts in business. However, we observe that from 2011 through 2013, MAB frequently encountered capacity constraints managed by a combination of stylist overtime, extended studio hours, and perhaps a more crowded studio and less time per order.

Following Michael's change in strategy to focus on clients seeking the full custom wardrobe experience, order volume has decreased to a manageable range and hovers right at order capacity for the current studio (Figure CS.2).

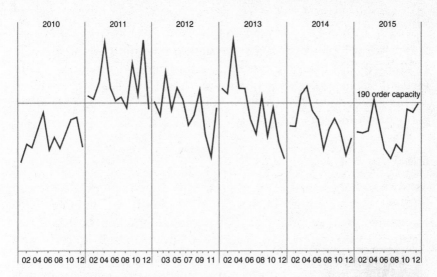

| 2010 | 2011 | 2012 | 2013 | 2014 | 2015 |

190 order capacity

| 02 04 06 08 10 12 | 02 04 06 08 10 12 | 03 05 07 09 11 | 02 04 06 08 10 12 | 02 04 06 08 10 12 | 02 04 06 08 10 12 |

Figure CS.2    Monthly Orders Relative to Estimated Capacity

### Client Performance

MAB has served over 5,000 clients since it began business. Clients returning after their initial purchase account for about 50 percent of its business and on average order about 2.5 times per year, spending approximately $5,000 per year. The remaining 50 percent of clients explore a relationship with MAB, spending about $2,500 in their initial order.

From 2012 to 2013, spend per client plateaued, threatening overall revenue growth as MAB was operating at full capacity with respect to studio space. Due to the high cost of studio space in New York City and minimum time to fit a client, Michael shifted his acquisition strategy to focus on clients purchasing wardrobe packages versus individual items. In this way, he could improve resource efficiency and continue to grow revenue without having to make expensive investments in additional studio space. Furthermore, MAB's target clients are discerning customers, placing a high value on service and product quality given the investment they are making. Continuing to pursue a high-transaction strategy versus an annuity business would likely impact repeat sales.

### Acquisition

Following retooling of its marketing strategy and stylist force in 2013, MAB has been successful in attracting and retaining clients focused on investing in a quality wardrobe and seeking a trusted partner to service their needs. Average spend per existing client continues to increase (Figure CS.3).

### Retention

As MAB's client base ages in tenure with the company, it has been successful at engaging clients in a long-term relationship, with returning clients accounting for 50 percent of its client base by 2016. Figure CS.4 shows the retention rate, year-over-year, from returning clients. To elaborate, in 2012, 29 percent of the sales came from clients from prior years and 71 percent of orders came from new clients. In 2015, 50 percent of orders came from clients from prior years and 50 percent of orders came from new clients.

Figure CS.5 shows the client retention by year of first order, which tells us the percentage of clients by retention category: *multiyear client, one-year client,* or *onetime client.* Each year is a cohort, that is, 2015 represents clients who first ordered with MAB in that year.

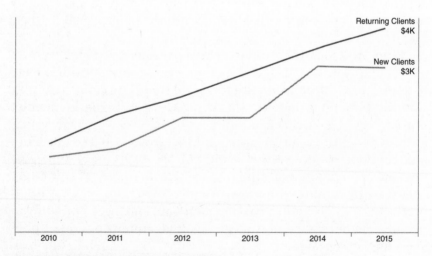

Figure CS.3    Average Annual Spend by Client Type

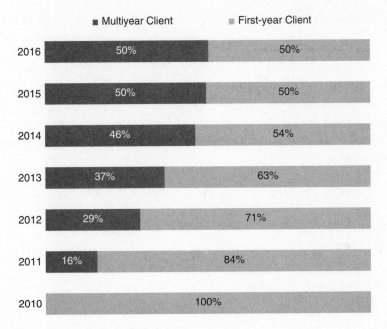

Figure CS.4    Client Retention by Order Year

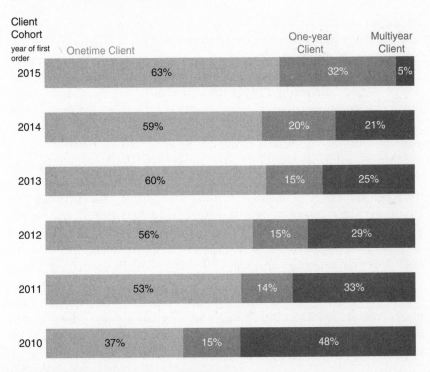

Figure CS.5    Client Retention by Year of First Order

To explain further, from the 2010 class, 48 percent are still clients today, 15 percent were clients for just one year, and 37 percent were clients just once.

For the 2014 class, 21 percent of the clients are still customers today, 20 percent were customers for just one year, and 63 percent of them were customers just once. The ending report period for this dataset is July 2016, so the 2015 class of customers have not yet had a full additional year to reorder; hence, the low multiyear client percentage.

One insight we draw from this analysis is that in 2010, MAB had a great crop of clients that have remained loyal and are still clients. In addition, with each passing year the number of returning clients is increasing, building a solid base for MAB to expand upon.

### Business Levers for Monetization

Next we identify the monetization business levers available to Michael to achieve his revenue growth objective. We have learned that Michael's business is a top-line business so we focus on the Revenue branch of our Business Lever framework. We have also learned that clients typically order about twice a year, much of which is driven by spring and fall seasons. Custom clothing ordering is an involved process requiring a significant commitment of time for fitting, refitting, and waiting for production and delivery, a process that is not easy to fit into clients' busy schedule on a more frequent basis.

While price is a potent lever in every business, the market for custom clothing is not as price sensitive as other retail clothing segments, and as we learned in discovery, Michael has capacity constraints that are expensive to expand. Driving more volume through lower price will likely have a negative impact on profitability. Channel expansion is an action to be considered as well, but we are drawn first to the opportunity to grow revenue organically. We have learned that approximately 50 percent of MAB's first-time clients only purchase one time and 15 to 20 percent of clients do not return after the first year of ordering. We believe there may be an opportunity to drive revenue growth organically through proactive targeted marketing focused on retaining and engaging more clients in a long-term relationship. Figure CS.6 calls out the Business Levers we believe Michael can consider in developing revenue-driving actions.

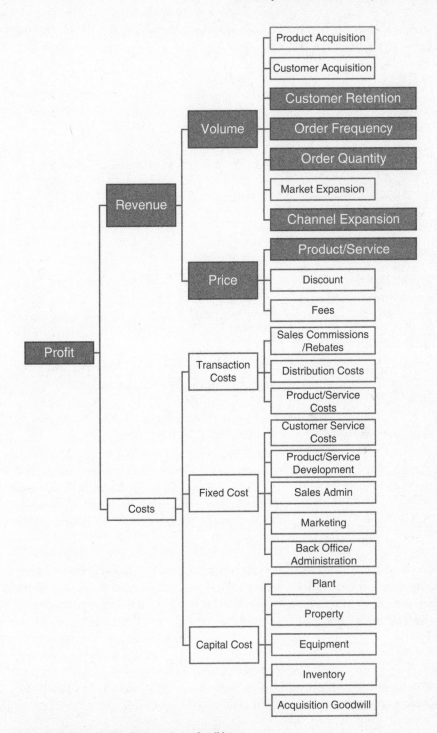

**Figure CS.6    Monetization Business Lever Candidates**

Further analysis will determine which of these levers will deliver the most promising results.

### Hypothesis

With these insights, we are ready to articulate our hypothesis to guide development of our Decision Architecture.

> MAB has a strong asset in its client base that it can leverage to drive organic revenue growth through targeted marketing activities focused on retention and increased frequency of engagement.

### Next Steps

Upon the completion of the Discovery phase we have achieved a good understanding of client types and life-cycle stages. Looking forward, we can apply data science to MAB's data to estimate purchase patterns to understand the degree to which MAB has been successful in acquiring, committing, and retaining clients.

We can use insights to seek out untapped opportunities for organic revenue growth through increased engagement and retention of its existing client base, the most cost-effective sales channel there is. This analysis can help MAB develop effective strategies to retain strong clients and grow high-potential clients.

Lastly, we can identify KPIs and success metrics that MAB can use to monitor the performance of its monetization strategies and act quickly on opportunities to improve through Guided Analytics. In sum, we can help MAB monetize its data.

## Decision Analysis Phase

We begin the Decision Analysis phase by conducting several working sessions to create our Question Analysis, Category Tree, Key Decisions, Action Levers, and Success Metrics. Following is a review of each of the outputs of our work.

### Question Analysis

Our Question Analysis helps us determine how Michael thinks of the business when solving a problem or trying to find an opportunity.

Q1 How are sales performing over last month and this time last year?

Q2 Who are our high-value clients and are we getting the most from our current business?

Q3 Which clients do we believe are undervalued?

Q4 Which clients offer the best opportunity to improve?

**Figure CS.7    Questions from Working Session**

Through our Question Analysis, we align to the base hypothesis that MAB's strongest growth engine is its client base, through which it can grow business organically through retention, engagement, and referrals. Figure CS.7 summarizes the key questions that arose from the working session.

The first question Michael asks is, how are they performing? To gauge the health of the business Michael wants to know if business sales are up or down over this time last year and how sales are trending overall. This performance-based questioning is part of the Inform level of questions in our analytical cycle.

In continuation with this line of questioning, Michael wants to know the number of appointments, as this is a key indicator of the health of the organization. For example, if Michael were to only look at sales for a given weekend, a large order resulting in a big sale may mask the fact that not many clients made appointments, hinting at a bigger issue.

The next set of questions can be grouped into several categories: Orders, Client Segmentation, Client Engagement, and Client Retention. All four of these categories are at the Diagnose level in our analytical cycle as Michael is trying to problem-solve for issues or generate opportunities.

### Category Tree

From our Question Analysis, we develop our Category Tree. Figure CS.8 shows the categories and hierarchy of the question groupings.

We also capture the types of analysis Michael would like to perform in the Inform stage.

**Performance**—The first analysis is centered on helping Michael answer the set of questions on how the store is performing today and over time. Is MAB improving performance over

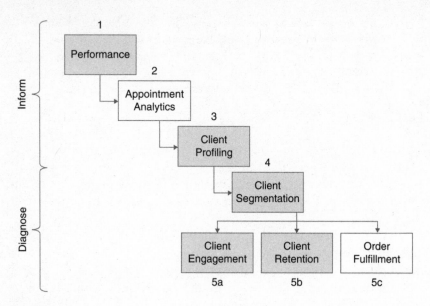

**Figure CS.8 MAB Category Tree**

same time last year? Is customer spend per order healthy? Are
we encountering capacity constraints, and if so, how often?

**Client Profile**—This analysis is focused on client profiles to
understand the mix of business and types of clients against
several segment attributes.

**Client Segmentation**—For the Client Segmentation analysis, we
would like to know if MAB's client base can be segmented
into groups of clients based on similar attributes and behavioral characteristics that can be used to identify opportunities
for improvement. By comparing segment order history, we
would like to know whether MAB's share of clothing spend
can be improved through a greater scope of purchases, such
as sport jackets and pants, in addition to suits and shirts. What
indicators can MAB use to be more targeted in identifying
prospects who have the potential to develop into a fuller partnership for their garment needs with respect to variety, value,
and quantity of garment purchases?

In the Diagnostic stage of the analytical cycle, we would like to
perform three diagnostics:

**Client Engagement**—The first diagnostic is centered on opportunities for various marketing activities. As MAB expands

its client base it will increasingly encounter constraints with showroom capacity and stylist availability. Located in the heart of New York City, expanding studio space and the stylist force represents a significant investment in space and overhead costs. Michael is anxious to invest in the growth of his business but at the same time he would like to optimize his existing investment and ensure the business grows profitably. With better targeting of client engagement through unique marketing activities, Michael would like expansion needs to be driven by clients who have a sustaining value for the MAB experience.

**Client Retention**—About 50 percent of MAB's business in a year is new clients. Michael would like a diagnostic centered on the high-potential clients who are not likely to return the following year based on data science efforts of a threshold time period in order to target them for engagement marketing. In addition, he would like to know if signs of possible attrition of his best clients can be identified in order to implement preventative measures.

**Order Fulfillment**—The final diagnostic is based on the process to fulfill orders. In this diagnostic, Michael would like to know the status of orders to better determine scheduling and optimization of the appointment calendar.

In working with Michael, we decide to focus on the following analytics: Performance, Client Segmentation, Client Engagement, and Client Retention.

### Key Decisions

After framing Michael's questions and building our Category Tree, we develop key decisions that came from our working sessions. As we learned in our discussion on Decision Analysis, decisions are developed through diagnostic analysis and usually come at the end of the root-cause analysis set of questions. Following is a list of questions with the resolving decision. (Please note that decisions are denoted by *D*.)

Q1 How are sales performing over last month and this time last year?

Q2 Who are our high-value clients and are we getting the most from our current business?

Q3 Which clients do we believe are undervalued?

Q4 Which clients offer the best opportunity to improve retention and engagement?

>D1 Which clients among my high-value clients show a risk of leaving?

>D2 Which exploratory clients should I work to engage in a long-term relationship?

Let's see how the decisions we have identified map back to our Business Levers (Figure CS.9).

### Action Levers

Next we want to understand the possible actions we can take from our decisions. These should be actions that Michael can execute to drive a decision. From our two decisions, the team developed the following actions. (Please note that actions are denoted by *A*.)

>D1 Which clients among my high-value clients show a risk of leaving?

>>A1 For multiyear clients who have not been to the studio in over 6 months, offer a free shirt to come back in as part of a "test a new style" campaign.

>D2 Which exploratory clients should I work to engage in a long-term relationship?

>>A2 For multiyear clients not in the high-value spend tier, target a marketing event to drive to a more engaged relationship.

>>A3 For newer clients who have placed large orders, conduct a group dinner to incent a multiyear relationship.

We return to our Business Lever framework once again and map the actions we will execute through our Monetization Strategy to the levers we selected (Figure CS.10).

### Success Metrics

Now that we have our decisions and actions, we need to understand the major metrics that drive these decisions. Let's see what metrics we have for each of these decisions. (Please note that Success Metrics are denoted by *SM*.)

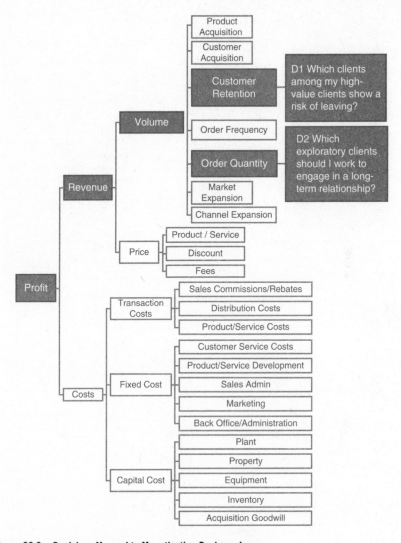

**Figure CS.9    Decisions Mapped to Monetization Business Levers**

D1 Which clients among my high-value clients show a risk of leaving?

    A1 For multiyear clients who have not been to the showroom in over 6 months, offer a free shirt to come back in as part of a "test a new feature" campaign.

        SM Clients not ordering in 6 months or greater as a percentage of total

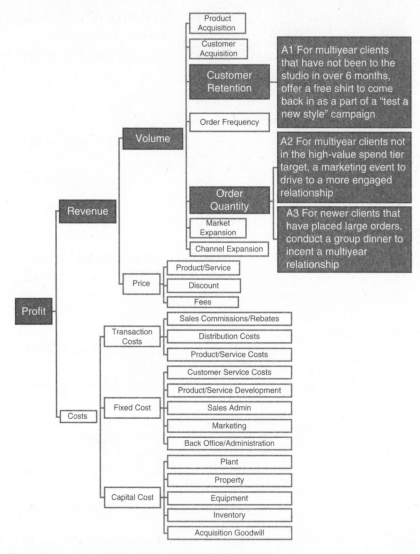

Figure CS.10   Actions Mapped to Monetization Business Levers

D2 Which exploratory or one-year clients should I work to engage in a long-term wardrobe relationship?

A2 For high-value clients, target a marketing event to drive to a more committed relationship.

A3 For newer clients who have placed large orders, conduct a group dinner to incent a multiyear relationship.

SM Distribution of high-potential clients by Engagement Score

### Decision Architecture

At this point, we have completed the Decision Analysis section of our Decision Architecture template. To recap:

| | |
|---|---|
| **Business Objective** | Grow revenue by 10 percent. |
| **Hypothesis** | MAB has a strong asset in its client base that it can leverage to drive organic revenue growth through frequency of engagement and retention performance. |

**Decision Analysis**

| | |
|---|---|
| Questions | Q1 How are sales performing over last month and this time last year? |
| | Q2 Who are our high-value clients and are we getting the most from our current business? |
| | Q3 Which clients do we believe are undervalued? |
| | Q4 Which clients offer the best opportunity to improve retention and engagement? |
| Decisions | D1 Which clients among my high-value clients show a risk of leaving? |
| | D2 Which exploratory clients should I work to engage in a long-term relationship? |
| Metrics | SM 1 Clients not ordering in 6 months or greater as a percentage of total |
| | SM 2 Distribution of high-potential clients by Engagement Score |
| Actions | A1 For multiyear clients who have not been to the studio in over 6 months, offer a free shirt to come back in as part of a "test a new style" campaign. |

A2 For multiyear clients not in the high-value spend tier, target a marketing event to drive to a more engaged relationship.

A3 For newer clients who have placed large orders, conduct a group dinner to incent a multiyear relationship.

## Monetization Strategy, Part I

We now have two components of the steps needed to develop our Monetization Strategy. We have decided to develop *customer engagement and retention* strategies and have selected the Business Levers of *customer retention* and *order quantity* as the target of our actions.

The next steps assess availability of competitive and marketing information and evaluate our strategy against our Guiding Principles. Following more discussion with Michael Andrews we capture the following requirements:

**Competitive & Market Information**

| | |
|---|---|
| Industry Information | None |
| Competitive Intelligence | Through competitive websites we know our competitions' prices and that many of them are moving to annuity relationships with multiyear clients. |
| Market Information | None |

**Monetization Framework Components**

| | |
|---|---|
| Quality Data | The data is acceptable for initial analysis. |
| Be Specific | We want to target our actions to specific clients to increase engagement and improve retention. |
| Be Holistic | The types of marketing and promotional activities need to fit with the overall brand of MAB. |

| | |
|---|---|
| Actionable | Specific actionable events and marketing activities need to be developed. |
| Grounded in Data Science | Develop a segmentation technique to group like customers.<br>Perform analytics to create an Engagement Score and Potential Lift. |
| Monetary Value | Generate expected revenue lift. |
| Confidence Factor or Probability | We do not plan to provide a confidence factor. |
| Decision Matrix | We plan to leverage a Decision Matrix. |
| Measurable | We will be able to measure based on specific client sales. |
| Drives Innovation | We are innovating our marketing activities based on a new client segmentation methodology and directly targeting specific clients. |

We will continue to develop our Monetization Strategy as we progress through the project.

## Agile Analytics

To develop the analytics to answer the questions in our Decision Architecture methodology, we gather the relevant data and develop the analytic structure necessary to expose the trends and patterns that will guide our analysis.

Using an extract from MAB's CRM system containing all orders since 2010, we have data that provides information with respect to date, type, quantity, and value of items purchased per order. Even with the relatively small number of order attributes we are able to develop an analytic structure that will provide a rich analytic dataset to data-mine.

In this next section we walk through the development of the various metrics, discuss Data Development, and review the analytic structure we put in place to facilitate analysis of MAB's client opportunities.

## *Data Analysis*

Having identified the success metrics that measure our strategy, we turn our attention to the following metrics to enable diagnostic analysis and performance monitoring.

- Operating metrics
- Diagnostic metrics
- Performance metrics

### Operating Metrics

Operating metrics, the most basic of business metrics, measure the ebb and flow of core business processes and resources, capturing the interactions between the key assets of the business. In the case of MAB, key assets include its client base, stylist base, New York showroom, product offering, and production processes. In order to measure the capacity of the stylist network and the showroom to support increased business volume, we need to understand metrics that relate client purchases to stylist servicing time as well as available servicing capacity in the showroom.

We use operational benchmarks based on Michael's expert knowledge of the business to analyze relationships between clients, orders, and stylist. If further refinement is needed, Michael could choose to employ operational research methods to gain a deeper understanding of MAB operations.

### Product Operating Metrics

| | |
|---|---|
| Typical wardrobe order package | 6 suits, 3 jackets, 5 pants, 20 shirts |
| Typical wardrobe order value | $20,000 to $40,000 |

### Stylist Operating Metrics

| | |
|---|---|
| Stylist client hours per order | 3 hours |
| Stylist time on admin | 15% per month |
| Available stylist hours per month (including vacation, holiday, and personal time off) | 147 hours |

| | |
|---|---|
| Stylist client-servicing capacity (no overtime) | 42 orders per month |
| Stylist base (4 full-time stylists, 1 stylist 50% management) | 4.5 |
| **Stylist base capacity benchmark** | **189 orders per month 2,268 per year** |

## Studio Capacity Metrics

| | |
|---|---|
| Client available appointment hours per month | 142 hours |
| Simultaneous client-servicing capacity | 4 clients |
| Studio hours per client | 3 hours |
| Studio servicing capacity benchmark | **190 orders per month 2,280 per year** |

Based on our current analysis, MAB may encounter capacity constraints with respect to studio space and current stylist load when client orders exceed 190 per month. With MAB's location in New York City, increasing studio space is not a trivial decision. We can use Appointment Analytics to help evaluate options to increase studio capacity incrementally and cost effectively. In addition, we can use it to monitor capacity utilization and anticipate when to implement options like overtime during particular seasons.

### Diagnostic Metrics
We utilize diagnostic metrics when we employ data science to analyze the current client base. Our diagnostic analysis can deliver valuable insights into the behavioral aspects of the client types by life-cycle stage.

It is helpful to segment clients by descriptive and behavioral attributes, allowing us to examine similarities and differences in performance trends and patterns among segments of the client base. With meaningful and behavioral-based segments, examination of the internal structure of the performance metrics can guide us to actions that can be taken to improve overall results.

## MAB Performance Diagnostic Metrics

| | |
|---|---|
| Year of first purchase (cohort year) | Calendar year of first purchase with MAB |
| Client tenure at order | On the date of the order, years or months since month of first purchase |
| Attrition rate | Percent of clients active in the prior year but not active in the current year |
| Retention rate | Percent of clients active in the current year who ordered in prior years |
| Client monthly spend | Total monthly spend per client Spend on core garment types: suits, shirts, jackets, pants, tuxedos, including accessories, net of discount, not including gift cards purchased |
| Client lifetime spend | Cumulative amount of spend per client from first purchase through reporting period |
| Client order tenure | Number of years the client has ordered core garment types |
| Client order scope | Cumulative number of core garment types ordered per client |
| Acquisition channel | Marketing channel through which the client contacted MAB, customer referral, paid media, Internet search, other |

### MAB Performance Metrics

Clients and orders are the heartbeat of MAB's business, so the performance metrics will focus on client orders and spend on a monthly basis.

### Revenue Metrics

| | |
|---|---|
| Average spend per client per month | Average value of all orders in a month net of discounts |
| Average spend per client per order | Average value of all orders per client net of discounts |

## Client Metrics

With the focus of our Monetization Strategy on organic revenue growth, our client performance metrics measure how good MAB is at retaining existing clients and acquiring new ones.

| | |
|---|---|
| Client retention rate (annual) | Percent of clients in the current year with purchase activity in the prior year |
| Client acquisition rate | Percent of clients in a month or year who are first-time clients, total and by channel |

## MAB KPIs

KPIs measure progress on goals and are the top-line metrics that monitor overall performance of the business.

| | |
|---|---|
| Total Client Spend | Total spend by clients on core garment items (suit, shirts, jacket, pants, tuxedo) Annual, monthly; year-over-year variance |
| Total Client Orders | Total count of orders by clients, which include core garment items (suit, shirts, jacket, pants, tuxedo) Annual, monthly; year-over-year variance |

### Data Development

Data produced by operational systems is rarely found in the form and quality needed for analytics. The MAB data is not a complex dataset and comes from a well-organized CRM system, but it still requires some cleansing and transformations in order to prepare it for our analytic purposes. The following are some issues typical of many analytic projects.

## Field Names

The field names in the dataset are not user friendly or intuitive so we apply transformations to field names to make them more useful.

| Original Field Name | Transformed Field Name |
|---|---|
| Invoice__r.Client__r.Occupation__c | Client Occupation |
| Invoice__r.Date__c | Order Date |
| Invoice__r.Invoice_Number__c | Order Number |
| Invoice__r.QB_Stylist_Initials__c | Stylist |
| InvoiceName__c | Invoice Name |
| Item_Name__c | Item Type |
| Order_Item__r.Price__c | Price |
| Order_Item__r.RecordType.Name | Item Category |

## Hierarchies

Product or service hierarchies are among the most difficult elements to manage in reporting systems. For example, core items in a wardrobe are suits, shirts, jackets, pants, and tuxedos. The CRM system has a field to categorize item types, but the Shirt category has two groupings and the Tuxedo category has four, introducing a lower level of granularity than the other items in the same list. In order to ensure a complete analysis of shirts, we add an additional field—item category—to group shirt and tuxedo types to a similar level as the other item types.

| Item Category | Order Item Type |
|---|---|
| Suit | Suit |
| Shirt | Shirt |
| | Casual Shirt |
| Jacket | Jacket |
| Pants | Pants |
| Tuxedo | Tuxedo |
| | Tuxedo Jacket |
| | Tuxedo Pants |
| | Tuxedo Vest |

## Inconsistent Values

Occupation is the field where we encounter the greatest incidence of inconsistent field values. However, Occupation is a field that is important to our segmentation analysis, so we group and standardize the values into a meaningful set. The original dataset has 889 unique values for occupation. In our final set, we reduce the list to three categories and 16 types.

**Sample of Original Values**

Occupation
Web design
Web designer
Web developer
Web development
Website analyst
Trial attorney
Trial lawyer
Trucking/Art
TV—reporter
TV executive
TV reporter

**Cleansed Values**

| Occupation Category | Occupation Type |
| --- | --- |
| Finance | Finance |
| Legal | Legal |
| Personal | Advertising and Media |
| | Arts and Design |
| | Business |
| | Education |
| | Hospitality |
| | Lifestyle |
| | Medical |
| | Military |
| | Politics |
| | Real Estate |
| | Retail |
| | Sports |
| | Technology |
| | CEO |
| Other | Not Listed |

### Analytic Structure

While sorting out data issues, we also study the inherent structure of the data and the transformations we need to uncover insightful patterns.

The MAB dataset is extracted from a CRM system that we import into our analytic database to produce the data layer. We apply transformations to create a set of views in the analytic layer to develop the metrics we need for analysis. We then bring the views together in the reporting layer to create the analytic dataset we need for analysis, diagnostics, and reporting. The completed analytic data mart structure is shown in Figure CS.11.

We next connect our visual analytic tool to the Client Order analytic dataset and develop the metadata to organize the data as shown in Figure CS.12.

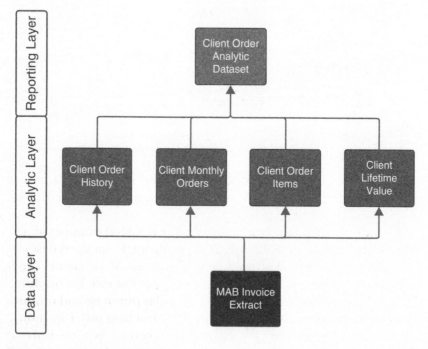

**Figure CS.11   MAB Analytic Data Mart**

**Figure CS.12    MAB Metadata**

## Transformations

As we explore the data for structure, we also develop the transformations needed to develop the diagnostic and Success Metrics for analysis and reporting.

Creating fields to measure client tenure is a good example of typical transformations needed to support analytics. From the dataset we have a field that captures the date of the order. Many clients order two or three times a year but in different calendar months on different days. As custom clothing is not an everyday purchase and requires six to eight weeks to complete the process, tracking order by month will be sufficient for our purposes. Client tenure is a measure of the number of months from the initial order for subsequent orders.

For example, the year and month of a first order date in January 2016 is tenure month 0. A subsequent order by the same client in June 2016 is tenure month 5.

This is important as we want to look for patterns when we contrast clients in comparable periods in their order experience, for example, comparing a client's order metrics, such as quantity of items, number of item types, and value of order, for clients in their initial tenure month and their second tenure month.

First we create a metric to calculate client tenure month:

Client tenure months at time of order

= Year and month of order − Year and month of initial order

Next we transform the metric to tenure years:

Client tenure years at time of order

= (Client tenure months at time of order)/12

As time progresses, we keep track of the maximum value of the client tenure as of the latest date of reporting:

Maximum client tenure years at time of order

= max((Client tenure months at time of order)/12)

Finally, we identify tenure segment to use for analysis:

Client tenure segment =

| If | Maximum Client tenure years at time of order = 0 then Onetime Client |
|---|---|
| Else | Maximum Client tenure years at time of order = 1 then One-year Client |
| Else | Multiyear Client |

We perform a similar transformation for the diagnostic and Success Metrics we identified earlier.

### Data Science

To help provide more insights into the data, we employ several data science techniques. These include building attribute-level segmentations that provide flexibility to group like customers based on various client descriptive and behavioral characteristics. In addition, we perform a statistical box-plot analysis to gain insights into natural cohorts to help create the segmentation groupings.

### Attribute Segmentation

In our Decision Analysis and Monetization Strategy phases, we developed monetization strategies and actions to drive organic growth through improved client engagement and increased retention. Applying engagement and retention strategies to each and every client could be overwhelming for MAB financially. MAB needs to be smart about which clients to target in order to create a profitable growth engine.

Using tools of Data Science, we develop a segmentation model for MAB to help Michael develop strategies and focus resources on client engagement and retention monetization strategies most likely to deliver a financial return.

A valuable client will purchase a variety of garment types (suits, shirts, jackets, pants, and tuxedo) yearly. Such clients are investing in a custom wardrobe because they view it as an extension of their occupation and/or their personal expression. With these characteristics in mind, we identify three attributes—occupation, purchase scope, and tenure—to build our segmentation model.

---

**Client Descriptive Attributes**

| | |
|---|---|
| Occupation | Industry/position with custom of wearing suits |
| | Industry/position without custom of wearing suits |
| Client Tenure | Years since the date of first order |

**Client Behavioral Attributes**

| | |
|---|---|
| Purchase Scope | Number of different garment types purchased (suit, jacket, pants, shirt, tuxedo) |

---

### Behavioral Segmentation

We choose a standard tool of statistical analysis, the box-plot, a technique that visualizes descriptive statistics of mean, spread, and outliers, as the method to determine the segmentation level for the behavioral attributes. Given the relatively small number of data points and high degree of variation in the dataset, we prefer to measure client behavior using the median, a measure of central tendency, instead of the average in order to reduce sensitivity to outliers. Using box-plot charts, we look for natural breaks between values of our segmentation attributes to inform our grouping of clients by similar behavioral characteristics.

### Purchase Scope

The first attribute we examine is purchase scope, a measure of the variety of garment types the client purchases. Suits, shirts, jackets, and pants are foundational garment types for a complete wardrobe, with tuxedos a frequent add-on for more formal occasions.

Using a box-plot analysis, we determine there is a meaningful difference in lifetime value of client spend between two and three garment types purchased. While clients purchasing two garment types have a wider range of lifetime spend, the median spend is half that of clients purchasing three garment types. This translates to clients spending, on average, 50 percent more than those who only purchase two garment types. These individuals have selected MAB as their partner to create a fuller wardrobe than just suits and shirts. This is a big epiphany for us and can drive many of our actions.

While clients purchasing four garment types spend more than those purchasing three, the difference in median spend is only 30 percent. We decide to group clients with purchases of three or more garment types into a scope segment labeled Wardrobe and group those with two or less as Ad Hoc.

We also identify a segment labeled Wedding to track clients who purchase for special events and are less likely to return for other items. These are clients with a onetime order that includes a tuxedo, although there may be other garment types on the order.

The box-plot diagram in Figure CS.13 is segmented based on how many garment types clients ordered. When reading the box-plot, the darker-shaded dots represent individual customers and the line between the light and dark-gray boxes is the median lifetime spend for that group.

### Descriptive Attribution Segmentation

Descriptive attributes are easier to segment than behavioral attributes because the segments are defined by intrinsic characteristics

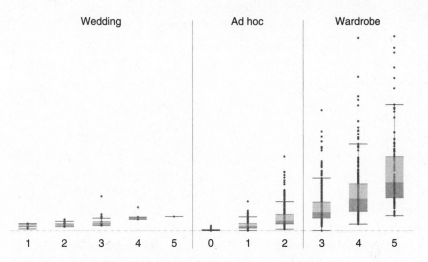

**Figure CS.13     Client Order Variety of Products Ordered Statistical Analysis**

of the analysis target. We identify two descriptive characteristics that we believe are meaningful to our analysis: occupation and tenure.

**Occupation**

When a client opens an account, MAB attempts to collect information with respect to their occupation in order to better tailor their design selection. As demonstrated earlier in the Data Development section, this information is not standardized or complete, but we can work with what we have.

Clothing standards in the business world have relaxed greatly over the past several decades, particularly with the growth in technology and startup firms. However, two occupations, Finance and Legal, especially in New York City, have sustained the custom of wearing suits every day in their work. Comprising 44 percent of MAB's client base and accounting for 53 percent of spend, we take these two occupations as individual segments.

Examining the client base, we find a wide range of client occupations not in Finance and Legal, but in areas that we take as an indicator of a client's interest in custom clothing as a personal expression. We group these clients into a category labeled Personal. Finally, we note a large number of clients with no occupation indicated and group these clients into a category labeled Other. We assign clients to one of these occupation types based on their designated Occupation/Position.

| Occupation Segment | |
|---|---|
| **Occupation Type** | **Occupation/Position** |
| Finance | Finance |
| Legal | Legal |
| Personal | Advertising and Media |
| | Arts and Design |
| | Business |
| | CEO |
| | Education |
| | Hospitality |
| | Lifestyle |
| | Medical |
| | Military |
| | Politics |
| | Real Estate |
| | Retail |
| | Sports |
| | Technology |
| Other | Not Listed |

**Tenure**

We already touched on client tenure when we discussed attrition and retention. We know that segmenting the base by client tenure helps to identify targets for engagement and retention strategies. As mentioned earlier, because clients do not typically order on a monthly basis, we define tenure segments based on years of relationship with MAB since the initial order.

| Tenure Segment | |
|---|---|
| Onetime client | Ordered only during the first month of the date of the initial order |
| One-year client | Ordered only during the first year of the date of the initial order |
| Multiyear client | Ordered more than one year from the date of the initial order |

| Segment Type | Segment Description | Segment Elements |
|---|---|---|
| Client Attribute Segments | | |
| Occupation | Industry/position with custom of wearing suits | Finance |
| | | Legal |
| | Personal preference to wear suits | Personal |
| | Occupation not known | Unknown |
| Tenure | Years of order activity | Onetime client |
| | | One-year client |
| | | Multiyear client |
| Client Behavior Segments | | |
| Order scope | Types of clothing articles purchased (suit, jacket, pants, shirt, tuxedo) | Wardrobe > 2 garment types |
| | | Ad Hoc 1 to 2 garment types |
| | | Wedding, onetime order with a tuxedo |

**Figure CS.14    Client Segmentation Model**

### MAB Client Segmentation

Having completed our segment analysis, we summarize our segmentation model in Figure CS.14.

We validate our segmentation model by evaluating the distribution of clients in the various segments, seen in the next three figures. In these charts, the bars represent the number of clients and the circles represent the median lifetime spend.

In Figure CS.15, segmenting by order scope, we see that our Wardrobe clients, those who purchase more than three different types of garments, have a lifetime spend on average more than 50 percent larger than clients who only order two garment types. This tells us that when clients purchase three or more types of garments from MAB, they begin to see MAB as a solution for their wardrobe, not just for individual articles of clothing. An opportunity presents itself to target clients in the Ad Hoc segment, encouraging them to expand the scope of their garment purchases with MAB.

Figure CS.16 shows clients segmented by tenure. In the first cohort, the clients only ordered once and their median lifetime spend was $3,000. In the second cohort, the client ordered only during their first year with MAB with a median lifetime spend of

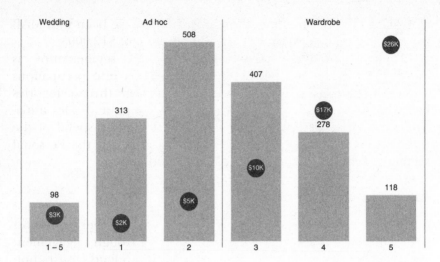

**Figure CS.15    Segment by Order Scope**

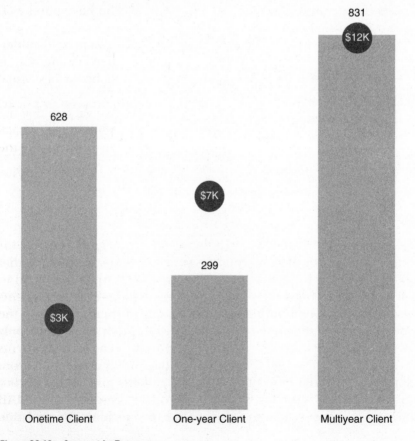

**Figure CS.16    Segment by Tenure**

$7,000. In the last grouping, those clients who have been with MAB for multiple years have a median lifetime spend of $12,000.

The last of our charts to validate our segmentation is Figure CS.17. In this analysis we group clients into occupations segmented as Personal, Finance, and Legal. The three categories have distinctive attributes for targeting marketing and sales initiatives. The Finance segment has the highest lifetime spend of the three segments (considering the overall average for the Personal segment), which validates our initial assumption.

## Monetization Strategy, Part II

At this point we are ready to bring our analysis together to support our monetization strategy of organic growth through engagement and retention. First, let's look at our Client and Spend Distribution based on our segmentations (Figure CS.18). In order to keep the analysis relevant, we limit our charts to clients who have purchased within the last 24 months.

Next we create a consolidated segmentation matrix to understand the distribution of the client base and their key metrics, as shown in Figure CS.19. However, this table may not be the best visual representation of this information.

To help Michael spot the opportunities quickly, we leverage the principles of UI discussed in earlier chapters to create a more impactful visualization, as shown in Figure CS.20. (Note that the width of the bars is relative to number of clients.)

Let's deconstruct the chart.

### One-time Clients

Examining our Client Segmentation Matrix (Figure CS.18) for clients active with MAB during the past two years, we observe that clients ordering from MAB only one time, not surprisingly, tend to fall in the lower third of lifetime spend. One-time–Wardrobe clients have a higher spend but there are not many of them. Clients in the one-time order segment represent 36 percent of clients but only 12 percent of spend. There are a number of reasons that clients order only one time. Some clients value the quality and fit of custom clothing but have limited budgets. Some clients give MAB a try but opt for another preferred partner, or other reasons. While MAB welcomes all clients passionate about custom clothing, the probable

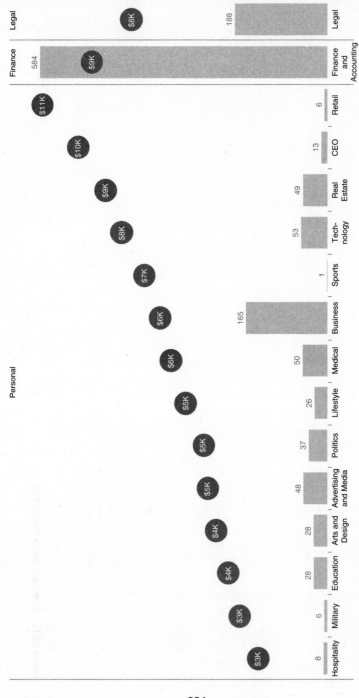

**Figure CS.17 Segment by Occupation**

| Client Tenure | Client Order Scope | Client Occupation | Percent of Total Clients | Percent of Client Spend |
|---|---|---|---|---|
| Multiyear Client | Wardrobe | Finance | 15% | 29% |
| | | Personal | 8% | 17% |
| | | Other | 5% | 9% |
| | | Legal | 4% | 8% |
| | Ad hoc | Finance | 5% | 4% |
| | | Personal | 4% | 3% |
| | | Other | 4% | 3% |
| | | Legal | 2% | 1% |
| One-year Client | Wardrobe | Finance | 3% | 3% |
| | | Personal | 3% | 3% |
| | | Other | 2% | 2% |
| | | Legal | 1% | 1% |
| | Ad hoc | Finance | 3% | 1% |
| | | Personal | 2% | 1% |
| | | Other | 2% | 1% |
| | | Legal | 1% | 0% |
| Onetime Client | Wardrobe | Personal | 1% | 1% |
| | | Other | 1% | 1% |
| | | Finance | 1% | 1% |
| | | Legal | 0% | 0% |
| | Ad hoc | Other | 11% | 3% |
| | | Personal | 8% | 3% |
| | | Finance | 5% | 2% |
| | | Legal | 3% | 1% |
| | Wedding | Finance | 2% | 1% |
| | | Personal | 2% | 1% |
| | | Other | 1% | 0% |
| | | Legal | 1% | 0% |

**Figure CS.18  Client and Spend Distribution**

|  |  | | Wardrobe | | | Ad hoc | |
| --- | --- | --- | --- | --- | --- | --- | --- |
|  |  | Finance | Legal | Personal | Finance | Legal | Personal |
| **Multiyear Client** | Avg Lifetime Spend | $16K | $14K | $17K | $7K | $10K | $6K |
|  | Clients | 32 | 13 | 26 | 19 | 5 | 15 |
| **Onetime Client** | Avg Lifetime Spend | $9K | $11K | $7K | $3K | $2K | $3K |
|  | Clients | 9 | 3 | 10 | 51 | 22 | 102 |
| **One-year Client** | Avg Lifetime Spend | $10K | $12K | $7K | $6K | $5K | $5K |
|  | Clients | 48 | 13 | 40 | 37 | 10 | 31 |

Figure CS.19    Client Segmentation Table

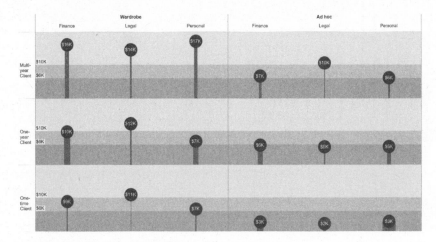

Figure CS.20    Client Segmentation Chart

return on investment for clients in this segment does not justify the expense of a proactive marketing strategy.

### One-Year Clients

The one-year cohort provides some interesting opportunities. Clients in this group, representing 17 percent of the total clients and 15 percent of spend, present a value opportunity. One-year clients in the wardrobe segment are in the top two-thirds lifetime spend tiers and are good candidates for a retention strategy. Selective marketing actions targeted at this segment are likely to produce increases in client value and conversion to multiyear clients. One-year clients in the Ad Hoc segment fall in the lower third of lifetime spend and may present some selective opportunities.

| | Wardrobe | | | Ad Hoc | | | Wedding | | |
|---|---|---|---|---|---|---|---|---|---|
| | Finance | Legal | Personal | Finance | Legal | Personal | Finance | Legal | Personal |
| Multi-year Client | Retain | | | Engage | | | | | |
| One-year Client | Engage | | | | | | | | |

Figure CS.21    Recommended Marketing Strategies

### Multiyear Clients

Multiyear clients are MAB's best clients, representing 47 percent of clients but 73 percent of spend. Multiyear–Wardrobe clients represent 33 percent of clients and 63 percent of revenue. MAB offers discounts for high-spend orders and various marketing activities targeted at this high-value segment. However, it would be helpful to MAB if clients showing early signs of possible attrition could be proactively addressed to prevent attrition.

Clients in the Multiyear–Ad Hoc segment fall into the top two-thirds of client spend and represent a rich opportunity for marketing programs to encourage increased engagement and expanded scope.

Figure CS.21 summarizes our recommended marketing strategies based on the opportunities by segmentation attributes that we have uncovered. The areas highlighted represent segments where MAB should target monetization strategies for retention and engagement to drive revenue.

### Monetization Strategy Requirements

With our segments for targeted marketing strategies identified, we are ready to complete our Monetization Strategy requirements.

| | |
|---|---|
| **Business Objective** | Grow revenue by 10 percent. |
| **Hypothesis** | MAB has a strong asset in its client base that it can leverage to drive organic revenue growth through frequency of engagement and retention performance. |

**Decision Architecture**

| | |
|---|---|
| Questions | Q1 How are sales performing over last month and this time last year? |
| | Q2 Who are our high-value clients and are we getting the most from our current business? |
| | Q3 Which clients do we believe are undervalued? |
| | Q4 Which clients offer the best opportunity to improve retention and engagement? |
| Decisions | D1 Which clients among my high-value clients show a risk of leaving? |
| | D2 Which exploratory clients should I work to engage in a long-term relationship? |
| Metrics | Clients not ordering in six months or greater as a percentage of total distribution of high-potential clients by Engagement Score |
| Actions | A1 For multiyear clients who have not been to the studio in over six months, offer a free shirt to come back in as part of a "test a new style" campaign. |
| | A2 For multiyear clients not in the high-value spend tier target, conduct a marketing event to drive to a more engaged relationship. |
| | A3 For newer clients who have placed large orders, conduct a group dinner to incent a multiyear relationship. |

**Competitive & Market Information**

| | |
|---|---|
| Industry Information | None |
| Competitive Intelligence | Through competitive websites we know our competition's prices and that many of them are moving to annuity relationships with their multiyear clients segment. |
| Market Information | None |

## Monetization Framework Components

| | |
|---|---|
| Quality Data | The data is acceptable for initial analysis. |
| Be Specific | We want to target our actions to specific clients to increase engagement and improve retention. |
| Be Holistic | The type of marketing and promotional activities need to fit with the overall brand of MAB. |
| Actionable | Specific actionable events and marketing activities need to be developed. |
| Grounded in Data | Develop a segmentation technique to group like customers. |
| Science | Perform analytics to create an Engagement Score and Potential Lift. |
| Monetary Value | Generate expected revenue lift. |
| Confidence Factor or Probability | We do not plan to provide a confidence factor. |
| Decision Matrix | We plan to leverage a Decision Matrix. |
| Measurable | We will be able to measure based on specific client sales. |
| Drives Innovation | We are innovating our marketing activities based on a new client segmentation methodology and directly targeting specific clients. |

### Decision Matrix

We move on to develop two decision matrixes to help us implement the actions identified in our Decision Analysis and Agile Analytics phases.

### Engagement Monetization Decision Strategy Matrix

To enable Michael to make decisions on the first set of actions around Engagement, we develop a Decision Matrix to support an Engagement Monetization Strategy (Figure CS.22). This strategy will focus on moving clients from two segments, Multiyear–Ad Hoc and One-year–Wardrobe, to the Multiyear–Wardrobe segment.

Next, we focus on clients who have ordered within the past 24 months. As shown in Figure CS.23, MAB has 421 clients in these

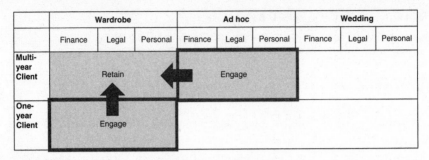

Figure CS.22   Engagement Monetization Decision Strategy Matrix

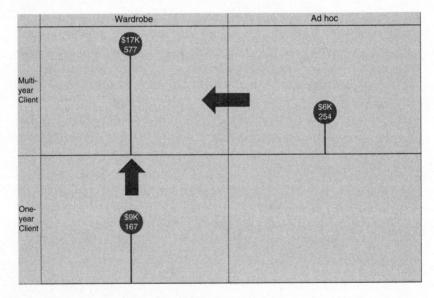

Figure CS.23   Engagement Monetization Strategy

two segments with median lifetime spend ranging from $6,000 to $9,000. The median lifetime spend for Multiyear–Wardrobe segment clients is about $17,000, which we use for our target goal.

We would like to develop engagement actions to migrate "likely to move" clients from these two segments and capture a part of the $8,000 to $11,000 lift per client in lifetime spend from the segment shift.

However, not all clients are likely to move segments for a variety of reasons. In order to implement a more effective strategy, we develop

Table CS.1    Scoring Rubric for the Engagement Score

| Percent Spend Diff | Time Since Last Order | Score Assigned | Likely to Migrate Probability |
|---|---|---|---|
| > 0 and < 30% | 0 to 6 months | High | 80% |
| > = 30% and < 60% | 0 to 6 months | High | 80% |
| > = 60% | 0 to 6 months | Low | 20% |
| > 0 and < 30% | 7 to 12 months | High | 80% |
| > = 30% and < 60% | 7 to 12 months | Med | 50% |
| > = 60% | 7 to 12 months | Low | 20% |
| > 0 and < 30% | 13 to 18 months | Med | 50% |
| > = 30% and < 60% | 13 to 18 months | Low | 20% |
| > = 60% | 13 to 18 months | Low | 20% |

an Engagement Score based on recency of the client's last order and difference in lifetime spend from the $17,000 target. We reason that clients with more recent order activity and already close in lifetime spend to the $17,000 target are more likely to respond to marketing incentives. Our scoring rubric is shown in Table CS.1.

Our goal is to develop two strategies for moving clients to the Multiyear–Wardrobe segment. In order to develop our strategy, we will develop a Decision Matrix as shown in Table CS.2. As a reminder, acts, events, outcomes, and payoffs are the four building blocks of decision theory. Acts are the actions or decisions that a person may take. Events are the occurrences taking place, usually with a level of uncertainty. Outcomes are the results of the occurrences, and payoffs are the values the decision maker is placing on the occurrences.

We outlined two actions in our requirements:

- A2 For multiyear clients not achieving the spend target, conduct a marketing event to drive to a more engaged relationship.
- A3 For newer clients who have placed large orders, conduct a group dinner to incent a multiyear relationship.

Let's build a potential monetization strategy targeting the entire segment. When we get to the final solution, we will decide on whom we target and the actual spend. For our strategy, the Act is two events, a Scotch Event for invited guests only, and an Exclusive Dinner with Michael Andrews. Both events are geared to promote continued engagement with MAB. The Events are the percentage of clients that convert to full engagement. The Outcome is the number

**Table CS.2  Engagement Monetization Strategy Decision Matrix**

| Client Tenure | Client Order Scope | Engagement Score | Clients | Lifetime Spend | Target Lifetime Spend | Potential Lift | Opportunity—Migrate to Champaign Client | Events—Full Engagement | Outcomes—Clients | Outcome Opportunity |
|---|---|---|---|---|---|---|---|---|---|---|
| Scotch Event—Invite Only | | | | | | | | | | |
| Multiyear Client | Wardrobe | High | 97 | 16,463 | 20,000 | 3,370 | 326,850 | 50% | 49 | 163,425 |
| Multiyear Client | Wardrobe | Med | 21 | 16,346 | 20,000 | 3,717 | 78,055 | 50% | 11 | 39,028 |
| Multiyear Client | Wardrobe | Low | 182 | 8,933 | 20,000 | 11,210 | 2,040,183 | 20% | 36 | 408,037 |
| Multiyear Client | Ad hoc | High | 14 | 16,125 | 20,000 | 3,398 | 47,569 | 80% | 11 | 38,055 |
| Multiyear Client | Ad hoc | Med | 5 | 13,926 | 20,000 | 5,131 | 25,656 | 50% | 3 | 12,828 |
| Multiyear Client | Ad hoc | Low | 189 | 5,835 | 20,000 | 13,647 | 2,579,333 | 20% | 38 | 515,867 |
| TOTAL | | | 508 | 9,248 | 20,000 | 10,035 | 5,097,646 | 29% | 147 | 1,177,239 |
| Exclusive Group Dinner with Michael | | | | | | | | | | |
| One-Year Client | Wardrobe | High | 10 | 15,761 | 20,000 | 4,580 | 45,798 | 80% | 8 | 36,638 |
| One-Year Client | Wardrobe | Med | 4 | 15,069 | 20,000 | 4,121 | 16,484 | 50% | 2 | 8,242 |
| One-Year Client | Wardrobe | Low | 104 | 7,365 | 20,000 | 12,085 | 1,256,840 | 20% | 21 | 251,368 |
| TOTAL | | | 118 | 8,386 | 20,000 | 11,179 | 1,319,122 | 26% | 31 | 296,248 |
| TOTAL | | | 626 | 9,094 | 20,000 | 10,250 | 6,416,768 | 28% | 178 | 1,473,487 |

of clients who migrate to the full engagement level. The Payoff is the opportunity value from the actions.

From our payoff matrix we see that we can generate $1.5 million in additional revenue, assuming full participation. We do not expect to be able to generate the full amount but believe we can execute strategies to capture some of this opportunity.

### Retention Monetization Decision Strategy Matrix

The next monetization strategy is focused on client retention. MAB has a loyal base of Wardrobe clients who have ordered regularly over the years. These clients have a median lifetime spend of $17,000 and spend on average $5,000 per year. By monitoring the time since last order, MAB can proactively engage with these clients to ensure they continue to select MAB as their clothing partner.

As seen in Table CS.3, 283 of MAB's Multiyear–Wardrobe clients have not ordered in the last 7 to 24 months.

The Time Since Last Order metric can serve as a valuable alert drawing attention to clients who might be at risk of leaving. We develop a strategy to target a 50 percent-off shirt campaign to continue the relationship with these valuable clients.

Let's review our Decision Matrix for this Monetization Strategy (Table CS.4). Our Act is the Free Shirt Campaign. The Event is the "percent" of people who participate in additional orders. The Outcome is the actual number of clients that order. The Payoff is the revenue the action will generate, which in this case is $654,000 of potential revenue.

## Guided Analytics

Having identified how to tap into organic growth opportunities, Michael can execute and monitor his strategy using Guided Analytics. This is when the magic of a well-developed analytic data model

**Table CS.3   Multiyear–Wardrobe Clients**

| Client Tenure | Client Scope | Time Since Last Order | Clients | Lifetime Spend | Spend per Client per Year |
|---|---|---|---|---|---|
| Multiyear Client | Wardrobe | 0 to 6 months | 294 | $19,583 | 5,277 |
| Multiyear Client | Wardrobe | 7 to 12 months | 116 | $16,218 | 5,333 |
| Multiyear Client | Wardrobe | 13 to18 months | 111 | $13,662 | 4,259 |
| Multiyear Client | Wardrobe | 19 to 24 months | 56 | $10,274 | 3,759 |
| Total | | | 577 | $16,697 | 4,949 |

**Table CS.4    Retention Monetization Strategy Decision Matrix**

| Client Tenure | Client Scope | Time Since Last Order Range | Number of Clients in Segment | Cost of Campaign | Events—Additional Purchase | Outcomes—Number of Clients | Payoff—Amount of Potential Revenue | Opportunity—Additional Year of Orders |
|---|---|---|---|---|---|---|---|---|
| Multiyear Client | Wardrobe | 7 to 12 months | 116 | $2,650 | 60% | 70 | $348,000 | $5,000 |
| Multiyear Client | Wardrobe | 13 to 18 months | 111 | 2,650 | 40% | 44 | 222,000 | 5,000 |
| Multiyear Client | Wardrobe | 19 to 24 months | 56 | 2,650 | 30% | 17 | 84,000 | 5,000 |
| TOTAL | | | 283 | | 46% | 131 | $654,000 | |

comes into play, allowing MAB not only to monitor performance of the business at the highest level but also to identify specific clients to target for marketing actions within one seamless tool.

We map dashboards to corresponding nodes on our Category Tree (Figure CS.24) to guide the user through the analytic process.

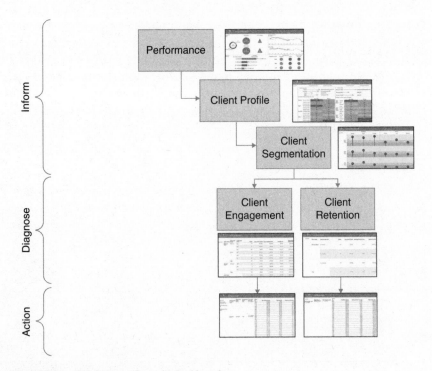

**Figure CS.24    MAB Category Tree with Dashboards**

The tree structure depicts the analytic flow Michael navigates when considering the various questions, decisions, and actions.

Let's walk through the guided experience to uncover the opportunities available to Michael to monetize his data. There are three dashboards in the Inform section that help Michael understand the health of the business and his clients. Based on issues or opportunities spotted, he navigates to one of two diagnostics: Client Engagement or Client Retention. Once in a diagnostic, he reviews the analysis in order to make a decision. From here, he moves to an Action dashboard that will help him find the right clients to target.

Making use of what we learned in the chapters on UI and UX, we design dashboards that are pleasant to view, quick to read, and easy to navigate.

### Performance Dashboard

The Performance dashboard helps Michael monitor progress of the company, providing a snapshot of the current sales and orders as well as monthly and annual comparisons.

On the Performance dashboard there are also Success Metrics providing a window into opportunities and issues. Success Metrics connecting performance to diagnosis are displayed on Inform dashboards as well as Diagnostic dashboards. These metrics alert a user that an opportunity or issue exists and they need to do further investigation in a Diagnostic dashboard to make a decision.

Success Metrics we implement include:

- Clients not ordering in 6 to 24 months as a percentage of total—This metric measures the number of clients who have not ordered within the past 6 to 24 months and therefore serves as an indicator of attrition. We apply this metric to high-value clients in the Multiyear–Wardrobe segment.

  An alert is signaled when the percentage of clients in an attrition risk exceeds 10 percent of total clients. The alert signals Michael that attrition risk is building and countermeasures should be considered. In our example dashboard in Figure CS.25, we see the metrics have turned a darker shade, alerting Michael to take further action.
- Distribution of high-potential clients by Engagement Score— This metric assesses the ability to increase a client's degree of

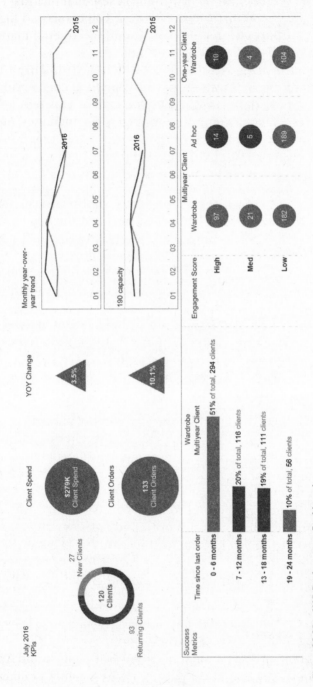

**Figure CS.25   MAB Performance Dashboard**

engagement with MAB. This metric scores individual clients on a scale of High, Medium, or Low. Clients scored high are expected to be more likely to respond to targeted marketing activities.

Clients in the Multiyear–Ad Hoc segment with a better than low potential and One-Year–Wardrobe clients with high potential are highlighted in Figure CS.25. This tells Michael that these clients are good candidates for increased engagement.

### Client Profile Dashboard

Once Michael has viewed the Performance dashboard, he may go directly to a particular diagnostic or navigate to the Client Profile dashboard (Figure CS.26). This dashboard is informational and provides a view in the various profile mixes of client base.

The profiles include clients by Occupation, Tenure, and Product Scope, allowing Michael to understand the composition of the client base.

From here, Michael will go to the Client Segmentation dashboard to see if there are groupings of like customers where he might have an engagement or retention opportunity.

### Client Segmentation Dashboard

The Client Segmentation dashboard (Figure CS.27) provides a quick view of the value of each of the client segments. On this dashboard, Michael can visually see if there are any opportunities of underserved segments that need additional engagement.

We know that we have a Monetarization Strategy that buckets various segments into Engage and Retain. The dashboard provides a quick visual into the health of this overall strategy as well.

At this point, Michael wants to build an engagement strategy and will navigate to the Client Engagement dashboard to determine which of the clients in the Engage segments would fit a particular strategy.

### Client Engagement Dashboard

There are two Client Engagement dashboards: Diagnose and Action. From our monetization strategy and our client segmentation, we are

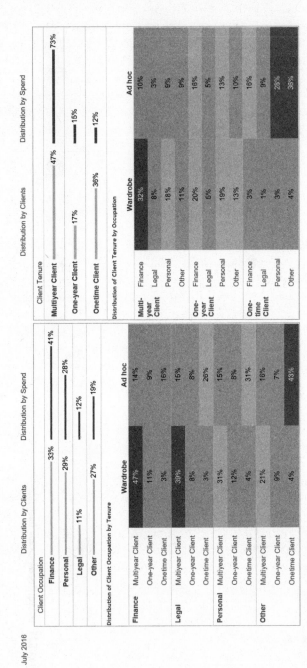

**Figure CS.26  Client Profile Dashboard**

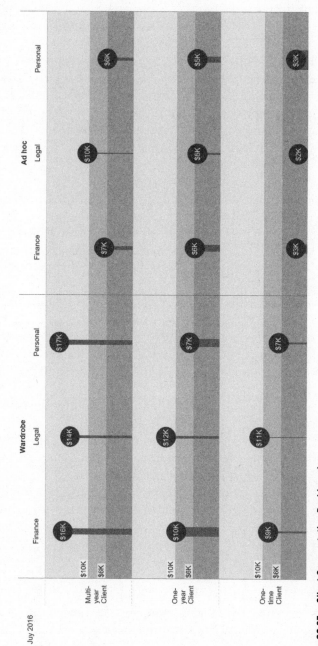

**Figure CS.27  Client Segmentation Dashboard**

going to focus on moving clients to the Multiyear–Wardrobe seg-ment, our highest-value segment.

We developed two actions that we would like to execute on:

A2 For high-value clients, target a marketing event to drive to a more committed relationship. MAB has determined a Scotch tasting, invite-only event at a cost of $100 per attendee.

A3 For newer clients who have placed large orders, conduct a group dinner to incent a multiyear relationship. MAB has determined a host group dinner with Michael Andrews at a cost of $200 per attendee.

From here, we need to determine who and how many clients we want to target for both events. We start with our Diagnose dashboard (Figure CS.28), which points us to the two segments. Michael decides that he will only take one action, the Scotch tasting event. He navigates to the Action dashboard to decide on the individual clients to invite.

The Action dashboard (Figure CS.29) provides specific informa-tion to help Michael take action. On the dashboard we see Client Number, Average Lifetime Spend, Potential Lift, and Potential Lift Percentage. This information provides Michael with the most attrac-tive clients to pursue based on the likelihood of the client generating revenue for MAB.

The highest-potential clients identified on the Performance dashboard are sorted to the top and highlighted.

Michael decides to invite everyone in the Multiyear–Wardrobe segment and Ad Hoc segments with high engagement scores. This is a total list of 111 clients. If everyone attends, the cost of the event will be $11,100. From the event, Michael expects that 49 of the clients will increase their engagement with MAB, delivering an estimated revenue lift of $201,480.

### Client Retention Dashboard

The next set of diagnostics Michael wants to see is focused on helping him execute a retention campaign of the clients that are at risk of leaving. Michael goes to the Client Retention diagnostic (Figure CS.30).

July 2016

| Client Tenure | Client Order Scope | Engagement Score | Clients | Avg Lifetime Spend | Target Lifetime Spend | Potential Lift | Gross Value Opportunity |
|---|---|---|---|---|---|---|---|
| Multiyear Client | Wardrobe | High | 97 | $16,463 | $20,000 | $3,370 | $326,850 |
| | | Med | 21 | $16,346 | $20,000 | $3,717 | $78,055 |
| | | Low | 182 | $8,933 | $20,000 | $11,210 | $2,040,183 |
| | Ad hoc | High | 14 | $16,125 | $20,000 | $3,398 | $47,569 |
| | | Med | 5 | $13,926 | $20,000 | $5,131 | $25,656 |
| | | Low | 189 | $5,835 | $20,000 | $13,647 | $2,579,333 |
| | Total | | 508 | $9,248 | $20,000 | $10,035 | $5,097,646 |
| One-year Client | Wardrobe | High | 10 | $15,761 | $20,000 | $4,580 | $45,798 |
| | | Med | 4 | $15,069 | $20,000 | $4,121 | $16,484 |
| | | Low | 104 | $7,365 | $20,000 | $12,085 | $1,256,840 |
| | Total | | 118 | $8,386 | $20,000 | $11,179 | $1,319,123 |
| Grand Total | | | 626 | $9,094 | $20,000 | $10,250 | $6,416,768 |

**Figure CS.28  Client Engagement Diagnostic**

| July 2016 | Client Tenure | Client Order Scope | Engagement Score | Time Since Last Order | Client ID | Avg Lifetime Spend | Potential Lift | Potential Lift Percent |
|---|---|---|---|---|---|---|---|---|
| Client Tenure Multiyear Client | Multiyear Client | Ad hoc | High | 0–6 months | 1034 | $19,782 | $218 | 1% |
| Client Order Scope All | | | | | 1065 | $18,218 | $1,782 | 10% |
| | | | | | 1113 | $18,443 | $1,557 | 8% |
| | | | | | 1116 | $16,628 | $3,372 | 20% |
| Engagement Score High | | | | | 1146 | $13,475 | $6,525 | 48% |
| | | | | | 1164 | $15,180 | $4,820 | 32% |
| | | | | | 1179 | $17,361 | $2,639 | 15% |
| | | | | | 1264 | $15,622 | $4,378 | 28% |
| | | | | | 1376 | $18,620 | $1,380 | 7% |
| | | | | | 1423 | $14,054 | $5,946 | 42% |
| | | | | | 1490 | $14,736 | $5,264 | 36% |
| | | | | | 1672 | $15,227 | $4,773 | 31% |
| | | | | | 1843 | $15,465 | $4,535 | 29% |
| | | | | 7–12 months | 2100 | $19,617 | $383 | 2% |
| | Multiyear Client | Wardrobe | High | 0–6 months | 1003 | $15,648 | $4,352 | 28% |
| | | | | | 1054 | $18,201 | $1,799 | 10% |
| | | | | | 1061 | $15,148 | $4,852 | 32% |
| | | | | | 1063 | $17,387 | $2,613 | 15% |
| | | | | | 1119 | $18,200 | $1,800 | 10% |
| | | | | | 1120 | $17,693 | $2,307 | 13% |
| | | | | | 1133 | $18,430 | $1,570 | 9% |
| | | | | | 1138 | $10,235 | $3,765 | 23% |
| | | | | | 1142 | $14,734 | $5,266 | 36% |
| | | | | | 1165 | $13,337 | $6,663 | 50% |
| | | | | | 1166 | $14,075 | $5,925 | 42% |
| | | | | | 1175 | $15,171 | $4,830 | 32% |
| | | | | | 1182 | $13,247 | $6,753 | 51% |
| | | | | | 1198 | $19,939 | $61 | 0% |
| | | | | | 1228 | $13,966 | $6,035 | 43% |
| | | | | | 1231 | $16,065 | $3,935 | 24% |
| | | | | | 1242 | $15,769 | $4,231 | 27% |
| | | | | | 1244 | $16,152 | $3,848 | 24% |
| | | | | | 1250 | $18,163 | $1,837 | 10% |

**Figure CS.29   Client Engagement Action**

July 2016

| Client Tenure | Time Since Last Order | Clients | Avg Lifetime Spend | Spend per Client per Year | Opportunity Value |
|---|---|---|---|---|---|
| **Multiyear Client** | 0–6 months | 294 | $19,694 | 5,272 | $3,099,719 |
| | 7–12 months | 116 | $16,124 | 5,186 | $1,203,165 |
| | 13–18 months | 111 | $13,862 | 4,245 | $942,362 |
| | Total | 521 | $17,693 | 5,052 | $5,263,783 |

**Figure CS.30  Client Retention Dashboard**

On this dashboard, Michael is able to view the clients by segment to determine groups at risk by the number of clients in the segment who have not purchased within a particular period of time. Michael decides to focus on the clients in the 7 to 12 months since last order window to attract them back into the store and refresh the relationship (Figure CS.31).

The MAB staff develops a Try a New Style Shirt campaign to entice these high-value clients to come back into the studio. The campaign will cost $100 per client, for a total of $11,600 in costs if all 116 clients take them up on their offer. The team expects to generate $6,000 in orders from 20 percent of the clients, yielding $63,600 in additional revenue.

## Closing

We have gone through the entire Decision Architecture methodology to create an analytical solution for MAB. The process started with Discovery and understanding the business of Michael Andrews Bespoke and fine custom tailoring. We also reviewed the business objective and developed a hypothesis to take advantage of the business opportunity. We selected business levers to act as the common thread through our project, tying the business problem to the hypothesis to the actions.

In the Decision Analysis phase, we developed our Decision Architecture requirements comprising our Category Tree, Question Analysis, Key Decisions, Action Levers, and Success Metrics. The requirements help us figure out how to solve the hypothesis and what data we will want to use for our analytical solution.

The Monetization Strategy was developed concurrently with the Decision Analysis and Agile Analytics phases. In the Decision Analysis phase, we developed the requirements that came from the Decision Analysis. In the Agile Analytics phase we developed our specific Monetization Strategies.

In the Agile Analytics phase, we completed our solution through the development of the Data Development and Analytical Structure. We used Decision Theory and Data Science to create Success Metrics to drive the decisions and action execution. In addition, we built our Decision Matrix to guide Michael to the various decisions. Finally, we utilize the principles of Guided Analytics to build our final solution.

July 2016

| Time Since Last Order | Client Tenure | Time Since Last Order |
| 7–12 months | Multiyear Client | 7–12 months |

| Client ID | Avg Lifetime Spend | Spend per Client per Year | Opportunity Value |
| --- | --- | --- | --- |
| 2095 | $72,631 | 11,979 | $23,958 |
| 2057 | $66,318 | 10,152 | $20,304 |
| 2263 | $61,011 | 28,019 | $56,037 |
| 2144 | $55,628 | 10,219 | $20,437 |
| 2158 | $53,762 | 9,927 | $19,854 |
| 1418 | $53,066 | 15,553 | $31,105 |
| 2236 | $45,444 | 8,348 | $16,696 |
| 2309 | $45,075 | 7,315 | $14,629 |
| 2155 | $43,694 | 10,033 | $20,066 |
| 2076 | $39,190 | 9,101 | $18,202 |
| 2093 | $37,480 | 6,913 | $13,825 |
| 2225 | $37,131 | 6,922 | $13,844 |
| 2119 | $36,503 | 5,564 | $11,128 |
| 2235 | $35,053 | 3,701 | $7,402 |
| 2336 | $35,036 | 6,436 | $12,872 |
| 2064 | $34,551 | 15,867 | $31,735 |
| 2280 | $32,916 | 10,078 | $20,155 |
| 2266 | $32,633 | 5,493 | $10,985 |
| 2019 | $30,834 | 9,509 | $19,019 |
| 2230 | $30,433 | 4,631 | $9,262 |
| 2127 | $30,271 | 5,925 | $11,849 |
| 2181 | $30,097 | 4,891 | $9,783 |
| 2232 | $30,044 | 4,134 | $8,268 |
| 2173 | $27,785 | 6,569 | $13,137 |
| 2012 | $27,518 | 4,144 | $8,288 |
| 2267 | $26,753 | 4,085 | $8,171 |
| 2334 | $25,844 | 11,869 | $23,738 |
| 2072 | $25,142 | 5,748 | $11,496 |
| 2063 | $25,014 | 5,744 | $11,488 |
| 2143 | $24,606 | 11,045 | $22,090 |
| 2211 | $23,626 | 10,788 | $21,575 |
| 2115 | $23,527 | 5,714 | $11,427 |
| 1883 | $23,515 | 5,315 | $10,630 |

**Figure CS.31   Client Retention Dashboard by Client**

The analytical solution we developed enables Michael to monitor the health of his business through the Inform dashboards (Performance, Client Profile, Client Segmentation). Once an issue or opportunity is spotted, Michael is able to diagnose the situation and map a plan of action down to the client level for retention or engagement actions.

It is these types of solutions that help companies take advantage of the troves of information they are flooded with and enable decisions that drive revenue through monetization strategies. We hope you have already begun your journey to build these solutions for your company. Let's continue the dialog at monetizingyourdata.com.

# Bibliography

Anderson, Chris. *The Long Tail: Why the Future of Business Is Selling Less of More*. New York: Hyperion, 2006.

Arthur, Brian. *Increasing Returns and Path Dependence in the Economy*. Ann Arbor: University of Michigan Press, 1994.

Baron, Jonathan. *Thinking and Deciding*, 3rd edition. New York: Cambridge University Press, 2007.

Benartzi, S., and R. Thaler. "Naive Diversification Strategies in Defined Contribution Saving Plans." *American Economic Review* 91, No. 1 (March 2001).

Beshears, John, and Francesca Gino. "Leaders as Decision Architects." *Harvard Business Review* (May 2015).

Bonabeau, Eric. "Don't Trust Your Gut." *Harvard Business Review* (May 2003).

Brant, Ana. "Using an Algorithm to Figure Out What Luxury Customers Really Want." *Harvard Business Review* (July 18, 2016).

Brown, C.L., and A. Krishna. "The Skeptical Shopper: A Metacognitive Account for the Effects of Default Options on choice." *Journal of Consumer Research* (2004).

Butler, Shawn A. "Improving Security Technology Selections with Decision Theory." www.cs.cmu.edu/afs/cs/project/vit/ftp/pdf/improv.butler.pdf. September 10, 2016.

Cameron, Kim S., and Robert E. Quinn. *Diagnosing and Changing Organizational Culture: Based on the Competing Values Framework*. Jossey-Bass Business & Management, 2nd edition.

Cederholm, Teresa. "Measuring Delta Air Lines' Performance with Key Operating Metrics" (June 18, 2014). http://marketrealist.com/2014/06/measuring-delta-airlines-performance-key-operating-metrics/. December 10, 2016.

Clark, Brian. Copyblogger (September 20, 2015). www.copyblogger.com/rule-of-three/ (retrieved October 30, 2016).

Davenport, Thomas H. "How P&G Presents Data to Decision-Makers." *Harvard Business Review* (April 4, 2013).

Einstein, Albert. "On the Method of Theoretical Physics." *Philosophy of Science* 1, no. 2 (1934): 163–169. http://www.jstor.org/stable/184387 (retrieved October 4, 2016), p. 165. September 10, 2016.

Few, Stephen. *Information Dashboard Design.* Sebastopol, CA: O'Reilly, 2006, p. 101.

Fuller, R. Buckminster. *Critical Path.* New York: St Martin's Press, 1981.

Gavett, Gretchen. "What You Need to Know About Segmentation." *Harvard Business Review* (July 9, 2014).

Gino, Francesca. "Don't Make Important Decisions Late in the Day." *Harvard Business Review* (February 23, 2016).

Gourley, Sean. "Vision Statement: Locating Your Next Strategic Opportunity." *Harvard Business Review* (March 2011).

Griffin, Robert. "When Pirates Meet Advanced Analytics." *Harvard Business Review* (October 12, 2012).

Hardman, David. *Judgment and Decision Making: Psychological Perspectives.* Wiley-Blackwell, 2009.

Harrington, Richard J., and Anthony K. Tjan. "Transforming Strategy One Customer at a Time." *Harvard Business Review* (March 2008).

Harvard Business Review Analytical Services. "Analytics That Work: Deploying Self-Service and Data Visualization for Faster Decisions." *Harvard Business Review* (July 27, 2016).

Hey, Tony. "The Big Idea: The Next Scientific Revolution." *Harvard Business Review* (November 2010).

Holmes, Jr., Oliver Wendell. *Holmes-Pollock Letters: The Correspondence of Mr. Justice Holmes and Sir Frederick Pollock, 1874–1932, Two Volumes in One,* 2nd edition. Harvard University Press, 1961, p. 109.

Iyengar, Shenna S., and Mark R. Lepper. "When Choice Is Demotivating: Can One Desire Too Much of a Good Thing?" *Journal of Personality and Social Psychology* 79, no. 6 (2000): 995–1006.

Johnson, Eric J., S.B. Shu, B.G.C. Dellaert, C. Fox, D.G. Goldstein, G. Haeubl, R.P. Larrick, J.W. Payne, D. Schkade, B. Wansink, E.U. Weber. "Beyond Nudges: Tools of a Choice Architecture." *Marketing Letters* (2012).

Joshi, Aditya, and Eduardo Giménez. "Decision-Driven Marketing." *Harvard Business Review* (July–August 2014).

Kahneman, Daniel. *Thinking, Fast and Slow* Farrar, Straus and Giroux; 1st edition (April 2, 2013)

___, Andrew M. Rosenfield, Linnea Gandhi, and Tom Blaser. "Noise: How to Overcome the High, Hidden Cost of Inconsistent Decision Making." *Harvard Business Review* (October 2016).

___, and Amos Tversky, "Prospect Theory: An Analysis of Decision Under Risk." *Econometrica* 47, no. 2 (March 1979): 263–291.

Kimball, Ralph. *Data Warehouse Toolkit.* Wiley, 3rd edition (July 1, 2013)

King, Brett. "Too Much Content: A World of Exponential Information Growth." www.huffingtonpost.com (retrieved May 25, 2011).

Koffka, Kurt. *Principles of Gestalt Psychology*. New York: Harcourt, Brace, 1935, p. 176.

Kumar, V., Rajkumar Venkates, and Werner Reinart. "Knowing What to Sell, When, and to Whom." *Harvard Business Review* (March 2006).

LaRiviera, Jacob, Preston McAfee, Justin Rao, Vijay K. Narayanan, and Walter Sun. "Where Predictive Analytics Is Having the Biggest Impact." *Harvard Business Review* (May 25, 2016).

Lidwell, William, Kritina Holden, and Jill Butler. *Universal Principles of Design*. Beverly, MA: Rockport Publishers, 2003, p. 178.

Paterson, Martin. *An Introduction to Decision Theory*. Cambridge University Press (May 25, 2009).

Peters, E., et al. "Numeracy Skill and the Communication, Comprehension, and Use of Risk and Benefit Information." *Health Affairs* (2007).

Martin, J.M., and M.I. Norton. "Shaping Online Consumer Choice by Partitioning the Web." *Psychology and Marketing* (2009).

Mcginty, Jo Craven. "As Forecasts Go, You Can Bet on Monte Carol." *Wall Street Journal* (August 12, 2016).

Nagle, Thomas, Joseph Zale, and Reed Holden. *The Strategy and Tactics of Pricing*. Pearson Prentice Hall, 4th edition (December 14, 2005).

Parmar, Rashik, Ian Mackenzie, David Cohn, and David Gann. "The New Patterns of Innovation." *Harvard Business Review* (January–February 2014).

Power, Brad. "Drive Performance by Focusing on Routine Decisions." *Harvard Business Review* (January 10, 2014).

Ritter, David. "When to Act on a Correlation, and When Not To." *Harvard Business Review* (March 19, 2014).

Rockrohr, Phil. "Thaler Explains How 'Choice Architecture' Makes the World a Better Place." www.chicagobooth.edu/news/2008ManCon/01-thaler.aspx (retrieved September 10, 2016).

Samson, Alain. "An Introduction to Behavioral Economics." www.behavioraleconomics.com/introduction-to-be/ (retrieved September 10th, 2016).

Schilling, David Russell. "Knowledge Doubling Every 12 Months, Soon to Be Every 12 Hours." www.industrytap.com (retrieved April 19, 2013).

Schwartz, Barry. *The Paradox of Choice: Why More Is Less*. New York: Harper Perennial, 2005.

Smith, N.C., D. Goldstein, and E. Johnson. "Choice Without Awareness: Ethical and Policy Implications of Defaults." *Journal of Public Policy* (2013).

St. Elmo Lewis, E. "Catch-Line and Argument." *The Book-Keeper* 15 (February 1903): 124. Detroit.

Sweller, John. "Cognitive Load During Problem Solving: Effects on Learning." *Cognitive Science* 12, Wiley-Blackwell-Journal (1988): 257–285.

Sutherland, Stuart. *Irrationality*. Pinter & Martin Ltd., 21st anniversary edition (November 7, 2013).

Thaler, Richard, and Cass Sunstein. *Nudge: Improving Decisions About Health, Wealth, and Happiness*. Penguin Books, Revised & Expanded edition (February 24, 2009).

Tufte, Edward. *The Visual Display of Quantitative Information*. Cheshire, CT: Graphics Press, 2001, p. 93.

Tugend, Alina. "Too Many Choices: A Problem that Can Paralyze." *New York Times* (February 26, 2010).

van den Driest, Frank, Stan Sthanunathan, and Keith Weed. "Building an Insights Engine." *Harvard Business Review* (October 2016).

Ware, Colin. *Information Visualization, Second Edition: Perception for Design*. San Francisco: Morgan Kaufman, 2004.

Wilson, H. James, Sharad Sachdev, and Allan Alter. "How Companies Are Using Machine Learning to Get Faster and More Efficient." *Harvard Business Review* (May 3, 2016).

Winquist, Eric. "How Companies Can Learn to Make Faster Decisions." *Harvard Business Review* (September 29, 2014).

Womack, James, and Daniel T. Jones. *Lean Thinking*. New York: Free Press, 2003, pp. 50–66.

Wood, Jennifer M. "20 Cognitive Biases That Affect Your Decisions." www.mentalfloss.com (retrieved October 10, 2016).

Yeomans, Mike. "What Every Manager Should Know About Machine Learning." *Harvard Business Review* (July 7, 2015).

# Index

Page references followed by f indicate an illustrated figure; followed by t indicate a table.